THE VEST-POCKET MBA

Jae K. Shim, Ph.D.
Joel G. Siegel, Ph.D., CPA
Abraham J. Simon, Ph.D., CPA

Prentice-Hall, Inc.
Englewood Cliffs, New Jersey

Prentice-Hall International, Inc., *London*
Prentice-Hall of Australia, Pty. Ltd., *Sydney*
Prentice-Hall Canada, Inc., *Toronto*
Prentice-Hall of India Private Ltd., *New Delhi*
Prentice-Hall of Japan, Inc., *Tokyo*
Prentice-Hall of Southeast Asia Pte. Ltd., *Singapore*
Whitehall Books, Ltd., *Wellington, New Zealand*
Editora Prentice-Hall do Brasil Ltda., *Rio de Janeiro*
Prentice-Hall Hispanoamericana, S.A., *Mexico*

© 1986 *by*

PRENTICE-HALL, INC.
Englewood Cliffs, N.J.

20   19   18   17   16   15   14   13   12   11

Library of Congress Cataloging-in-Publication Data

Shim, Jae K.
  The vest-pocket MBA.

  Includes index.
  1. Managerial accounting. 2. Business enterprises—
Finance. I. Siegel, Joel G. II. Simon, Abraham J.
III. Title.
HF5635.S55295   1986   658.1′5   86-497

ISBN 0-13-941709-5

PRINTED IN THE UNITED STATES OF AMERICA

Dedication

TO OUR WIVES
CHUNG, ROBERTA, AND MARILYN
For the love, patience, and
assistance they have given us

TO THE MEMORY OF OUR FATHERS
We miss them so much

Acknowledgments

We wish to specially thank our editors at Prentice-Hall for their invaluable input in the preparation of the manuscript. Bette Schwartzberg provided encouragement and outstanding editorial comments and suggestions that were of immeasurable benefit. Her efforts are greatly appreciated. Patricia Virga, our developmental editor, did an excellent job of going over the entire manuscript to assure technical accuracy and appropriate writing style. Her earnest and helpful efforts are greatly recognized. Thanks also to Cathy Johnson, our production editor, for her help in the production process.

About the Authors

JAE K. SHIM, Ph.D., is a professor of accounting and computer science at California State University. Dr. Shim received his Ph.D. in operations research from the University of California at Berkeley. He is the author of several professional publications and books. His articles have appeared in many accounting, financial, and quantitative journals, including *Decision Sciences, Management Science, Econometrica,* and *International Journal of Systems Science.* He is actively involved in computer consulting.

JOEL G. SIEGEL, Ph.D., CPA, is a professor of accounting and finance at Queens College of the City University of New York and a financial consultant to management. He is the author of 13 published and about-to-be-published books and over 100 articles. Dr. Siegel's articles have appeared in professional journals, including *The Financial Executive, The Financial Analysts Journal, The CPA Journal, The National Public Accountant, Credit and Financial Management,* and the *International Journal of Management.* He has served as consultant and/or adviser to numerous organizations, including the AICPA, Citicorp, and ITT. He was affiliated with Coopers and Lybrand, CPAs, and Arthur Andersen, CPAs. In 1972 Dr. Siegel was the recipient of the Outstanding Educator of America award. He is listed in Who's Where Among Writers and in Who's Who in the East.

ABRAHAM J. SIMON, Ph.D., CPA, is professor of accounting and information systems at Queens College of the City University of New York. He has served as consultant to several organizations and the City of New York. He has authored professional books for the AICPA and the Council on Municipal Performance. Dr. Simon's articles have appeared in many journals, including the *International Journal of Accounting Education and Research, the National Public Accountant,* and *Credit and Financial Management.* Professor Simon has practiced extensively as a CPA.

Contents

Introduction

Here is a handy pocket problem-solver for today's busy executive. It's a working guide to help you quickly pinpoint

- What to look for
- What to do
- What to watch out for
- How to do it

in the complex world of business. You'll find ratios, formulas, guidelines, and rules of thumb to help you analyze and evaluate any business-related problem. Throughout, you'll find this book practical, quick, and useful.

Uses for this book are as varied as the topics presented. Part I (Chapters 1, 2, and 3) takes you through accounting principles and guidelines for evaluating a company's financial health. You'll learn techniques for analyzing another company's financial position should you wish to invest, extend credit, or compare. We present internal accounting applications to help you evaluate your own company's performance, profitability, marketing effectiveness, and budgeting process. You'll learn how to highlight problem areas with variance analysis.

Part II (Chapters 4, 5, and 6) takes a look at financial and economic measures for decision making. Through breakeven and sensitivity analysis, you'll be able to move your company toward greater profits. For investment purposes, this part presents guidelines for evaluating proposals, whether they be short or long term, for profit potential and risk–return comparisons. You'll learn management and financing techniques to ensure the best possible strategies for maximizing and acquiring cash.

Part III (Chapters 7 and 8) takes you through the seemingly complex world of quantitative analysis. You'll use statistics for forecasting and validity testing. Decision theories include linear programming, learning curve theory, and queuing models; these are presented concisely and comprehensively to help you use such sophisticated techniques with relative ease. And, you'll learn how computer applications facilitate the many complex procedures.

This book has been designed in question-and-answer format in order to address the pertinent issues that come up during the course of business. The questions are typical of those asked by persons like yourself. The answers are clear, concise, and to the point. In short, this is a veritable cookbook of guidelines, illustrations, and "how-to's" for you, the modern decision maker. Keep it handy for easy reference throughout your busy day.

Jae K. Shim   Joel G. Siegel   Abraham J. Simon

PART I
ACCOUNTING TOOLS AND GUIDELINES

1

How to Evaluate a Company's Financial Position: Part I

Financial analysis of other companies is important if you are

- An investor who needs to formulate portfolio decisions
- A creditor who must make sure he gets paid
- An auditor who needs to appraise her client's financial astuteness
- A financial manager who wants to evaluate and improve areas of inadequacy and improvement
- A marketing manager who wants to establish product line strategies

Here are your guidelines for conducting a financial analysis.

1.1 THE INCOME STATEMENT ANALYSIS

1.1.1 Evaluating Earnings Quality

What is the importance of earnings quality?

Earnings quality refers to *realistic* earnings, or monies earned after various factors have been taken into account. The following factors will have a bearing on the earnings quality of the company:

- The P/E ratio (market price per share divided by earnings per share) used in equity financing decisions. A low P/E ratio means lower earnings quality.

3

- Effective interest rate in credit decisions. Compensating balance requirements and the cost of borrowing will be higher when earnings quality is lower.
- Availability of future financing sources. Poor earnings quality may put fewer funds at the company's disposal.
- The bond rating. Poor earnings quality means a lower bond rating, and this may lower the market price of bonds.

WARNING: Beware the "high accounting risk" company. Many fall under this category, including:

- "Glamour" companies, known for profitability growth
- Companies in the public eye
- Companies with problems getting adequate financing
- Companies whose management might previously have been dishonest

How do accounting policies affect earnings quality?

You should compare the company's accounting policies with industry standards. If the firm's policies are more liberal, earnings quality is likely to be lower. Realistic policies as determined by industry standards can be found in American Institute of Certified Public Accountants (AICPA) industry audit guides, AICPA statements of position, and CPA firm publications.

WHAT TO DO: Compare reported earnings based on the most realistic accounting principles with the principles used by the firm. If realistic policies would have resulted in less profit, then the earnings quality would be lower. For example, the deferred method of accounting for investment tax credit is more realistic than the flow-through method. The deferred method amortizes the tax credit against tax expense over the life of the asset. The flow-through method reduces tax expense in full for credit in the year of acquisition, thus, companies using this method would have lower earnings quality.

What constitutes accurate revenue recognition?

Revenue recognition means recording revenues when earned, either at the time of sale or rendering of services. Make sure that revenue is being recognized *only* when warranted. For example, a company might record credit sales without adequate provision for bad debts even if the risk of not collecting is high. Revenue should not be recognized when material services have not yet been performed, for example, if a correspondence school claims revenue before the student has begun work. On the other hand, revenue recognition may be deferred unjustifiably, in which case consider net income to be improperly understated.

How do I interpret over- or underaccrued expenses?

Underaccrued or overaccrued expenses, that is, those that are recorded too low or too high, result in poor earnings quality. For example, a warranty provision that does not adequately address problems with product quality would result in an underaccrued expense. WHAT TO DO: Adjust net income based on realistic normal charges.

EXAMPLE 1.1

Bad debts were recorded at $12,000. The analyst finds this to be an overestimated expense, and believes bad debts should have been estimated to be $9,000. Net income, hence, should be increased by $3,000.

What about accounting changes?

An accounting change is appropriate if it is made to conform to a new Financial Accounting Standards Board (FASB) statement, AICPA industry audit guide, or Internal Revenue Service (IRS) regulation. An unwarranted accounting change, either in principle (method) or estimate, detracts from earnings quality. Often, these changes can mislead earnings growth estimates. WARNING: If a firm makes many accounting changes, you will not be able to use current period earnings as a reliable base for predicting future earnings.

How should I interpret income smoothing?

Income smoothing occurs when earnings are reported artificially, and it results in lower earnings quality. Why? Because net income does not portray economic results as they are, but rather as management wants them shown. WARNING TO CREDIT AND LOAN OFFICERS: A weak relationship between sales and net income may be a sign of income smoothing.

EXAMPLE 1.2

Company J's ratio of net income to sales for the period 19X1 to 19X4 is given as follows:

19X1	19X2	19X3	19X4
0.10	0.05	0.18	0.02

The trend shows a weak relationship between net income and sales. This may mean possible income smoothing.

What do discretionary costs tell me?

Management can alter at will such discretionary costs as advertising, repairs, research, and training. Ask yourself, "Does the amount of discretionary costs for this period conform to previous trends, industry norms, future expectations?" Remember, an unjustified decrease in discretionary costs means lower earnings quality. Why? Because management is depriving its business of required expenditures. SUGGESTION: Take particular note of decreasing trends in these ratios: discretionary costs to sales and discretionary costs to assets.

FOR CREDIT AND LOAN OFFICERS: Use index numbers to compare discretionary costs with base year amounts. Example 1.3 shows how to do it.

EXAMPLE 1.3

The relationship between research and sales for 19X1 to 19X3 is given as follows:

	19X1	19X2	19X3
Sales	$120,000	$150,000	$80,000
Research	12,000	18,000	6,000
Ratio of research to sales*	0.10	0.12	0.075

*19X1 is the base year.

Since 19X1 is the most typical year, it is assigned an index number 100. In 19X2, the index number is 150 ($18,000/$12,000). In 19X3, the index number is 50 ($6,000/$12,000).

A negative trend is indicated here. Research is lower than in previous years, but it should have been increased to ensure future success.

EXAMPLE 1.4

Company F gives the following information regarding its fixed assets:

	19X1	19X2
Fixed assets	$6,000	$6,300
Less accumulated depreciation	(3,300)	(3,700)

	19X1	19X2
Book value	$2,700	$2,600
Repairs	400	300
Replacement cost of fixed assets	8,000	8,900
CPI value of fixed assets	8,600	9,400
Sales	47,000	55,000
Working capital	4,000	3,400
Cash	1,000	930
Debt-to-equity ratio	0.42	0.68
Downtime of fixed assets in terms of available capacity	2.1%	5.3%

The following observations point to inadequate maintenance of capital:

- The ratio of repairs to gross fixed assets went from 0.067 ($400/$6,000) in 19X1 to 0.048 ($300/$6,300) in 19X2. For the same period, there was a reduction of repairs to sales from 0.0085 ($400/$47,000) to 0.0055 ($300/$55,000).

- From 19X1 to 19X2 there was a widening difference between replacement cost and book value as well as between CPI value and book value. These trends reflect growing obsolescence of assets. NOTE TO MARKETING MANAGERS: Production problems may be in store; these can adversely affect future sales.

- Increased downtime indicates growing equipment problems.

- There were minimal purchases of fixed assets in 19X2 ($300). In this year, the ratio of new acquisitions to the gross fixed asset base was 0.05 ($300/$6,000). There will be a problem replacing the assets when required owing to the firm's weakening cash and working capital position. In turn, the higher replacement cost will hurt liquidity. A high debt-to-equity ratio means the company will have a problem getting adequate financing, particularly when there is a tight money market.

Here are some other signposts to look for regarding discretionary costs:

- *Cost-reduction program.* A cost-control program lowers earnings quality when material cutbacks in discretionary costs occur.

- *Proper reductions in discretionary costs.* A decline in discretionary costs is not *always* unwarranted. A reduction may be required when the prior corporate policy was inadequate.

- *Boost in discretionary costs.* A material boost in discretionary costs will likely enhance future earnings.
- *Income management.* If discretionary costs fluctuate relative to revenue, income smoothing may be occurring.

How do I measure cash flow?

Net income is better in quality when backed up by cash because it can be used to pay debt, expand, etc. WHAT TO DO: Look at the trend in cash flow from operations to net income.

EXAMPLE 1.5

A partial income statement of Company H is given as follows:

Sales		$1,600,000
Less cost of sales		(600,000)
Gross margin		$1,000,000
Less operating expenses		
Wages	$150,000	
Rent	220,000	
Utilities	40,000	
Depreciation	70,000	
Amortization expense	50,000	
Total operating expenses		(530,000)
Income before other revenue and expenses		$ 470,000
Interest expense	$ 60,000	
Less amortization of deferred income	(20,000)	
Total other revenue and expense		(40,000)
Net income		$ 430,000

The ratio of cash flow from operations to net income is computed as follows:

Cash flow from operations

Net income		$ 430,000
Add noncash expenses:		
Depreciation	$ 70,000	
Amortization expense	50,000	

Total noncash expenses	120,000
Less noncash revenue: Amortization of deferred income	(20,000)
Cash flow from operations	$ 530,000

$$\frac{\text{Cash flow from operations}}{\text{Net income}} = \frac{\$530,000}{\$430,000} = 1.23$$

Cash revenue and expenses are more factual than estimated revenue and expenses. For example, salary expenses are more certain than depreciation, and thus are more reliable.

How do I analyze taxable income?

In general, taxable income is lower than net income because firms use more conservative policies for tax reporting. However, if book income greatly exceeds taxable income, the earnings quality may be lower. WHAT TO LOOK FOR: A widening disparity between the two is reflected in a trend toward increasing the deferred income tax credit account.

EXAMPLE 1.6

ABC Company furnishes the following information:

	19X1	19X2	19X3
Deferred income tax credit	$200	$230	$350
Sales	12,000	13,500	14,200
Net income	3,000	3,200	2,600
Deferred income tax credit to sales	0.017	0.017	0.025
Deferred income tax credit to net income	0.067	0.072	0.135

The increase in the deferred account in base dollars was 115 ($230/$200) for 19X2 and 175 for 19X3 ($350/$200). The increase in deferred income tax credit to both sales and net income indicates a widening difference between book income and taxable income.

Take note of these special circumstances:

Foreign earnings. Many businesses earn profits in low-tax foreign countries. Such profits are often not repatriated back to the United States because they would be subject to U.S. taxes. If you consider net income as funds available to stockholders, then net income that includes foreign profits would be overstated.

Effective tax rate. The effective tax rate relates tax expense to before-tax income. A reduction in the effective tax rate arising from a one-time source (such as an investment tax credit for a major plant expansion) causes overstated earnings from the point of view of the investment analyst. These tax benefits will not continue in future years.

Domestic International Sales Corporation (DISC). Net income is overstated when DISC tax deferrals exist.

1.1.2 Using Accounting Estimates

**How does uncertainty
in accounting estimates
affect earnings quality?**

The more subjective the estimates used to determine earnings are, the more uncertain are the results. For example, a ship builder uses a percentage-of-completion accounting method because of its long-term activities. There would be a significant amount of uncertainty associated with the earnings, especially if a great amount of estimates is involved. WHAT TO DO: You should compare estimated and actual losses over the years. A significant difference points to lower earnings quality. WARNING: Material gains and losses on the disposition of assets may imply that improper estimates were used to compute depreciation. REMEMBER THIS: The greater the percent of assets involving many accounting estimates is, the more uncertain the reported results will be.

EXAMPLE 1.7

Company S's provision for expense warranties came to $80,000 in 19X1 and $120,000 in 19X2. Actual warranty costs were $110,000 in 19X1 and $180,000 in 19X2. The unfavorable difference in 19X1 was $30,000, or 37.5% of the original estimate ($30,000/$80,000). In 19X2, the unfavorable difference grew to $60,000, or 50% of the estimate ($60,000/$120,000). You cannot rely on this company's estimation process.

Additionally, earnings for 19X1 and 19X2 are overstated by virtue of the underestimated expense provisions.

You should distinguish between revenue and expense items that are cash related versus those that are based on estimates. CREDIT AND LOAN OFFICERS: Pay attention to trends indicated from these ratios:

- Cash expenses to total revenue
- Estimated expenses to total revenue
- Cash revenue to total revenue
- Estimated revenue to total revenue
- Cash expenses to net income
- Estimated expenses to net income
- Cash revenue to net income
- Estimated revenue to net income

Trends should always be compared over the years within the same company, with competing companies, and with industry norms. The following example shows some of these ratios.

EXAMPLE 1.8

Company A provides the following information for the period 19X1 and 19X2:

	19X1	19X2
Cash and near-cash revenue	$ 80,000	$ 95,000
Noncash revenue	160,000	210,000
Total revenue	$240,000	$305,000
Cash and near-cash expenses	$ 30,000	$ 70,000
Noncash expenses	80,000	140,000
Total expenses	$110,000	$210,000
Net income	$130,000	$ 95,000
Estimated revenue to total revenue	0.67	0.69
Estimated revenue to net income	1.23	2.21
Estimated expenses to total expenses	0.73	0.67
Estimated expenses to total revenue	0.33	0.46
Estimated expenses to net income	0.62	1.47

You can see that there is greater uncertainty regarding the net income for 19X2 because of higher ratios in nearly every category—the only ratio that decreased was estimated expenses to total expenses.

What is residual income and how do I measure its effects?

Residual income can be calculated using the following formula:

Net income − (cost of capital × total assets)
= residual income

The higher the ratio of residual income to net income, the better the earnings quality. Why? Because the company is earning a sufficient amount to cover its minimum rate of return on assets. This measure tells the real earnings of the business. FOR ECONOMISTS: You would like to know what a company really earns after taking into account the minimum return on assets (cost of capital). Example 1.9 tells you how to find out.

EXAMPLE 1.9

A company's cost of capital is 12%, its net income is $800,000, and its assets total $4,000,000. Residual income is calculated as follows:

Net income	$800,000
Less cost of capital times total assets (12% × $4,000,000)	(480,000)
Residual income	$320,000
Ratio of residual income to net income ($320,000/$800,000).	0.40

Persons preparing and using the financial statement must determine the cost of capital based on data in the annual report. The cost of capital considers the cost of various financing instruments and their weights (percentages) in the capital structure. For example, the cost of debt is interest and the cost of stock is dividends. The weights of debt and stock in the capital structure depend on the ratio of each in dollars to the total debt and equity.

The cost of financing may depend on current market prices rather than book value. Cost of capital determination is of interest to you if you are a

- *Financial manager* who wants to determine the best mixture of new financing that lowers overall cost of financing

- *Managerial accountant* who needs to compute the discount rate for capital budgeting decisions

- *Creditor* or *investment analyst* who needs to ascertain the riskiness of the company on the basis of the rate change in the cost of capital

1.1.3 Analyzing Acquisitions

What accounting methods are used for business combinations?

Two methods of accounting used for business combinations are pooling and purchase. You must carefully evaluate pooling because it can portray artificial earnings growth. Here, the purchaser recognizes the earnings of the acquired business for an entire year, even though the acquisition was made some time during the year. WHAT YOU SHOULD DO: Eliminate that part of the reported results that includes the profit of the acquired firm before the date of acquisition.

Bring forth the net assets of the acquired company at book value, *not* market value. Since book value is typically less, the understated assets (e.g., fixed assets) will result in understated expenses (e.g., depreciation). The result is overstated earnings. You should adjust the net assets of the acquired business from book value to market value and also adjust the expenses to determine a realistic earnings figure comparable to what the earnings would have been using the purchase method.

Bringing forth net assets at book value will suppress such asset valuations. Thus, upon the sale of those assets, earnings will be overstated. You should adjust net income downward to account for the difference between the reported and probable gain if the asset valuation was based on market value.

The purchase method is more realistic than pooling. Here, net income of the acquired business is recognized from the date of acquisition to year-end. Market value shows the worth of the assets better than outdated historical cost. Take note of the reasonableness of the market value used.

WARNING: Even under purchase, weak companies may still show strong operating results by buying very profitable businesses. Hence, you should look at the trend and dollar effect upon profitability of purchase transactions.

CHECKLIST OF QUESTIONS REGARDING ACQUISITIONS

- Is earnings growth illusory?
- In pooling, is book value of acquired assets significantly understated relative to market value?

- In pooling, were there one-time gains on the sale of low-cost basis assets?
- In purchase, were the fair values assigned to assets realistic?
- In purchase, were equity securities issued at an unusually high price?

How do I handle construction contracts?

TO LOAN OFFICERS AND CREDITORS: Watch closely if the company classifies period costs as construction costs so as not to lower reported results. Also note whether cost overruns on contracts are occurring but are not being recognized in the statements.

Does income from discontinued operations affect earnings quality?

Income from discontinued operations is typically of a one-time nature and should be ignored when forecasting future earnings. Also, a discontinued operation implies that the business is in a state of decline or that a poor management decision is responsible for the company's entering the discontinued line of business. REMEMBER: Income from continuing operations is the most representative earnings figure applying to the company's current operating performance.

What are signs of unreliable earnings?

Look for these signs of unreliable earnings:

- Poor internal control (This implies possible undetected accounting errors.)
- Material error corrections relating to prior years
- A history of income smoothing as evidenced by accounting and financial publications (e.g., brokerage reports)
- Liberal accounting policies
- Skyrocketing audit fees owing to problems in the company's accounting system
- High turnover rate in using CPA firms

What does the audit report mean?

FOR INVESTMENT AND CREDIT ANALYSTS: Consider carefully the audit report for a company; in particular, remember that earnings quality is highest if the firm has received an unqualified opinion. With a qualified opinion, the CPA states that "except for" (a limitation placed on the scope of the audit) or "subject to" (an uncertainty, like a lawsuit), the financial statements present financial position and operating results fairly. A disclaimer means the CPA cannot render an opinion, which generally occurs when he or she did not conduct the necessary audit procedures. An adverse opinion means the CPA believes the statements do not conform to generally accepted accounting principles (GAAP).

NOTE: A material event occurring after year-end but before the issuance of the audit report (for example, a catastrophe loss) may be disclosed in the audit report.

1.2 APPRAISING THE FINANCIAL STRUCTURE

1.2.1 Evaluating Earnings Stability

How do I compute growth rate?

A company's growth rate equals

$$\frac{\text{Net income} - \text{dividends}}{\text{Common stock equity}}$$

A high ratio indicates a company's ability to generate internal funds and a minimal reliance on external sources. WHAT TO DO: Compare the company's growth rate with those of major competitors and with industry norms.

How do I define stability of earnings?

Stable earnings, that is, those that remain relatively constant, are of higher quality because you can project future earnings more readily. Less instability is also associated with corporate operations. You should compute the following ratios:

- One-time gains and losses to net income
- One-time gains and losses to sales

How Do I Measure Earnings Stability? A lack of stability indicates riskiness associated with the business. WHAT TO DO: Evaluate trends in earnings stability by examining a long interval of time, say ten years. The more vacillation in earnings, the lower the earnings quality. You can use the following measures:

- *Average net income.* The computation of average net income for a ten-year period smooths out erratic income statement elements and cyclical impacts on the business. Average net income therefore is a good indicator of earning power.

● *Average pessimistic earnings.* This represents the average earnings based on the worst possible situation with the business. FOR CREDIT AND LOAN OFFICERS: To measure risk, use the minimum earnings figure in cases where the business is very risky.

Standard Deviation (SD) in Earnings

$$SD = \sqrt{\frac{\Sigma(y - \bar{y})^2}{n}}$$

where

y = net income for period t
$\bar{y}$ = average earnings
n = number of years

A high standard deviation indicates low earnings quality.

Coefficient of Variation (CV) in Earnings

$$CV = \frac{SD}{\bar{y}}$$

This is useful in appraising relative earnings instability. A high coefficient means high risk.

Instability Index (I) of Earnings

$$I = \sqrt{\frac{\Sigma(y - y^T)^2}{n}}$$

where

y^T = trend earnings for period t, computed as follows:
$y^T = a + bt$

where

a = dollar intercept
b = slope of trend line
t = time period

Trend earnings are best determined with a computer. The instability index shows the variation between actual and trend earnings. A high index points to low earnings quality.

Beta. Beta, which may be determined by computer, is equal to

$$r_{jt} = a_j + \beta \bar{r}_{mt} + E_{jt}$$

where

r_{jt} = return on security j for period t
a_j = constant

β_j = Beta for security j
r_{mt} = return on a market index (like Dow Jones)
E_{jt} = error term

Beta measures the riskiness of a stock. A high beta shows that the company's stock price fluctuates more than the market index. For example, a beta of 1.7 means that the company's stock price can increase or decrease 70 percent *faster* than the market. A beta of 0.6 means that the company's stock price can increase or decrease 60 percent *less* than the market. Various financial services (e.g., Standard & Poor's) will provide beta values for specific companies.

Over a number of years, a company's stock may have a positive beta during some periods and a negative beta during others.

EXAMPLE 1.10

Company *P* shows the following earnings trend:

19X0	$80,000
19X1	75,000
19X2	70,000

The standard deviation in earnings is computed as follows:

$$SD = \sqrt{\frac{\Sigma (y - \bar{y})^2}{n}}$$

$$y = \frac{\Sigma y}{n} = \frac{\$80,000 + \$75,000 + \$70,000}{3}$$

$$= \frac{\$225,000}{3} = \$75,000$$

Year	$(y-\bar{y})$	$(y-\bar{y})^2$
19X0	$+5,000	$25,000,000
19X2	0	0
19X3	$-5,000	$25,000,000
Total		$50,000,000

$$SD = \sqrt{\frac{\$50,000,000}{3}} = \sqrt{16,666,666}$$

= $4,082.48 (rounded)

The coefficient of variation in earnings is computed as follows:

$$CV = \frac{SD}{\bar{y}} = \frac{\$4,082.48}{\$75,000} = 5.4\%$$

What is the significance of gross profit percentage?

IMPORTANT FOR MANAGEMENT EXECUTIVES: A high gross profit percentage (gross profit divided by sales) reflects positive earnings quality. Usually it means the business can control its manufacturing costs, a task sometimes difficult to achieve. NOTE: Operating expenses are easier to control because they are internal and can be subject to cost control programs.

What is operating leverage?

Operating leverage refers to the extent that fixed costs are contained in the company's cost structure. Use these ratios to measure operating leverage:

- Fixed cost to total cost
- Percent change in operating income to the percent change in sales volume
- Net income to fixed costs

An increase in the first two or a decrease in the third indicates higher fixed costs. These may cause earnings to vacillate, thereby suggesting lower earnings quality.

ATTENTION FINANCIAL MANAGERS: The company's cost structure affects earnings as volume changes. Companies with high operating leverage will have high risk because fixed cost cannot be lowered when revenue declines.

A high ratio of variable cost to total cost shows earnings indicate stability. Variable costs may be adjusted more easily than fixed cost during a decline in product demand. MARKETING MANAGERS REMEMBER: The cost makeup of products affects product line profitability.

What are the advantages of original sales generating further revenue?

When a company can obtain additional revenue from its initial sale, this means greater earnings stability. For example, the sale of a TV may lead to further business (such as a service contract, tubes, etc.). FOR MARKETING MANAGERS: When setting policy, note trends as reflected in the following ratios:

- Replacement and maintenance revenue to new sales
- Replacement and maintenance revenue to total revenue
- Replacement and maintenance revenue to net income

Rising trends point to better earnings quality.

How do I recognize an opportunist market?

Short-term schemes (such as single government contracts) increase profit temporarily and thus are of poor earnings quality. FOR MARKETING MANAGERS: Be sure to compute the following ratios:

- Short-lived income to total revenue
- Short-lived income to net income

How do I evaluate the product line?

In terms of marketing strategy, companies whose product line demand is relatively constant are minimally affected by the business cycle. Companies with product lines that relate closely to gross national product show more fluctuation in earnings. SUGGESTION: To stabilize operations, products should be added that have different seasonal peaks. The following factors should be considered when evaluating the product line.

Nature of the Product. Certain products enhance earnings stability by performing well in recessionary as well as growth periods. Such products include necessity items and retail trade.

MARKETING MANAGERS: The product mix selection is vital. Some products detract from earnings stability. These include novelty goods, high-priced items, excluding those that appeal to a select marketing (e.g., Rolls Royces), heavy goods, and raw materials. Higher earnings quality would be associated with new, similar products that can be developed easily from the company's basic manufacturing operations or new products that produce supplementary demand instead of eating into existing product lines.

Variances in the Product Line. Volume, price, and cost may vary throughout a company's product line. The more variability in these elements, the greater the earnings vacillation.

SUGGESTION TO THE MANAGEMENT EXECUTIVE: You should evaluate the fluctuation in quantity, selling price, and cost for each major product. Try charting graphs. Also, compute the standard deviation by product. MARKETING MANAGERS: You may wish to compute sales mix, cost, and quantity variances.

Product Line Diversification. A single-product firm possesses less earnings stability because it is more susceptible to earnings vacillation and runs higher risk of product obsolescence.

ADVICE FOR MARKETING MANAGERS: Diversification in the product line coupled with negatively correlated products is best.

In appraising the product line, you should determine the correlation coefficient between products (refer to Section 7.6). SUGGESTION: Use a computer-determined correlation matrix. Also, measure product demand elasticity as follows:

Percent change in quantity
Percent change in price

If the ratio exceeds 1, this indicates elastic demand. Poor earnings quality occurs when products are positively correlated with elastic product demand.

EXAMPLE 1.11

The correlation matrix of Company I's product line is given as follows:

Product	A	B	C	D	E	F
A	1.00	0.13	−0.02	−0.01	−0.07	0.22
B	0.13	1.00	−0.02	−0.07	0.00	0.00
C	−0.02	−0.02	1.00	0.01	0.48	0.13
D	−0.01	−0.07	0.01	1.00	0.01	−0.02
E	−0.07	0.00	0.48	0.01	1.00	0.45
F	0.22	0.00	0.13	−0.02	0.45	1.00

Of course, perfect correlation exists with the same product. For example, the correlation between Product A and Product A is 1.00. High positive correlation exists between Products E and C (0.48) and E and F (0.45). Since these products are closely tied to each other, risk is indicated.

Low negative correlation exists between Products A and D (−0.01) and Products A and C (−0.02).

No correlation exists between Products B and E (0.00) and Products B and F (0.00).

It would have been better for Company I if it had some products that had significant negative correlations (e.g., −0.60). Unfortunately, it does not.

Unusual Product Demand. Extraordinary product demand coupled with skyrocketing prices detracts from earnings quality. MARKETING MANAGERS TAKE NOTE: This causes an unusual situation that is not likely to be repeated.

Consumer Taste. A company with a product line vulnerable to rapid shifts in consumer taste has lower earnings stability.

Product Introduction. A company that introduces new products to replace old ones has better earnings stability.

FINANCIAL MANAGERS: Examine the number of patented products being introduced to the total product line.

Product Mix. MARKETING MANAGERS: You should determine the degree to which the product line can be considered growth, mature, declining, and/or developing. You should also evaluate the risk in the life cycle. Prefer mature and growth products to declining or developing ones.

1.2.2 Recognizing Revenue Stability

How does product demand affect revenue stability?

Product demand susceptible to outside forces detracts from revenue stability. WARNING TO MARKETING MANAGERS: Export sales to a foreign country may disappear as that country develops its own manufacturing capability.

When a company sells to diversified industries that are susceptible to contrasting cyclical factors, greater revenue stability results. HINT: To reduce the effects of economic cycles, the company should enter noncyclical or countercyclical business lines. ANOTHER SUGGESTION: Geographic diversification reduces vulnerability to economic downturns.

What about costs of raw materials?

Vulnerability in raw material cost causes earnings vacillation. FINANCIAL ACCOUNTANTS: Look at trade publications to appraise cost instability.

A company without alternative raw material sources experiences greater uncertainty regarding future earnings. Dependence on potentially unreliable supply sources (e.g., oil) increases risk. HINT TO MANAGEMENT EXECUTIVES: To curtail a company's price and supply risk of raw materials, you should vertically integrate.

How do I assess risk and uncertainty?

Net income is affected by both controllable (e.g., management decisions) and uncontrollable (e.g., shortage in money supply) factors. The more uncontrollable the factors influencing operations, the greater the uncertainty in earnings. Be sure to appraise the degree of influence uncontrollable factors have over operations.

Riskiness can be measured by the degree of frequency with which abnormal events occur. If uncertainties are great, net income will be less predictable.

There is a trade-off between risk and return. The higher the risk, the greater should be the return (see also Section 5.3).

Corporate Risk. WARNING TO MANAGEMENT EX-ECUTIVES: Corporate risks are plentiful. For example, a company may be overly dependent on a select few employees or there may be a militant union.

Political Risk. Political risk applies to fund repatriation, exchange shifts, local customs, and regulations.

Operations in politically unstable foreign countries point to poor earnings quality. FINANCIAL MANAGERS: You should ascertain the profit and assets for each foreign country considered to be high risk. Examine these relevant ratios:

- Questionable foreign revenue to total revenue
- Questionable foreign profit to total profit
- Export revenue to total revenue
- Export profit to total profit
- Total assets in each questionable foreign country to total assets
- Total assets in foreign countries to total assets

Companies who depend on government contracts and subsidies may have lower earnings stability because governmental spending is susceptible to hostile events and the whims of legislators. FINANCIAL ACCOUNTANTS: Compute the percent of profit derived from government contract work and the extent to which the work is nonrepetitive.

MANAGEMENT EXECUTIVES: Appraise the strictness of governmental regulation. What is the level of current and potential governmental interference? FINANCIAL MANAGERS: Here you should review current and proposed laws and regulations of governmental agencies. Make note of legislative hearings and information from trade publications. Know the impact of current and contemplated tax legislation. Stringent environmental and safety regulations may also be involved (e.g., pollution control devices for equipment). Also, be familiar with the attitudes of the regulatory agency; rate increases may take too long.

CHECKLIST OF
POLITICAL FACTORS TO CONSIDER
IN APPRAISING EARNINGS QUALITY

- Operations in foreign trouble spots
- Regulatory environment
- Environmental and safety legislation
- IRS areas of attack, such as tax shelters

1.2.3 Determining Quality of Earnings

What is the significance of adequate insurance?

If assets are insured improperly, there will not be adequate compensation for losses. A company having a high-risk product line without proper insurance risks uncertainty. SUGGESTION TO MANAGEMENT EXECUTIVES: Where companies within an industry have difficulty obtaining insurance, try pooling your risks by setting up mutual insurance companies. This way, equity interests are retained and insurance premiums are paid.

WARNING SIGNS TO FINANCIAL MANAGERS

- A declining trend in the ratio of insurance expense to fixed assets
- Repeated drops by insurance companies
- Significantly rising insurance rates
- Unusual losses that point out inadequate coverage

What is a segmental disclosure?

Segmental disclosure relates to specific business-line performance, and is required when a company obtains 10 percent or more of its revenue or profit from an industry, product line, geographic area, single customer, or domestic government contract. MANAGEMENT EXECUTIVES: This disclosure helps management executives in appraising risk and corporate earning power. For example, if a high percent of revenue is obtained from "problem" foreign areas, this indicates high risk.

Of what importance is management?

Management quality affects investors' confidence in the firm. Look for these tipoffs to poor management:

- Past mismanagement of corporate affairs
- Previous bankruptcy
- Exaggerations in the annual report
- Inability to adjust to changing times

What do employee relations tell me about the company?

Poor employee relations lower earnings stability. Take note of these indicators:

- Number and duration of prior strikes
- Extent of union militancy

- Expiration date of union contracts
- Employee turnover

Should I take note of interest rates?

FOR FINANCIAL MANAGERS: Interest depends on the prime rate, magnitude of financing, and type of financing. Interest on short-term debt changes with the prime rate, and this changes with the business cycle. Interest on long-term debt has greater stability.

How do I evaluate the type of industry?

In appraising earnings quality, you should take into account whether the industry is growing or declining. Earnings have superior value if they come from a healthy, expanding industry. For example, a firm in a technological industry has greater uncertainty owing to possible obsolescence.

Companies in a staple industry have more earnings stability by virtue of inelastic product demand.

Since labor-intensive businesses have a higher percentage of variable cost within the total cost structure, they have more stability than capital-intensive ones.

FOR MARKETING MANAGERS: Consider the degree of competition by looking at the ease of entry, price wars, and lower-cost imports from foreign markets.

CHECKLIST OF INDUSTRY CHARACTERISTICS BEARING UPON EARNINGS QUALITY

- Technological
- Labor- or capital-intensive
- Staple
- Competition
- Regulation
- Industry cycle

1.2.4 Measuring External Forces

What should I know about inflationary measures?

Consider inflation-adjusted profits a superior indicator than net income when gauging either management performance or amount of funds available to meet cash requirements. NOTE TO INVESTORS AND CREDITORS: Examine the inflation footnote. This tells you what net income would be on a Consumer Price Index (CPI)-adjusted and replacement-cost basis.

Net income is overstated to the extent that it includes inflationary earnings. Why? Because the profits arise from price levels and replacement costs, not operational performance. WHAT TO DO: To see the effect of inflation on net income, you should compare:

- CPI-adjusted net income to net income
- Replacement cost net income to net income
- Monetary assets to monetary liabilities

If net income is reported significantly higher than the inflation figure would indicate, consider earnings quality to be poor. The greater the difference, the poorer the earnings quality. A high ratio of monetary assets to monetary liabilities is not advantageous because of the resulting net purchasing power loss.

1.3 WAYS TO COUNTERACT INFLATION

FOR FINANCIAL MANAGERS, MARKETING MANAGERS, AND FINANCIAL ACCOUNTANTS: You can combat the adverse effects of inflation in the following ways.

Selling Price. Selling prices may be increased at short intervals to improve profit margins. Price catalogues and sales literature should be changed quickly. Keep price quotations for only a short time.

Selling prices should be on a next-in, first-out (NIFO) basis in order to keep replacement costs as the basis for new selling prices.

When a long interval exists between the time an order is received and the merchandise shipped, you should increase prices up to the time of shipment. As work is being done, progress payments should be received.

For long-term contracts, there should be a "cost plus" provision tied to the price index.

Cost Control. You should find cheaper ways of performing operations. Avoid product components that have excessive price increases. Try to enter into long-term purchase agreements.

If inflation is expected to worsen, engage in futures contracts to obtain raw materials at present prices.

Get competitive bids from insurance companies and change carriers periodically when it is cost beneficial.

Marketing. Deemphasize products significantly impacted by inflation and emphasize those that are inflation resistant.

Avoid projects with long payback periods. Do not introduce unprofitable products unless design changes can ultimately make the product profitable.

Labor Aspects. Automated companies utilizing minimal labor do better during inflation. Tie wage increases to improved productivity.

Financial consideration. In inflation, a business with a net monetary position (monetary assets minus monetary liabilities) will incur a loss in purchasing power. Therefore, you should hold a minimum in cash and receivables.

Debt results in increased purchasing power since you will be paying creditors back in cheaper dollars. However, debt should not be excessive.

Real estate is a good investment during inflation. You can also borrow from insurance companies against the cash surrender value of life insurance; these loans are likely to be available at lower interest than the prevailing rate.

During inflationary periods, dividends should be cut back to retain earning power and required cash flow. Do not pay dividends that exceed inflation-adjusted net income.

Asset Management. Efficient asset management reduces cost and risk. For instance, cash management should accelerate cash inflow and defer cash outflow.

Put projects into self-contained economic units. Why? The ultimate success would not be contingent on completion of the entire project. This assists in controlling escalating costs.

HINT: To minimize risk, try joint ventures.

Accounting Aspects. With regard to taxes, companies dependent on depreciation are in a worse position than those depending on research and development. Depreciation is charged gradually, and thus the tax saving comes ratably. Research and development is expensed immediately; thus a full tax deduction is possible.

SUGGESTION: During inflationary periods, use the last-in, first-out (LIFO) inventory method to achieve maximum tax savings.

1.4 WHAT IS THE IMPACT OF FOREIGN OPERATIONS?

When the dollar is devalued, foreign assets and income in countries with strong currency are worth more dollars, provided foreign liabilities do not exceed the value.

When foreign assets are appropriately balanced against foreign liabilities, the company is better protected from changes in exchange rates; this tends to stabilize earnings. WHAT TO DO: You should evaluate the company's exposed position for each foreign country in which a major operation is located.

FOR INVESTMENT ANALYSTS: When evaluating foreign operations, consider the following:

- The degree of intercountry transactions
- Varying year-ends of foreign subsidiaries
- Foreign restrictions on fund transfer
- The foreign country's tax structure

WARNING: Beware of erratic foreign exchange rates. The magnitude of vacillation in the exchange rate is measured by its percent change over time and/or its standard deviation.

According to FASB Statement 52, foreign currency gains and losses are reported as a separate item in stockholders' equity. Look at the trend in the ratio of foreign exchange gains and losses to net income to evaluate the degree of stability.

A forward exchange contract applies to an agreement to buy or sell identifiable foreign currency when the delivery of such currency occurs at a later time. It is used to hedge against exchange risks arising from foreign currency transactions. FINANCIAL MANAGERS: Consider such a contract positively because the company is attempting to minimize its foreign currency exposure.

WARNING TO INVESTMENT ANALYSTS: You should frown upon forward exchange contracts used for purposes of speculation. Why? It indicates that management likes to take risks.

2

How to Evaluate a Company's Financial Position: Part II

2.1 BALANCE SHEET ANALYSIS

This chapter continues where Chapter 1 left off. In the sections to follow, you will learn how to complete your analysis of a company's financial health.

2.1.1 Examining the Balance Sheet

How are assets evaluated?

If assets are overstated, net income is likewise overstated because a loss has not been reflected. Similarly, when liabilities are understated, net income is overstated because an expense provision has not been made.

FOR CREDIT AND LOAN OFFICERS: To adjust for overstated assets and understated liabilities, you should use realistic rather than reported values for balance sheet analysis. Example 2.1 shows you how.

EXAMPLE 2.1

Company X reports total assets of $7,000,000, total liabilities of $2,000,000, and stockholders' equity of $5,000,000. Specific accounts are given as follows:

Long-term investments (lower of book or market)	$600,000
Goodwill	200,000
Deferred pension credit	300,000

NOTES

Investments have a market value of $900,000.

With regard to acquired companies, superior earnings have not been generated.

The present value of future pension benefits exceeds pension fund assets by $400,000.

Restated total assets are as follows:

Reported total assets	$7,000,000
Increase on investments	300,000
Decrease in goodwill	(200,000)
Realistic total assets	$7,100,000

Restated total liabilities are given as follows:

Reported total liabilities	$2,000,000
Increase in pension deficiency	400,000
Realistic total liabilities	$2,400,000

Asset quality depends on the degree of certainty of their cash realization with regard to amount and timing. A decline in inventory turnover, for instance, suggests future inventory write-offs.

SUGGESTION: Segregate assets by risk category. For example, receivables have a higher probability of realization than deferred charges. The more dollars in a high-risk category, the lower the earnings quality. FOR THE INVESTMENT ANALYST: Check trends in the following ratios:

● High-risk assets to total assets

● High-risk assets to sales

EXAMPLE 2.2

Company Y reports total assets of $8,000,000 and sales of $10,000,000.

High-risk items	
Deferred charges	$300,000
Receivables from very financially troubled companies	200,000
Inventory of technological items that are obsolete	100,000
Total high-risk assets	$600,000
Relevant ratios	
High-risk assets to total assets	
($600,000/$8,000,000)	0.075

High-risk assets to sales

($600,000/$10,000,000)   0.06

Risk should be evaluated within each major asset category. NOTE: Ratios are relative only in comparison to other companies.

EXAMPLE 2.3

Company Z reports receivables of $3,000,000. Included are the following high-risk receivables:

Notes receivable resulting from an
extension of unpaid balances from
delinquent customers $200,000

Advances to politically unstable foreign
countries   300,000

You can thus conclude that $500,000 of the $3,000,000 in receivables, or 16.7%, are of poor quality.

NOTE: Single-purpose or specialized assets are of lower quality than multipurpose ones. Assets without separable value cannot be sold easily and thus would have high risk associated with them. An example: work-in-process inventory.

CHECKLIST OF FACTORS
TO CONSIDER WHEN ANALYZING
THE BALANCE SHEET

• The impact of changing political, economic, industry, and corporate conditions on the balance sheet
• Percent of high-risk assets to total assets
• Multipurpose or single-purpose assets
• Effect of government policies on asset realization

2.1.2 Evaluating Operations

What should I look for in the cash account?

FOR FINANCIAL MANAGERS: You should determine whether part of the cash account is restricted and unavailable for use. Examples of this would be a compensating balance required for a bank loan or cash held in a politically unstable country.

EXAMPLE 2.4

Company Z reports cash of $3,000,000.

NOTES

The company has a $10,000,000 bank loan that requires a 5% compensating balance.

Cash amounting to $200,000 has been expropriated by the foreign government.

Thus, of the cash balance $300,000,000, $700,000, or 23.3% is not available for use.

How do I appraise receivables risk?

INVESTMENT ANALYSTS: You can appraise receivables risk by examining the nature of the receivable balance. For example, a high-risk receivable would be one due from a country experiencing severe financial problems.

Companies that depend on one or two customers are more vulnerable than those with many equally important accounts.

Since fair-trade laws protect consumers, receivables from another company are safer than those from consumers.

NOTE: Factoring accounts receivable, a higher-cost financing alternative, may mean the company has liquidity difficulties.

When sales are lagging, the business might boost receivables by shipping unneeded merchandise to customers, sometimes giving generous credit terms. This is a game because the merchandise may well be returned. CREDIT AND LOAN OFFICERS: Be sure to note the following "red flags":

- A significant increase in revenue in the last quarter of the present year

- A significant amount of sales returns in the first quarter of the following year

- A material decline in sales for the first quarter of the following year

Four Indicators of Receivable Risk. You can determine realization risk in receivables by calculating the following four ratios:

- *Annual credit sales to average accounts receivable.*

Accounts Receivable Turnover =
$$\frac{\text{annual credit sales}}{\text{average accounts receivable}}$$

If sales vary greatly throughout the year, average accounts receivable should be computed as a weighted average based on a monthly or quarterly accounts receivable balance.

- *Days in collection period.*

$$\text{Collection period} = \frac{365}{\text{accounts receivable turnover}}$$

The longer receivables are past due, the higher the risk of not collecting. A longer collection period may be justified, however, when credit terms have been liberalized, for example, with new product introduction or as a competitive reaction.

- *Accounts receivable to total assets.*
- *Accounts receivable to sales.* A larger receivable balance compared to the prior year may point to realization risk.

EXAMPLE 2.5

Company A shows the following financial data:

	12/31/X1	*12/31/X2*
Sales	$420,000	$530,000
Total assets	610,000	670,000
Accounts receivable	60,000	100,000
(On Jan. 1, 19X1, accounts receivable were $50,000.)		
Accounts receivable turnover	7.64	6.63
Collection period	47.78 days	55.05 days
Accounts receivable to total assets	0.098	0.149
Accounts receivable to sales	0.143	0.189

Note that all ratios deteriorated in 19X2. Thus, there is a higher realization risk in accounts receivable in 19X2.

Bad Debts. An unjustified lowering of bad debts overstates earnings. This occurs, for example, when bad debts are reduced even while sales are made to riskier customers and/or actual bad debts are increasing.

Be sure to examine the following ratios:

- Bad debts to accounts receivable
- Bad debts to sales

Here are some items to note:

- Overstatement of bad debts sets up an accounting cushion, and this results in understatement of net income.

- When there is a substantial bad debts provision in the current period owing to inadequate provisions in earlier periods, the trend in net income has been distorted.

EXAMPLE 2.6

Company B presents the following financial data:

	19X1	19X2
Sales	$90,000	$120,000
Accounts receivable	28,000	39,000
Bad debts	3,000	3,500
(Sales are being made to more marginal customers.)		
Ratio of bad debts to sales	0.033	0.029
Ratio of bad debts to accounts receivable	0.107	0.09

Because the company is selling to riskier customers, bad debts should be going up. Instead, they are going down as they relate to sales and accounts receivable. By understating bad debts, net income and accounts receivable are overstated, and net income should be reduced for the increased earnings. If you conclude that the realistic ratio of bad debt to sales in 19X2 should be 3.2%, then bad debts should be $3,840 (3.2% × $120,000) rather than $3,500. Thus, reported earnings should be reduced by another $340.

Sales Returns. A large number of sales returns indicates a quality problem with the merchandise. When there is increasing liability for returns and a significant reduction in the ratio of sales returns to sales, this indicates an inadequate quality provision and net income has been overstated.

Loans Receivable. ATTENTION LOAN OFFICERS: Take note of the following indicators, which point to high realization risk in the loan portfolio:

- An inadequate loss provision
- Interest not received on loans or interest rate downwardly adjusted

You should determine

- The trend in the loan loss provision to total outstanding loans
- The market value of collateral to the loan balance

- The difference over time of the loan loss provision to the eventual loan loss amount
- The ratios of loans receivable to total assets and loans receivable to stockholders' equity

What significance does inventory play?

At the plant, wholesaler, or retailer, an inventory buildup reflects a realization problem. Take note when inventory rises at a faster rate than sales.

EXAMPLE 2.7

Finished goods increased by 60% while total inventory increased by 45%. Sales went up by only 15%.

A future production slowdown may be possible since there is a decline in raw materials coupled with an increase in work-in-process and finished goods.

EXAMPLE 2.8

Company C shows the following inventory components:

	19X1	19X2
Raw materials	$100,000	$90,000
Work-in-process	60,000	110,000
Finished goods	15,000	30,000

Over the year, raw materials went down by 10% ($10,000/$100,000), work-in-process went up by 83.3% ($50,000/$60,000), and finished goods increased by 100% ($15,000/$15,000). The inconsistent trend between raw materials compared to work-in-process and finished goods indicates a production slowdown. It also indicates a high probability of obsolescence in inventory due to the buildup.

REMEMBER THIS: When the increase in sales significantly exceeds the increase in inventory, good management is indicated.

EXAMPLE 2.9

Company D shows the following inventory:

	19X1	19X2
Sales	$300,000	$400,000
Inventory	50,000	60,000

Sales went up by 33.3% while inventory increased by 20%. This means good inventory management.

A turnover rate should be computed for each inventory category by department. To compute:

$$\text{Inventory turnover} = \frac{\text{cost of sales}}{\text{average inventory}}$$

Also, determine the number of days inventory is held:

$$\text{Age of inventory} = \frac{365}{\text{inventory turnover}}$$

Poor turnover may suggest potential obsolescence, perhaps from problems with the product line or advertising. IMPORTANT FOR FINANCIAL MANAGERS: A high turnover rate may point to insufficient inventory balances, and this can cause a loss in business. There are cases, however, where proper justification exists for a low turnover rate, for example when prices of raw materials are expected to rise.

When a company uses its "natural year-end," the turnover rate may be very high because the inventory level will be quite low at that time.

EXAMPLE 2.10

The following data are given for Company E:

	19X1	19X2
Finished goods	$11,000	$17,000
Cost of sales	73,000	85,000
(As of Jan. 1, 19X1, finished goods total $8,000)		
Inventory turnover	7.7	6.1
Age of inventory	47.4 days	59.8 days

The deteriorating ratios point to higher realization risk in inventory.

Higher realization risk in inventory exists when merchandise is subject to fluctuation in price or with fad, specialized, and perishable items. Low realization risk applies to standardized, staple, and necessity merchandise. Raw materials are of lower risk than finished goods owing to their universal and multiple uses.

Inventory secured to creditors under loan agreements has higher realization risk as does inadequate insurance coverage for inventory.

Since inventory is reported at the lower of book or market value, the amount shown in the financial statements could be significantly less than the inventory is worth. For credit decision-making purposes, you should always use market value.

During a rapid inflationary period, first-in-first-out (FIFO) may cause exaggerated earnings because older costs are being matched against current revenue.

CHECKLIST OF INVENTORY RISK

- Buildup at plant, wholesaler, or retailer
- Comparing the trend in raw materials to work-in-process to finished goods
- A high ratio of work-in-process to total inventory
- Inventory that fluctuates widely in price
- Inventory used as collateral
- Inadequately insured inventory
- Inventory prone to political risk

CHECKLIST OF WARNING SIGNS FOR EVALUATING INVENTORY

- Unusual costs reflected in inventory
- A change in inventory policy that boosts earnings
- Fourth-quarter adjustments that significantly affect inventory valuation
- Inventory valuation dependent on internal cost records
- Sudden inventory write-offs

2.1.3 Assessing Accounting Practices

What do increased prepaid expenses mean?

A significant increase in prepaid expenses may point to capitalization of items that were expensed in prior years.

How do I assess a company's investments?

Investments in equity securities are taken at cost or market value, whichever is lower. An investment portfolio having a market value exceeding cost constitutes an undervalued asset.

NOTE TO INVESTMENT ANALYSTS: If, in the prior period, an unjustified change occurred from current to noncurrent classification, you should adjust earnings downward for unrealized losses on noncurrent investments (shown as a reduction to stockholders' equity).

Higher realization risk in the investment portfolio is indicated when the ratio of revenue (dividend income, interest income) to the carrying value of investments declines. You should also note that debt securities may be reported at cost even if they are higher than market value, provided the decline is considered temporary. HINT: See if there is a subsequent event disclosure concerning un-realized losses that have occurred in the securities port-folio. If so, you should adjust the investment account downward.

EXAMPLE 2.11

Company F reports the following information:

	19X1	19X2
Investments	$40,000	$45,000
Income from investments	5,000	4,000

The 19X2 annual report footnote titled "Subsequent Events" reported a decline of $7,000 in the portfolio.

Income to investments decreased from 12.5% ($5,000/$40,000) in 19X1 to 8.9% ($4,000/$45,000) in 19X2, thereby pointing to a higher realization risk in the port-folio. Post-balance-sheet disclosure indicates that the 19X2 investment amount of $45,000 is overstated by $7,000.

Higher realization risk in the investment portfolio exists with volatile securities, even though such securities may be more profitable in a bull market. WHAT TO LOOK FOR: The portfolio should be diversified by industry, economic sector, and geographic location. Be sure to appraise the extent of diversification and stability associated with the portfolio. Less realization risk exists with negatively or noncorrelated securities than with positively correlated ones. A vacillating trend of market value to their cost over a period of time indicates instability in the portfolio. Reali-zation risk can also be measured by computing the stan-dard deviation in the rate of return.

CHECKLIST FOR APPRAISING THE INVESTMENT ACCOUNT

- A portfolio having a market value exceeding cost
- Trend in investment income to investments
- Subsequent event disclosure indicating a decline in market value of securities
- Purchasing securities of another company in order to gain a controlling interest when the other company has negative attributes (e.g., high risk)

How are fixed assets analyzed?

Failure to replace or maintain old assets, especially within technological companies, will result in operational defi-ciency and breakdown.

MANAGEMENT EXECUTIVES: You should determine the following:

- Age and condition of each major asset category
- Replacement cost compared to historical cost of the asset base
- Trend in fixed asset acquisitions to total gross assets
- Rate of return on fixed assets measured by net income to fixed assets and sales to fixed assets
- Disclosure in the footnotes of inactive and inefficient assets (e.g., references to downtime)

INVESTMENT ANALYSTS: You should determine earnings trend. Make sure fixed assets were written down at the proper time.

Here's a good sign: An appropriation of retained earnings for future capital expansion.

EXAMPLE 2.12

Company F reports the following information regarding fixed assets:

	19X1	19X2
Fixed assets	$120,000	$100,000
Repairs and maintenance	7,000	3,500
Replacement cost	200,000	230,000

Note an inadequate maintenance of fixed assets as reflected by the decline in repairs and maintenance to fixed assets from 5.8% to 3.5%, the widening difference between replacement and historical cost from $80,000 to $130,000, and the reduction in fixed assets.

If you believe that repairs and maintenance to fixed assets should realistically be 5% in 19X2, you would reduce earnings by an additional 1.5%, which amounts to $1,500 (1.5% × $100,000).

CHECKLIST OF FACTORS TO CONSIDER WITH FIXED ASSETS

- Repairs and maintenance to fixed assets
- Fixed asset acquisitions to total gross assets
- Net income to fixed assets
- Machinery output levels
- Specialized assets
- Equipment subject to governmental pollution requirements

Depreciation. Use the depreciation method that most realistically reflects the decline in service potential of the asset and that results in the best earnings quality.

FINANCIAL ACCOUNTANTS: In appraising the adequacy of the company's depreciation rate, you should compare it to industry standards and to the rate used for tax purposes.

INVESTMENT ANALYSTS: You should examine the trend in depreciation expense to fixed assets and depreciation expense to sales. Lower trends imply insufficiency in depreciation reflective of asset obsolescence.

EXAMPLE 2.13

Company G reports the following:

	19X1	*19X2*
Fixed assets	$520,000	$600,000
Sales	630,000	740,000
Net income	120,000	125,000
Depreciation expense per books	18,000	20,000
Depreciation expense per tax return	22,000	25,000
Depreciation expense to fixed assets	0.035	0.033
Depreciation expense to sales	0.029	0.027

The reduction in these ratios implies insufficiency in depreciation reflective of asset obsolescence.

The percent increase in fixed assets was 15.4%, but the percent increase in depreciation was only 11.1%, another sign of inadequate depreciation.

You conclude that tax depreciation is more representative, and a downward adjustment to 19X2 net income of $5,000 is warranted.

Lower earnings quality is indicated when a reduction in depreciation emanates from an unjustified change in the life or salvage value of fixed assets. In this situation, you should reduce net income by the reduction in depreciation expense.

CHECKLIST OF POOR DEPRECIATION POLICY

- Does not accurately reflect the decline in service potential of the asset
- The book depreciation rate is materially less than the tax depreciation rate

- Declining trend in depreciation expense to sales
- Moderate increase in depreciation expense coupled with a sizable increase in capital expansion

What about intangibles?

CREDIT AND LOAN OFFICERS: Intangibles are usually overstated when estimating their future income-generating capability. For instance, corporate goodwill might be overstated in a recessionary period.

You should carefully scrutinize realization risk as indicated by the following ratios:

- Intangible assets to total assets
- Intangible assets to stockholders' equity
- Change in intangibles to the change in net income (a material amount of the change coming from capitalization rather than expensing is a warning sign)

SPECIAL NOTE TO THE INVESTMENT ANALYST: Accounting Principles Board (APB) Opinion 17 allows for a 40-year period to amortize intangibles. Some companies ignore reality and use the maximum amortization period. Absurdly, intangibles placed on the books before the effective date of the Opinion (1970) do not have to be amortized at all.

EXAMPLE 2.14

Company I reports the following information:

	19X1	19X2
Intangible assets	$60,000	$200,000
Total assets	610,000	630,000
Sales	700,000	725,000
Net income	90,000	130,000
Intangible assets to total assets	0.098	0.317
Intangible assets to sales	0.086	0.276

Higher asset realization risk is indicated by the increasing ratios. Also, the 233% increase in intangibles coupled with the 44% increase in profit may show that net income is overstated. Why? Because of the failure to reflect items that should have been expensed rather than capitalized.

In some instances, intangibles may be considerably undervalued. Patents may be recorded at amounts significantly less than present value of related future cash flows.

NOTE: Patented items have less worth when they can be easily infringed upon by minor change or when they apply to a technological item. Also consider the financial capability of the business to defend the patent in court and take a look at patent expiration dates as well as new patents being issued.

Goodwill is only reported when a company buys another at a cost greater than fair market value of the acquired firm's net assets. FINANCIAL MANAGERS: Evaluate the reported value of goodwill by ascertaining whether the acquired company indeed has superior earning power. If not, goodwill is really of no value.

CHECKLIST FOR APPRAISING THE RISKINESS OF INTANGIBLES

- Ratio of intangible assets to total assets
- Ratio of intangible assets to net income
- Specific suspected intangible (e.g., goodwill) to total assets
- Ratio of change in intangibles to change in net income

What is the significance of deferred charges?

ATTENTION CREDIT AND LOAN OFFICERS: Watch the deferred charges closely. Why? These depend to a large extent on estimates of future probabilities rather than other assets. The probability that expectations will fail to be achieved is relatively high. Or, the company may defer a cost with no future benefit in order not to charge it against earnings. No cash realization can be applied to deferred charges, and consequently they cannot be used to meet creditor obligations. Dubious deferred charges include moving, start-up and plant rearrangement costs.

WARNING: A company may try to boost earnings by deferring costs that were expensed in previous years.

There are instances in which an increase in deferred charges is appropriate, for example, deferring start-up costs when beginning a lucrative new operation.

CREDIT AND LOAN OFFICERS: In gauging the realization risk in deferred charges, you should determine the following trends:

- Deferred costs to sales
- Deferred costs to net income
- Deferred costs (e.g., deferred advertising) to total expenditures (e.g., total advertising)

Remember, rising trends point to higher realization risk.

The higher the ratio of intangible assets and deferred charges to total assets, the greater the asset risk.

CHECKLIST OF PROBLEMS
WITH DEFERRED CHARGES

- Deferral of costs expensed in prior years
- Deferral of costs for book purposes that are expensed for tax purposes
- Increasing trend in deferred charges to total expenditures
- Sudden write-off of deferred charges

What do estimated liabilities show?

CAUTION FOR THE INVESTMENT ANALYST: Incorrectly estimated liabilities for future costs and losses may impair the significance of net income. WHAT TO DO: You should exclude arbitrary adjustments to estimated liabilities when ascertaining corporate earning power. If you conclude that estimated liabilities are being used to smooth earnings, add back the amounts credited to earnings. For instance, net income obtained by recouping previous year reserves may be invalid.

CREDIT AND LOAN OFFICERS: Be on guard: A firm with an unrealistically low provision for future costs has lower earnings quality. For instance, it is illogical for a business to lower its warranty provision when there are product deficiencies.

There may be an overprovision of an estimated liability when management wants to reduce excessive earnings. This also sets up an accounting cushion.

Lower earnings quality exists when more operating expenses and losses are charged to reserve accounts compared with the amounts charged in prior periods.

CHECKLIST OF QUESTIONS
CONCERNING ESTIMATED LIABILITIES

- Are reserve provisions properly stated?
- Has an accounting cushion been set up?
- Were reserve estimates modified?
- Was there an estimated liability established to offset a significant extraordinary gain?

2.2 LIQUIDITY

What is liquidity?

Liquidity refers to the company's ability to convert noncash assets to cash or to obtain cash to meet maturing obligations. CREDIT AND LOAN OFFICERS: You must appraise the current amount of liquid assets as well as future flows. A potential problem is indicated when expected cash outflows exceed inflows.

In appraising a seasonal business, year-end financial data may not be representative. Thus, use quarterly or monthly averages to level out seasonal effects.

SUGGESTION: In financing seasonal requirements, employ short-term credit to meet short-term cash problems. Seasonal firms also require open lines of credit.

How do I determine cash adequacy?

You can appraise cash adequacy by examining the following trends:

- Cash flow generated from operations (net income plus noncash expenses minus noncash revenue)
- Cash flow generated from operations less cash payments needed to pay debt on principal, dividends, and capital expenditures
- Cash flow generated from operations before interest expense

EXAMPLE 2.15

Company B reports the following information for the year ended December 31, 19X1:

Net income	$750,000
Depreciation	30,000
Amortization expense	15,000
Interest expense paid in cash	140,000
Amortization of a deferred credit	7,000
Gain on sale of fixed assets	20,000
Payments on debt principal	300,000
Dividends	90,000
Capital expenditures	280,000
Cash flow provided from operations	
Net income	$750,000
Adjustments	
Depreciation	30,000
Amortization expense	15,000
Amortization of a deferred credit	(7,000)
Gain on sale of fixed asset	(20,000)
Cash flow provided from operations	$768,000

The cash flow provided from operations prior to interest expense is $908,000 ($768,000 plus $140,000), a sufficient cash flow from operations to satisfy interest expense.

Cash flow provided from operations less cash payments needed for debt on principal, dividends and capital expenditures is computed as follows:

Cash flow provided from operations		$768,000
Less		
Payments on debt principal	$300,000	
Dividends	90,000	
Capital expenditures	280,000	(670,000)
Residual cash provided from operations		98,000

ATTENTION: Not much cash is left over!

FINANCIAL MANAGERS: You should evaluate the trend in sales to cash. A high ratio indicates inadequate cash, and this may lead to future financial difficulties. A low ratio points to excess cash where there is a return foregone on the excessive balance.

EXAMPLE 2.16

Company G reports the following information:

	19X1	*19X2*
Cash	$700,000	$600,000
Sales	7,000,000	8,000,000
Cash turnover	10	13.3

Cash inadequacy is apparent in 19X2, and this will lead to difficulties in liquidity.

CHECKLIST OF MEASURES
FOR GAUGING CASH ADEQUACY

- Amount and timing of cash flows
- Ability to delay cash payments
- Ability to get financing
- Closeness to cash of assets and liabilities
- Cash flow generated from operations
- Cash flow generated from operations less cash payments for debt principal, dividends, and capital expenditures

How do I examine current liabilities?

CREDIT AND LOAN OFFICERS: Examine the trend in current liabilities to total liabilities, current liabilities to stockholders' equity, and current liabilities to revenue. Higher trends may point to liquidity difficulties. BAD SIGN: Delays in paying creditors.

When evaluating current liabilities, you should ascertain whether they are "patient" (e.g., supplier with a long-standing relationship) or "pressing" (e.g., bank loan payable, taxes). Then examine the trend in pressing liabilities to patient liabilities. An increasing trend points to greater liquidity risk.

How do I appraise financial flexibility?

FINANCIAL MANAGERS AND FINANCIAL ACCOUNTANTS: In appraising a company's financial flexibility, you should evaluate how quickly assets can be converted to cash, the capability of getting additional financing, the extent of nonoperating assets, and the ability to change operating and investing activities.

WARNING TO MANAGEMENT EXECUTIVES: Excessive financial flexibility may reduce the rate of return. For instance, holding cash enhances liquidity but reduces the rate of return. Open lines of credit will ensure that funds are available when required, but remember there is usually a cost associated with this.

CHECKLIST FOR EXAMINING
FINANCIAL FLEXIBILITY

- Nearness of assets to cash
- Salability of assets
- Open credit lines
- Length of payback period
- Ability to modify policies in changing times

How do I undertake a funds flow evaluation?

CREDITORS AND INVESTORS: Here are 14 measures to use in appraising a company's funds flow status:

- *Current and acid-test ratios.*
- *Accounts receivable and inventory turnover.*
- *Working capital.* Substantial working capital is required if the business is not capable of borrowing on short notice. Working capital should be related to other financial statement accounts like revenue and total assets.

- *Revenue to current assets.* A high rate of turnover implies inadequate working capital. A low turnover means excessive current assets.
- *Working capital provided from operations to net income.* Greater liquidity exists when earnings are backed up by liquid funds.
- *Working capital provided from operations to total liabilities.* This shows the extent to which internally obtained working capital can meet liabilities.
- *Cash plus marketable securities to current liabilities.* This shows the cash immediately available to meet short-term debt.
- *Cost of sales, operating expenses, and taxes to average current assets.* This reveals the adequacy of current assets to meet ongoing business expenses.
- *Quick assets (cash plus receivables plus marketable securities) to year's cash expenses.* This shows the ability to meet expenses with highly liquid assets.
- *Sales to accounts payable.* This tells you whether the business can partly finance without incurring cost. When less trade credit is available, creditors think more negatively.
- *Net income to sales.* A declining profit margin means possible losses.
- *Fixed assets to current liabilities and current liabilities to noncurrent liabilities.* These ratios show possible precarious financing policies. Financing fixed assets with current debt may produce a problem. Why? The debt is due before the proceeds from the fixed assets are realized.
- *Accounts payable to average daily purchase.* Here you see the number of days required for the business to pay creditors.
- *Liquidity index.* This shows the number of days current asssets are away from cash.

EXAMPLE 2.17

	Amount	× Days from Cash	= Total
Cash	$ 40,000	—	—
Accounts receivable	90,000	25	$2,250,000

Inventory	120,000	30	3,600,000
	$250,000		$5,850,000

$$\text{Index} = \frac{\$5,850,000}{\$250,000} = 23.4 \text{ days}$$

What are important asset characteristics?

OF VITAL CONCERN TO FINANCIAL MANAGERS: A business that can sell assets without adversely affecting earnings of other assets has a financial advantage, particularly when the assets are not overly interdependent. For instance, the sale of a marketable security will not negatively affect other marketable securities. CAUTION: Certain assets may be so closely related that the disposition of one significantly affects others (e.g., the sale of a machine in a production network).

ATTENTION: Price characteristics of assets also relate to their marketability. Wide price fluctuation may prevent the business from selling assets when it is in financial difficulty.

Long-term assets (like machinery) are riskier than short-term assets (like inventory) because it will be more difficult to dispose of them.

What about availability and cost of financing?

Availability of funds is required for a business to grow. External considerations (like money supply) and internal considerations (like bank relationships) will affect the availability and cost of financing.

FINANCIAL MANAGERS: Take note of restrictions on the firm's ability to borrow and its ability to get financing at reasonable interest rates.

TO THE INVESTMENT ANALYST: What is the mixture of commercial paper and bank loans? Commercial paper costs less and can be used only by highly creditworthy businesses.

CREDIT AND LOAN OFFICERS BEWARE: The following red flags may appear in the debt footnote:

- Compensating balances have increased
- The effective interest rate has increased
- The weighted average debt for the year exceeds the year-end debt balance
- Loan acceleration clauses are in effect (failure to satisfy a current installment on debt may make the loan due immediately)

- There has been a near violation of loan restriction requirements

CHECKLIST FOR EVALUATING
A COMPANY'S FINANCING

- External and internal constraints on the business
- Ability to issue commercial paper
- Loan compliance requirements to actual financial position
- Collateral value of property to the principal balance of a loan

2.3 SOLVENCY

What is solvency?

Solvency is appraised to determine whether the business can meet long-term obligations when due. CREDIT AND LOAN OFFICERS: You should be concerned with long-term funds flow. Pay particular attention to

- Long-term funds available to meet long-term debt
- Long-term financial and operating status of the business
- The magnitude of long-term debt in the capital structure
- Realizability of noncurrent assets
- Earning power of the company

How do I measure financial solvency?

Here are nine ways to measure financial solvency. Where possible, use market value of assets rather than book value in computing these figures.

- *Ratio of long-term debt to stockholders' equity.* A high ratio points to riskiness.
- *Ratio of cash flow from operations to long-term debt.* This measures the sufficiency of funds to satisfy noncurrent obligation.
- *Ratio of net income, before interest and taxes, to interest.* This indicates the number of times interest expense is met and shows the extent of profit decline the company can handle.
- *Ratio of cash flow from operations plus interest to interest.* This ratio is superior because it reflects actual

cash available to satisfy interest. Remember, cash flow rather than profits is used to pay interest.

- *Ratio of net income, before fixed charges and taxes, to fixed charges.* This ratio evaluates a company's ability to meet fixed costs. A low ratio presents a problem.

- *Ratio of cash flow provided from operations plus fixed charges to fixed charges.* This is an excellent indicator because cash is needed to satisfy fixed costs.

- *Ratio of noncurrent assets to noncurrent liabilities.* Long-term obligations are ultimately paid from noncurrent assets. A high ratio points to greater protection from long-term creditors.

- *Ratio of retained earnings to total assets.* The trend here shows the company's earning capability over the years.

- *J. Wilcox's gambler's ruin prediction formula.* This shows a firm's liquidation value and hence is useful to appraise solvency. Liquidation value equals cash and marketable securities at market value plus inventory, accounts receivable, and prepaid expenses at 70 percent of the reported amount plus other assets at 50 percent minus current liabilities minus long-term liabilities.

What are unrecorded assets?

Unrecorded assets constitute resources of the business anticipated to have future benefit. They include tax loss carry-forward benefits or purchase commitments in which the business buys an item at a price materially below the going price.

What are unrecorded liabilities?

Unrecorded liabilities are not shown in the balance sheet, but they require future payment or rendering of services. Such liabilities include:

- Unfunded past service pension expense

- Excess of vested benefits over pension fund assets

- Operating lease commitments

- Lawsuits

NOTE TO CREDIT AND LOAN OFFICERS: FASB Statement 47 requires disclosure of long-term obligations. You should examine commitments under unconditional purchase obligations and future payments on long-term debt.

FINANCIAL ACCOUNTANTS: You can determine whether unrecorded liabilities are significant by comparing them to total liabilities and/or total assets.

How do I appraise noncurrent liabilities?

FOR CREDIT AND LOAN OFFICERS: You should evaluate carefully the deferred tax credit account. Deferred taxes applicable to depreciation may never be due when fixed assets are bought repeatedly. Hence, the account may not be payable for a long period of time. If the deferred tax account reverses, it is properly a long-term liability.

Even though the deferred investment tax credit account is reported as a liability, later tax payment may not be required. The deferred investment tax credit account is simply amortized against income tax expense. Therefore, you need consider no adverse impact on solvency.

WHAT TO DO: In appraising estimated liability accounts, you should examine their source and sufficiency of amount. For instance, estimated liabilities for litigation can ultimately mandate material payments.

Preferred stocks with a maturity date or sinking fund requirements are more like debt than equity, and will require future cash payment. On the other hand, reported liabilities need not really be such, such as, for example, convertible bonds with attractive conversion features.

Are consolidated financial statements truly representative?

A financially poor subsidiary may be combined with a healthy one, thereby resulting in a satisfactory net consolidated position. Analysis of the consolidated financial statements may point to financial difficulties within an individual subsidiary.

REMEMBER THIS: Liabilities shown in the consolidated balance sheet are not a lien on total assets. A creditor of a given subsidiary cannot be paid from the assets of that subsidiary unless the parent guarantees its debt. Hence, when evaluating a consolidated statement, you should concentrate on the financial capability and individual financial statements of the given subsidiary.

NOTE TO CREDIT AND LOAN OFFICERS REGARDING PENSION PLANS: In case of corporate liquidation, up to 30 percent of the company's net worth may be used to meet pension fund deficiency.

In defined-benefit pension plans, identified assets must comprise more than 5 percent of net assets available for benefits. Determine the extent to which such assets can be realized and their proportion to total assets. INVESTMENT ANALYSTS: You should view negatively a situation in which a significant percentage of available net assets are invested in financially deficient companies.

CHECKLIST FOR LOOKING AT CONSOLIDATED STATEMENTS

- Restrictions on the remission of earnings by the subsidiary to the parent
- Ascertaining whether a tax provision should be provided in the undistributed foreign subsidiary's earnings
- Change in year-end of subsidiary
- Parent guarantee for subsidiary loans

CHECKLIST FOR LOOKING AT PENSION PLANS

- Changes in actuarial assumptions affecting earnings
- The amount of unfunded past service cost
- The variance between pension fund net assets and vested benefits
- Present value of vested and nonvested benefits
- Asset quality in the pension fund

Should I examine the Statements of Changes in Financial Position?

A comparison of statements over several years can depict the present and future direction of the business; it can reveal investing and financing activities and allow better planning for future financing needs; and it can highlight unusual items as well as distorted relationships.

The statement of changes in financial position allows you to predict future profit on the basis of present asset structure as well as planned acquisitions. INVESTMENT ANALYSTS: You can appraise growth potential by taking into account the working capital level. CREDIT AND LOAN OFFICERS: Pay attention to the source of funds and applications.

Sources of Funds. Funds provided from operations are the best source because they result internally without the cost associated with financing in external markets. The higher the ratio of funds provided from operations to net income, the better. Also, look at the ratio of working capital provided from operations to total sources of funds. You should prefer a high ratio. Check working capital provided from operations to total applications of funds. The more the applications are met with funds from operations, the better.

CREDITORS AND INVESTORS: You should also evaluate external financing sources. To what extent is financing being done with long-term debt versus equity securities? What is the risk involved in financing? What is the cost of financing? Will the fund sources be available even in times of tight money?

SOME GOOD SIGNS: Conversion of bonds and preferred stock to common stock is looked upon favorably.

Converting short-term loans to long-term loans by refinancing may provide more stability because debt will not have to be paid back until a later date. This also facilitates planning, because interest rates are fixed for a long period of time.

On the other hand, sale of fixed assets brings a negative implication because the firm is viewed in a state of contraction. The reduction in such assets without adequate replacement adversely affects earning power.

Applications of Funds. In looking at the application of funds, you should note the assets acquired and how they were financed. Are the assets risky (e.g., specialized) or nonrisky (e.g., multipurpose)? WHAT TO DO: Evaluate the assets in terms of uncertainty and expected return. The type of assets bought indicates future direction of the company. Is the business moving into new product lines?

By not acquiring new assets, management may not be optimistic about the future. Is the industry in a downturn? Remember, improper maintenance of capital will negatively affect future earning power because of the possibility of equipment breakdown.

Investments in other companies might be beneficial if they result in diversification, either horizontally or vertically.

An upward trend in intangibles may be favorable. An increase in patents may point to the company's introducing "solid" products for future profit growth.

A reduction in long-term debt may imply less risk because it means less future cash payment. However, if matured, low-interest, long-term debt has been replaced with high-interest, long-term debt, the firm has lost a financial advantage.

INVESTMENT ANALYSTS: Examine the dividend trend to see if it is stable or variable, increasing or decreasing. Are dividends sufficient for stockholder needs? Does cash flow from operations adequately meet the dividends?

CAUTION: Acquisition of treasury stock may be prompted by a desire to boost earnings per share.

2.4 BUSINESS FAILURE

When must bankruptcy be reported?

AICPA Statement on Auditing Standards No. 34, titled "The Auditor's Considerations When a Question Arises About an Entity's Continued Existence," requires the auditor to recognize and report on possible business failure. When the company is expected to go out of business, assets must be on a liquidation basis. A lack in going concern may be indicated by operating losses, deficiency in working capital, and rejection of trade credit. If a business does fail and the auditor has not mentioned problems concerning the continuity of the business, a liability suit could be instituted.

How can I predict bankruptcy?

E. Altman's "Z-score" is a useful measure of predicting bankruptcy in the short run. Z-score equals

$$\left(\frac{\text{Working capital}}{\text{Total assets}} \times 1.2 \right)$$
$$+ \left(\frac{\text{Retained earnings}}{\text{Total assets}} \times 1.4 \right)$$
$$+ \left(\frac{\text{Operating income}}{\text{Total assets}} \times 3.3 \right)$$
$$+ \left(\frac{\text{Market value of common and preferred stock}}{\text{Total liabilities}} \times 0.6 \right)$$
$$+ \left(\frac{\text{Sales}}{\text{Total assets}} \times 1 \right)$$

Score	Probability of Failure
1.8 or less	Very high
1.81 to 2.7	High
2.8 to 2.9	Possible
3.0 or higher	Very low

Use the Z-score in forecasting failure and in telling management whether it should make cutbacks to retain needed funds.

ATTENTION CREDIT AND LOAN OFFICERS: In appraising an entity's susceptibility to failure, you should examine the trend in these ratios:

- Working capital to total assets
- Debt to equity
- Total liabilities to total assets

- Fixed assets to stockholders' equity
- Net income to total assets
- Cash flow from operations to total liabilities
- Net income plus interest to interest

FOR MANAGEMENT EXECUTIVES: Here are other indicators of possible failure:

- Material drop in market price of stock
- Material decline in cash flow from operations and in earnings
- Presence in an industry with a high probability of failure
- Young and/or small company
- Material contraction in dividends

Look to these financial and operating deficiencies to indicate financial distress:

- Inability to get further financing
- Inability to meet past-due obligations
- Poor financial reporting system
- Movement into business areas unrelated to the firm's basic business
- Failure to keep up to date
- Failure to control costs
- High degree of competition

SUGGESTION TO FINANCIAL MANAGERS: You can take the following steps to prevent failure:

- Have open lines of credit with banks
- Get rid of unprofitable product lines and divisions
- Improve asset management
- Engage in a cost-reduction program

3

Internal Accounting
Applications
for Your Company

In this chapter you will find measures and guidelines for internally evaluating your company's performance. There are discussions of

- Divisional and departmental performance analysis
- Selling price formulation and strategy
- Product line evaluation techniques
- Budgeting process and budget types
- Variance analysis for highlighting and correcting problem performance areas

As a management executive, your goals should be many. Among them include profitability, high market share, product leadership, personnel development, productivity, and employee satisfaction. The guidelines set forth in this chapter will help you to realize your company's potential in all these areas.

3.1 HOW TO ANALYZE DIVISIONAL AND DEPARTMENTAL PERFORMANCE

What criteria are used for measuring performance?

In evaluating how well a business segment is doing, use the following criteria:

- Budgeted versus actual cost
- Profitability—in order to arrive at the profit of a di-

vision, prices for internal transfers may have to be
established

- Return of investment
- Residual income

FOR MANAGERIAL ACCOUNTANTS: You can evalu-
ate adminstrative functions by preparing performance reports. Look at such dollar indicators as executive salaries
and service department costs as well as nondollar measures
like number of files handled, phone calls taken, and in-
voices processed. NOTE: It's more difficult for you to evaluate the performance of a marketing department than a
manufacturing department. Why? The former depends more
on external factors, which are more difficult to control than
internal ones.

When evaluating a division manager, you should look
at controllable profit; that is, controllable revenue less controllable costs. REMEMBER: The manager should not be
held accountable for factors (costs, for example) beyond
his or her control.

What is the cost center approach?

The cost center approach is an efficiency evaluation in
which budgeted cost is compared to actual cost. A cost
center is most often the smallest segment of activity or area
of responsibility for which costs are accumulated. This approach is typically used by departments rather than divisions. Departmental profit is difficult to derive because of
problems with revenue and cost allocations.

What is divisional profit?

Divisional profit equals a division's revenue less direct
and indirect costs. Since it is possible to determine divisional earnings, profit is the most often used method of
evaluation. The divisional profit concept allows for decen-
tralization, as each division is treated as a separate business
entity with responsibility for making its own profit.

How do I use transfer pricing?

In determining divisional profit, a transfer price may
be necessary. This is the price charged among divisions for
the transfer of an assembled product or service. MANA-
GERIAL ACCOUNTANTS: Possible transfer prices include:

- *Actual cost plus profit markup.* This allows cost inef-
  ficiencies to be passed on from the selling division to
  the buying division.

- *Negotiated market price.* This equals the outside market price less the amount saved (e.g., for transporta-

tion, salesperson salaries, and commissions) by working from within the organization. The negotiated market value for services may be based on a per-hour rate or a flat rate. If a negotiated price cannot be agreed upon, the transfer price would be established arbitrarily by a higher authority. This is the best price to use, because it reflects the true value of the item.

- *Budgeted cost plus profit markup.* This should be used when a negotiated market price is not available, say for a new product. Here, the selling division has an incentive to control its cost since credit will be applied on the basis of budgeted cost only.

EXAMPLE 3.1

Division A wants to transfer an assembled item to Division B. Division A can sell the item to an outside company for $100. Cost savings of transferring the item internally are $20 (i.e., shipping costs, insurance on delivery, sales commission). Thus, the transfer price should be $80.

SUGGESTION: Do not use a temporarily high or low market price. Rather, use the average market price for the given period.

RULE OF THUMB: The maximum transfer price is the price that the buying division can purchase the item for outside. Do not allow the selling division to charge a higher price. In fact, if the buying division can get the item from the outside for less than inside, you probably should consider the selling division quite inefficient.

EXAMPLE 3.2

The selling division wants to charge $50 for an internal transfer. The buying division can acquire the same item from outside for $45 . The transfer price should be $45.

SOMETHING TO THINK ABOUT: If the buying division can get the item at less than the selling division price, should the buying division be forced to buy inside (at the outside price, of course), or should it be permitted to buy outside? The answer depends on what would be best for overall corporate profitability.

EXAMPLE 3.3

The selling division wants to charge $70 for 100 assembled units. Current statistics for the selling division follow:

Units sold	10,000
Variable cost per unit	$50
Fixed cost	$100,000

Therefore, the selling division's fixed cost per unit is currently

$10 ($100,000/10,000)

Idle capacity (underutilization of facilities) exists. The buying division can buy the item outside for $55, so this should be the maximum transfer price. The buying division should buy from inside because it would be best for overall corporate profitability. Here's evidence:

Savings to selling division (variable cost × units): $50 × 100	$5,000
Cost to buying division (outside price × units): $55 × 100	$5,500
Disadvantage to company for buying division to go outside:	$500

CONCLUSION: There is no saving in fixed cost to the selling division if the buying division goes outside. Why? When idle capacity exists, fixed cost remains constant regardless of units produced.

How is divisional profit determined?

Now that you understand transfer pricing, you can determine the divisional profit.

EXAMPLE 3.4

XYZ Corporation has two production divisions (assembling and finishing) and one service division (maintenance). The assembling division assembles 800 units, 200 of which are sold to an outside concern for $40 each. The other 600 units are transferred to the finishing division, which in turn sells the units at $80 each. The negotiated market value is $35 each. The maintenance division earns revenue of $3,000 rendering services to the public. This division also renders repair services to the assembling division at a fair market value of $6,000 and to the finishing division at a fair market value of $8,000. The costs applicable to the divisions are

	Assembling	*Finishing*	*Maintenance*
Direct	$4,000	$5,000	$4,300
Indirect (allocated)	6,000	7,000	5,000

MANAGERIAL ACCOUNTANTS: You can now determine the profit of each division as shown in Schedule A on page 60. The total profit of XYZ Corporation equals the aggregate of its divisions, or $27,700 ($13,000 + $7,000 + $7,700), excluding nonallocated central costs. This is verified as follows:

Revenue to outside ($8,000 + $48,000 + $3,000)		$59,000
Less costs		
Direct ($4,000 + $5,000 + $4,300)	$13,300	
Indirect ($6,000 + $7,000 + $5,000)	18,000	
Total costs		(31,300)
Profit (before nonallocated costs)		$27,700

NOTE: Certain corporate costs are not allocated to any division. Examples of these include interest expense on corporate debt and the president's salary.

How do I measure return on investment (ROI)?

Return on investment equals net income divided by total assets.

This performance measure is superior to profit because it accounts not only for earnings, but also the assets to get those earnings.

EXAMPLE 3.5

Compare the following data for Divisions X and Y:

	Division X	Division Y
Net income	$ 100	$ 1,000
Assets	$1,000	$100,000
Return on investment	10%	1%

Division X is clearly the better division. Why? It earns a higher rate on assets employed.

MANAGERIAL ACCOUNTANTS: In deriving ROI for a division, you would assign revenue, expenses, and assets, including direct and indirect, for each division. Those belonging to the corporation are allocated to each division by some predetermined basis.

In using ROI you should value total assets at replacement cost or CPI-adjusted value. If you use book value or gross cost, ROI goes up artificially over time because total assets (the denominator) decrease.

SCHEDULE A

Assembling (A)		Finishing (F)		Maintenance (M)	
Revenue 200 × $40	$8,000	Revenue: 600 × $80	$48,000	Revenue	$3,000
Transfer price (F); 600 × $35	21,000			Transfer price (A)	6,000
Total revenue	$29,000			Transfer price (F)	8,000
				Total revenue	$17,000
Costs		Costs		Costs	
Direct	$ 4,000	Direct	$ 5,000	Direct	$ 4,300
Indirect	6,000	Indirect	7,000	Indirect	5,000
Transfer price (M)	6,000	Transfer price (A)	21,000	Total costs	$ 9,300
Total costs	$16,000	Transfer price (M)	8,000	Profit	$ 7,700
Profit	$13,000	Total costs	$41,000		
		Profit	$ 7,000		

When is residual income used to evaluate divisional performance?

Refer to Section 1.1 for a description of residual income.
INTERNAL AUDITORS: Consider the following advantages of residual income as a measure of divisional performance:

- It incorporates risk. The riskier the division, the higher the minimum required rate of return assigned to it.
- It uses different rates of return for different types of assets.
- It assigns different rates of return to different divisions depending on risk.
- It is expressed in dollars rather than as a percent. This leads to goal consistency between the corporation and the division.

WARNING: Since the assignment of risk is subjective, residual income will always have this basic limitation.

How should I weigh controllability?

When evaluating a divisional manager, you should look at the controllable profit for which he or she is responsible. WARNING: If you allocate uncontrollable costs to the manager, you'll breed resentment.

3.2 CONTRIBUTION MARGIN ANALYSIS

What is the contribution margin?

The contribution margin equals sales less variable costs. A detailed contribution margin income statement has the following components:
Sales
Less: Variable cost of sales
Manufacturing contribution margin
Less: Variable selling and administrative expenses
Contribution margin
Less: Fixed costs
Net income

EXAMPLE 3.6

The selling price of an item is $6; unit sales total 520,000; beginning inventory is 40,000; ending inventory is 60,000; unit variable manufacturing cost is $4; variable selling cost per unit is $1.20; fixed manufacturing overhead totals $200,000, and selling and administrative expenses come to $80,000.

With this information, the units produced for the period can be calculated as follows:

Sales	520,000
Ending inventory	60,000
Merchandise needed	580,000
Less beginning inventory	(40,000)
Production	540,000

The contribution margin income statement would be as follows:

Sales (520,000 × $6)		$3,120,000
Less variable cost of sales		
Beginning inventory (40,000 × $4)	$ 160,000	
Variable cost of goods manufactured (540,000 × $4)	2,160,000	
Variable cost of goods available	2,320,000	
Less ending inventory (60,000 × $4)	(240,000)	
Total		(2,080,000)
Manufacturing contribution margin		$1,040,000
Less variable selling and administrative expenses (520,000 × $1.20)		(624,000)
Contribution margin		$416,000
Less fixed costs		
Overhead	200,000	
Selling and administrative	80,000	
Total		(280,000)
Net income		$ 136,000

MANAGEMENT EXECUTIVES: Use contribution margin analysis to appraise the performance of your manager and program. CAUTION: This approach is acceptable only for internal reporting!

When should I sell a product below normal selling price?

A company should accept an order at below-normal selling price when idle capacity exists (since fixed cost remains constant), as long as there is a contribution margin on that order.

EXAMPLE 3.7

Ten thousand units are currently sold at $30 per unit. Variable cost per unit is $18, and fixed costs total $100,000. Therefore, the fixed cost per unit equals $10 ($100,000/10,000). Idle capacity exists. A prospective customer is willing to buy 100 units at a selling price of only $20 per unit.

Ignoring market considerations (for example, unfavorable reaction by customers paying $30 per unit), you should recommend the sale of the additional 100 units. Why? Because it results in a positive additional (marginal) profitability of $200, as indicated in the following example:

Sales (100 × $20)	$2,000
Less variable cost (100 × $18)	(1,800)
Contribution margin	200
Less fixed cost	0 *
Net income	$ 200

*Because of idle capacity, there is no additional fixed cost. If the order were to increase fixed cost by $50, say, because it required a special tool, it is still financially advantageous to sell the item at $20. The additional profit is now $150, as illustrated in this example:

Sales (100 × $20)	$2,000
Less variable cost (100 × $18)	(1,800)
Contribution margin	200
Less fixed cost	(50)
Net income	$ 150

EXAMPLE 3.8

Financial data for T Corporation are given as follows:

	Per Unit
Selling price	$5.40
Direct material	1.50
Direct labor	1.70
Variable overhead	0.40
Fixed overhead ($100,000/40,000 units)	2.50

Selling and administrative expenses are fixed except for sales commissions, which are 12% of the selling price. Idle capacity exists.

An additional order has been received for 600 units from a prospective customer at a selling price of $4.50. You should accept the order because, since fixed costs stay the same at idle capacity, a net profit results, as illustrated in this example:

Sales (600 × $4.50)	$2,700
Less variable manufacturing costs (600 × $3.60ᵃ)	(2,160)
Manufacturing contribution margin	$ 540
Less variable selling and administrative expenses (12% × $2,700)	(324)
Contribution margin	$ 216
Less fixed cost	(0)
Net income	$ 216

ᵃVariable manufacturing cost equals variable manufacturing cost per unit times number of units produced.

EXAMPLE 3.9

The marketing manager had decided that for Product A he wants a markup of 30% over cost. Particulars concerning a unit of Product A are given as follows:

Direct material	$ 4,000
Direct labor	10,000
Overhead	2,500
Total cost	$16,500
Markup on cost (30%)	4,950
Selling price	$21,450

Total direct labor for the year equals $1,200,000. Total overhead for the year equals 25% of direct labor ($300,000), of which 40% is fixed and 60% is variable. The customer offers to buy a unit of Product A for $18,000. Idle capacity exists. You should accept the extra order because it provides a marginal profit, as indicated in this example:

Selling price		$18,000
Less variable costs		
Direct material	$4,000	
Direct Labor	10,000	
Variable overhead ($10,000 × 15%)ᵃ	1,500	(15,500)
Contribution margin		$2,500
Less fixed overhead		(0)
Net income		$ 2,500

ᵃVariable overhead equals 15% of direct labor, calculated as follows:

$$\frac{\text{Variable overhead}}{\text{Direct labor}} = \frac{60\% \times \$300,000}{\$1,200,000}$$
$$= \frac{\$180,000}{\$1,200,000} = 15\% \text{ of direct labor}$$

MANAGEMENT EXECUTIVES: You can employ contribution analysis to see the optimum way of utilizing capacity.

EXAMPLE 3.10

A company produces a raw metal that can either be sold at this stage or can be processed further and sold as an alloy. Information on the raw metal and alloy are given as follows:

	Raw Metal	Alloy
Selling price	$150	$230
Variable cost	80	110

Total fixed cost is $300,000; either the raw metal, the alloy, or both can be manufactured; 800,000 hours of capacity are available; unlimited demand exists for both the raw metal and the alloy; two hours are required to make one ton of raw metal; and three hours are needed to produce one ton of alloy.

The contribution margin per hour is computed as follows:

	Raw Metal	Alloy
Selling price	$150	$230
Less variable cost	(80)	(110)
Contribution margin	70	120
Hours per ton	2	3
Contribution margin per hour	$ 35	$ 40

You should produce only the alloy, because it results in a higher contribution margin per hour. Fixed costs do not enter into the calculation because they are constant regardless of whether the raw metal or the alloy is manufactured.

FOR MANAGERIAL ACCOUNTANTS: Use contribution margin analysis to determine the bid price on a contract.

EXAMPLE 3.11

Travis Company has received an order for 6,000 units. The management executive wants to know the minimum bid price that would produce a $14,000 increase in profit. The current income statement follows:

Income Statement

Sales (30,000 units × $20)		$600,000
Less cost of sales		
Direct material	$60,000	
Direct labor	150,000	
Variable overhead (150,000 × 40%)	60,000	
Fixed overhead	80,000	(350,000)
Gross margin		$ 250,000
Less selling and administrative expenses		
Variable (includes transportation costs of $0.20 per unit)	15,000	
Fixed	85,000	(100,000)
Net income		$ 150,000

If the contract is taken, the cost patterns for the extra order will remain the same, with these exceptions:

- Transportation costs will be paid by the customer
- Special tools costing $6,000 will be required for just this order and will not be reusable
- Direct labor time for each unit under the order will be 10% longer

WHAT TO DO: Derive the bid price in this manner:

Current Cost Per Unit

Selling price	$20	($600,000/30,000)

Direct material	2	($60,000/30,000)
Direct labor	5	($150,000/30,000)
Variable overhead	40% of direct labor cost	($60,000/$150,000)
Variable selling and administrative expense	$0.50	($15,000/30,000)

See Schedule B on pages 68–69.

The contract price for the 6,000 units should be $80,000 ($680,000 − $600,000), or $13.33 per unit ($80,000/6,000).

The contract price per unit of $13.33 is less than the $20 current selling price per unit. Remember, by accepting the order, total fixed cost will remain the same except for the $6,000 cost of special tools.

MANAGEMENT EXECUTIVES: The contribution margin income statement approach can be used to evaluate the performance of department managers as well as their divisions.

EXAMPLE 3.12

Let's assume a three-division company. Relevant data are displayed in Schedule C on pages 70–71.

You can conclude from Schedule C that Division X shows highest profit.

3.3 PRICING TOOLS

What pricing method should I use?

Product pricing is a matter of concern to management executives, accountants, and marketing managers. Use either of the following two methodologies:

- *Absorption costing approach.* Here, pricing equals total cost plus profit markup. This approach covers all costs and should be employed when pricing new products and current business.

- *Contribution margin approach.* When a new order comes in and the prospective customer will buy only at a lower price, you should use the contribution margin approach, particularly when idle capacity exists. Here, the price is set at the variable cost plus profit markup. Remember, at idle capacity, fixed cost is constant. The order should only be accepted when selling price is greater than variable cost.

SCHEDULE B

INCOME STATEMENT

	30,000 Current	36,000 Projected	Computed last
Sales	$600,000	$680,000[a]	
Cost of sales			
Direct material	$ 60,000	$ 72,000	($2 × 36,000)
Direct labor	150,000	183,000	($150,000 + [6,000 × $5.50[a]])
Variable overhead	60,000	73,200	($183,000 × 40%)
Fixed overhead	80,000	86,000	($80,000 + $6,000)
Total	$350,000	$414,200	

Variable selling and administrative costs	$ 15,000	$ 16,800	($15,000 + [6,000 × $0.30])[b]
Fixed selling and administrative costs	85,000	85,000	
Total	$100,000	$101,800	
Net income	$150,000	$164,000[c]	

[a]$5 × 1.10 = $5.50

[b]$0.50 − $0.20 = $0.30

[c]$150,000 + $14,000 = $164,000

[d]Net income + selling and administrative expenses + cost of sales = sales

$164,000 + $101,800 + $414,200 = $680,000

SCHEDULE C

	Total	DIVISIONS		
		X	Y	Z
Sales	$500,000	$300,000	$150,000	$ 50,000
Less variable manufacturing costs[a]	(200,000)	(100,000)	(70,000)	(30,000)
Manufacturing contribution margin	$300,000	$200,000	$ 80,000	$ 20,000
Less variable selling and administrative expenses[b]	(60,000)	(25,000)	(30,000)	(5,000)
Contribution margin	$240,000	$175,000	$ 50,000	$ 15,000
Less controllable fixed costs[c]	(40,000)	(20,000)	(18,000)	(2,000)
Short-run performance margin[d]	$200,000	$155,000	$ 32,000	$ 13,000
Less uncontrollable fixed costs[e]	(60,000)	(50,000)	(9,000)	(1,000)
Segment margin[f]	$140,000	$105,000	$ 23,000	$ 12,000
Joint fixed costs[g]	30,000			
Net income	$110,000			

a Variable manufacturing costs equal direct material, direct labor, and variable overhead. The variable manufacturing costs are derived by multiplying the variable manufacturing cost per unit by the number of units produced.

b Variable selling and administrative costs equal variable selling and administrative cost per unit times number of units sold.

c Controllable fixed costs are controllable by the division manager, if, for instance, he or she is responsible for advertising.

d Short-run performance margin equals the profitability figure used to evaluate the division manager's performance.

e Uncontrollable fixed costs equal costs for which the division manager has no responsibility, such as property taxes and insurance.

f Segment margin is the profitability figure used to evaluate divisional performance. This is the last earnings figure shown for each division. The segment margin of all divisions is equal to the total segment margin of the company.

g Joint fixed costs are not allocated to divisions because it is not rational to do so since they do not apply to them. These might include professional fees, president's salary, and interest expense on corporate debt.

How do I analyze pricing policies if I am a managerial accountant?

Analyze the impact that economies of scale have on the costs and required production time. Evaluate the degree to which increased worker experience (i.e., the learning curve) will lower the per-unit cost with increased production.

You should determine different prices based on the segment involved, whether manufacturer, wholesaler, retailer, or consumer. The price to each segment will differ depending on the applicable marketing costs, such as advertising and distribution.

What price methods should I use if I am a marketing manager?

When you establish a price, take the following factors into account:

- Return on sales
- Share of market
- Age categorization
- Economic breakdown
- Regional location
- Social aspects
- Ethnic wants

Also, consider the customer's perception of prestige—higher may suggest a "quality" image to the consumer.

When you want to attract further business for other products or service contracts, you should prefer contribution margin pricing over full costing. However, do not use this approach if you think selling at a lower price will bring a negative reaction from existing customers.

CAUTION: When you decide to increase the price, do so only to the point that it does not cause a disproportionate decrease in volume. For instance, a 14-percent price increase may result in a 20-percent reduction in volume, thereby effecting overall lower earnings.

Set target rates of return for products that depend on risk, stage in the life cycle, and whether the initial sale generates subsequent business for other products or services. Ask to what extent the product line is affected by the learning curve (see Section 8.4).

3.4 EVALUATING THE PRODUCT LINE

What factors do I consider when evaluating a product line?

IF YOU'RE A MANAGEMENT EXECUTIVE: Appraise introduction of a new product according to its synergistic effects, that is, how the new product fits into the whole product line.

IF YOU'RE A FINANCIAL MANAGER: Decide whether to discontinue products that show losses. In making your decision, consider the following factors:

- Eliminating a product would reduce volume and sales commissions but would necessitate higher base salaries for salespeople
- Fixed costs must still be recovered

You may still keep products that show a net loss based on full costing but that show a contribution margin.

Inventory stockouts should be recorded along with lost sales. Back-order costs should likewise be determined (see also Section 8.5).

SUGGESTION: Finance risky product lines with less risky funding, thereby reducing overall business risk. For example, a fad item should be financed with equity.

IF YOU'RE A MARKETING MANAGER: You can appraise the riskiness of product lines by computing the probability distribution in price, volume, and cost for products (see also Section 8.3).

How should I prepare marketing analysis reports?

To make your reports clear, you should express them not only in dollars but in percentages, ratios, and graphs. You should also provide reasons for any problems along with appropriate recommendations.

3.5 HOW TO MEASURE MARKETING EFFECTIVENESS

How do I measure marketing effectiveness?

Here's what you can do within your job function:

- *Management executives*: Examine product warranty complaints and their disposition.
- *Managerial accountants*: Determine revenue, cost, and earnings by product line, customer, industry segment,

geographic area, distribution channel, type of marketing effort, and average order size.

- *Financial managers*: Prepare new product evaluations in terms of risk and profitability.

- *Marketing managers*: Appraise strengths and weaknesses of the competition as well as promotional effectiveness. Evaluate revenue, marketing costs, and profits before, during, and after promotion efforts. Also, know your competitor's reaction. Identify advertising costs by media, including newspaper, journal, direct mail, television, and radio.

How do I measure the effectiveness of the sales force?

GUIDE FOR MANAGERIAL ACCOUNTANTS: Gauge sales force effectiveness by looking at income generated by salespeople, call frequency, sales incentives, sales personnel costs (e.g., salary, auto, hotel), and dollar value of orders obtained per hour spent.

FINANCIAL MANAGERS: To gauge performance of your marketing employees, compute the following ratios:

- Revenue and/or net income per employee
- Marketing costs to sales

By doing so, you derive a proper selling price, identify poor marketing activities, and establish a proper discount.

FOR MARKETING MANAGERS: In determining salesperson profitability, subtract variable product costs and selling expenses from sales. Also, determine the profitability by type of sales solicitation (phone, mail, or personal visit). Find out the break-even point for each salesperson.

Establish an optimal commission plan for salespeople by incorporating the following strategies:

- Give a higher commission for original business than for repeat business.
- Vary commission rates depending on the territory and type of product being sold (e.g., a slow-moving item could have a higher commission).
- Base the commission on the product's profitability rather than on the selling price.
- Use a graduated commission rate on product sales that exceed the established quota.

SUGGESTION: Do not evaluate sales performance on actual sales generated but rather on profitability.

What financial measures should I use to evaluate success?

Financial measures of marketing success include

- Market share
- Sales
- Trend in inventory at wholesalers and retailers
- Profit margin

IF YOU'RE A MANAGEMENT EXECUTIVE: Look at marketing costs in terms of physical distribution, including inventory management, order processing, packaging, warehousing, shipping vehicle, and customer services.

IF YOU'RE A FINANCIAL MANAGER: Evaluate marketing costs according to the means of distribution, whether retailer, direct mail, or wholesaler. Examine the trend in the percentage of marketing cost to revenue as a basis for ascertaining the selling price.

3.6 BUDGETING TECHNIQUES

What is a budget?

A budget is a plan that quantifies the company's goals in terms of specific financial and operating objectives. Follow these steps in the budgeting process:

- Establish goals
- Develop strategies
- Formulate plans of action
- Evaluate the market
- Look at economic and political conditions
- Analyze competition
- Identify the life cycle of the product
- Appraise the company's financial strength
- Take corrective action

How do I formulate a budget?

Budgets may cover a long- or short-term period. The first step is to estimate future sales, and then production costs are based upon them.

A flexible budget employs budgeted figures at different capacity levels. Choose the best expected (normal) capacity level (100 percent) and assign pessimistic (80-percent), optimistic (110-percent), and full (150-percent) capacity levels.

MANAGEMENT EXECUTIVES: You can then see how the company's performance is at varying capacity levels. Fixed costs remain constant as long as the firm operates below full capacity.

What types of budgets must I prepare?

Many types of budgets should be prepared, including production, cash, sales, costs, profit, purchases, and forecasted financial statements.

Production Budgets. This type of budget tells how many units will be produced and their cost for a given period. If you're a financial manager, this budget will help you to find out your cash needs. MANAGERIAL ACCOUNTANTS: You need this budget for proper planning.

EXAMPLE 3.13

A company has a sales budget of 30,000 finished units. Beginning inventory is 6,000 units, and the expected ending inventory is 18,000 units. The cost per unit is $8. Budgeted production cost is estimated as follows:

Budgeted sales	30,000
Desired ending inventory	18,000
Need	48,000
Beginning inventory	(6,000)
Budgeted production	42,000
Budget cost of production (42,000 × $8)	$336,000

Assume three pieces of raw material are needed to produce one unit. There are 65,000 pieces on hand at the beginning of the period. Desired ending inventory is 80,000 pieces. Budgeted purchases of needed pieces are as follows:

Needed for production (42,000 × 3)	126,000
Desired ending inventory	80,000
Need	206,000
Beginning inventory	(65,000)
Budgeted purchases	141,000

If each piece costs $1.50, the budgeted cost of purchases is $211,500 (141,000 × $1.50).

Cash Budgets. In preparing a cash budget, start with beginning cash, add cash receipts, and subtract cash payments to arrive at ending cash. Cash receipts include anything that yields cash, like borrowing money or selling assets. CAUTION: Cash receipts are not necessarily the same as revenue (e.g., credit sales). Cash payments consist of cash disbursements, like buying assets or paying off debt. Not all expenses are cash payments (for example, depreciation).

OF SPECIAL NOTE: In many cases, cash collections will have to be predicted when a cash discount is given for early collection.

EXAMPLE 3.14

A company sells on terms of 3%/10 days, net/30 days. The following collection pattern has been observed:

- 60% of credit sales are collected within the discount period
- 30% are collected at the end of 30 days
- The balance is collected at the end of 60 days
- At the end of any month, 25% of sales on which cash discounts will be taken are still uncollected

Estimated sales are

	Oct.	Nov.	Dec.
Cash sales	$ 50,000	$40,000	$ 80,000
Credit sales	100,000	90,000	120,000

September credit sales are $110,000 and August credit sales are $85,000.

Schedule D is a table of collections on sales.

INTERNAL AUDITORS: To appraise performance of managers and programs, make a comparison between budgeted and actual revenue, cost, and time.

Zero-Base Budgeting (ZBB). With ZBB, each year's expected expenditure must be justified. Existing and new programs must have value and contribute to overall objectives of the firm. Each project is reexamined at the beginning of the period. When a project does not meet established criteria, it is dropped.

STEPS FOR FINANCIAL MANAGERS IN USING ZBB

- Appraise the activity of a division, department, or operation

SCHEDULE D

Month	COLLECTIONS ON CURRENT MONTH'S SALES		COLLECTIONS FROM PREVIOUS MONTH'S SALES		COLLECTIONS FROM CREDIT SALES MADE TWO MONTHS AGO[d]	TOTAL
	Cash	Credit[a]	Discount[b]	No Discount[c]		
October	$50,000	$43,650	$16,005	$33,000	$ 8,500	$151,155
November	40,000	39,285	14,550	30,000	11,000	134,835
December	80,000	52,380	13,095	27,000	10,000	182,475

[a] 0.6 × 0.97 × 0.75 × current sales
[b] 0.6 × 0.97 × 0.25 × credit sales from previous month
[c] 0.3 × credit sales from previous month
[d] 0.1 × credit sales from two months ago

- Analyze each activity from a cost-benefit perspective
- Formulate a decision package that accomplishes the specified goal
- Rank the decision packages in order of priority
- Assign limited funds to competing activities on the basis of merit

What should the decision package include?

The decision package describes the activity to be performed and consists of various ways in time and money to meet the objective. The manager indicates a recommended path as well as alternative possibilities. Then upper management decides which path to fund, assuming it wishes to accept the activity.

A decision package may be rejected, accepted at a minimal funding level, accepted at the minimal funding level plus an increment, or approved at the requested funding level.

3.7 HIGHLIGHTING PROBLEM AREAS WITH VARIANCE ANALYSIS

What is variance analysis?

Variance analysis is a comparison between standard and actual performance. If you are a managerial accountant, financial manager, production manager, or are in marketing, variance analysis will be useful to you.

Use variance analysis to

- Control costs
- "Red flag" present and prospective problems (this way, you can follow the "management by exception" principle)
- Identify responsibility so you know whom to "call on the carpet"
- Formulate corporate objectives
- Aid in decision making
- Provide a vehicle for better communication within the organization

You should prepare performance reports that focus on the difference between budgeted and actual figures. Look at these items:

- Production (cost, quantity, and quality), to gauge the foremen's performance

- Sales and market share, to evaluate marketing managers
- Profit, to appraise overall operations
- Return on investment, to evaluate asset utilization

***How do marketing managers compute
sales variances?***

EXAMPLE 3.15

Budgeted sales for 19X1

Product A: 8,000 units at $5.50 per unit	$ 44,000
Product B: 24,000 units at $7.50 per unit	180,000
Expected sales revenue	$224,000

Actual sales for the year

Product A: 6,000 units at $6.00 per unit	$ 36,000
Product B: 28,000 units at $7.00 per unit	196,000
Actual sales revenue	$232,000

A positive sales variance of $8,000 is composed of sales price and volume variances. The sales price variance equals actual selling price versus (minus) budgeted selling price times actual units sold.

Product A ($6.00 vs. $5.50 × 6,000)	$ 3,000 F[a]
Product B ($7.00 vs. $7.50 × 28,000)	14,000 U[b]
Sales price variance	$11,000 U

[a] Favorable.
[b] Unfavorable.

The sales volume variance equals actual quantity versus budgeted quantity times budgeted selling price.

Product A (6,000 vs. 8,000 × $5.50)	$11,000 U
Product B (28,000 vs. 24,000 × $7.50)	30,000 F
Sales volume variance	$19,000 F

Proof

Sales price variance	$11,000 U
Sales volume variance	19,000 F
Sales variance	
	$ 8,000 F

How do I apply standards and cost variances?

When actual cost exceeds standard cost, variance is unfavorable. Be sure to determine the reason behind the variance in order to facilitate appropriate corrective action.

Set standards according to their application as follows:

Job Function	Situation	Standard
Financial managers	Cost reduction	Stringent
Managerial accountants	Inventory valuation	Fair
Marketing managers	Pricing decision	Realistic
Buyers	Expensive purchases	Perfection

When should I do a variance analysis?

Standard prices (material price, wage rate) are determined at the beginning of the period.

Variance analysis can be performed by year, quarter, month, day, or hour depending on the importance of identifying a problem quickly.

MANAGERIAL ACCOUNTANTS: Because you do not know the number of units produced or services rendered until the end of the period, you cannot arrive at such variances until then.

How do I interpret a variance analysis?

Immaterial variance percentages (i.e., variance divided by standard cost) not exceeding 5 percent need not be investigated further unless they occur consistently and show a potential problem.

MANAGERIAL ACCOUNTANTS SHOULD DO THIS: When a product is made or a service is rendered, you need to compute these three measures:

- Actual cost equals actual price times actual quantity, where actual quantity equals actual quantity per unit of work times actual units of work produced.
- Standard cost equals standard price times standard quantity, where standard quantity equals standard quantity per unit of work times actual units of work produced.
- Control variance equals actual cost minus standard cost.

Control variance consists of the following components:

- Price (rate, cost) variance (standard price versus actual price times actual quantity)

- Quantity (usage, efficiency) variance (standard quantity versus actual quantity times standard price)

Compute these for both material and labor.

Material Variances. MANAGERIAL ACCOUNTANTS: The material price variance permits you to appraise the purchasing department function and examine the effect of raw material cost changes on overall corporate earnings. The material quantity variance is the responsibility of the production supervisor.

EXAMPLE 3.16

The standard cost of one unit of output (product or service) was $15: three pieces at $5 per piece. During the period, 8,000 units were produced. Actual cost was $14 per unit: two pieces at $7 per piece.

Material control variance

Standard quantity times standard price (24,000 × $5)	$120,000
Actual quantity times actual price (16,000 × $7)	112,000
	$ 8,000 F

Material price variance

Standard price versus actual price times actual quantity ($5 vs. $7 × 16,000)	$ 32,000 U

Material quantity variance

Standard quantity versus actual quantity times standard price (24,000 vs. 16,000 × $5)	$ 40,000 F

MANAGEMENT EXECUTIVES: You cannot control material price variances when higher prices arise from inflation or shortage situations or when rush orders are required by the customer who will bear the ultimate cost increase.

Look for possible causes of unfavorable material variances.

CHECKLIST OF UNFAVORABLE MATERIAL VARIANCE

Cause	*Responsible Entity*
Unnecessarily high prices paid	Purchasing

Purchased material differed from specifications	Purchasing
Inspection did not reveal defective goods	Receiving
Workers' incompetency	Foremen
Poor supervision	Foremen
Deficient mix in material	Production manager
Immediate delivery of materials by plane	Traffic
Unfavorable quantity variance	Foremen
Forced acquisitions	Purchasing
Unanticipated change in production volume	Sales manager

SOLUTIONS FOR MANAGEMENT EXECUTIVES: By examining the nature and degree of the material price variance, you may decide to

- Increase prices
- Substitute cheaper materials
- Change a production method or specification
- Implement a cost-reduction plan

Labor Variances. The standard labor rate should be based on the contracted hourly wage rate. Where wage rates are set by union contract, the labor rate variance will typically be minimal. Labor efficiency standards are normally established by engineers on the basis of an analysis of the manufacturing operation. Determine labor variance exactly as you would material variance.

EXAMPLE 3.17

The standard cost for labor is four hours times $9 per hour, or $36 per unit.

During the period, 7,000 units were manufactured.

The actual cost is six hours times $8 per hour, or $48 per unit.

Labor control variance

Standard quantity times standard price (28,000 × $9)	$252,000
Actual quantity times actual price (42,000 × $8)	336,000
	$ 84,000 U

Labor price variance

Standard price versus actual price
times actual quantity ($9 vs. $8 ×
42,000) $ 42,000 F

Labor quantity variance

Standard quantity versus actual
quantity × standard price (28,000 vs.
42,000 × $9) $126,000 U

INTERNAL AUDITORS: Examine reasons for an unfavorable labor price variance. Some examples are

Cause	Responsible entity
Use of overqualified or an excessive number of workers	Production manager or union contract
Improper work assignments from poor job descriptions	Personnel
Overtime	Production planning

NOTE: An unfavorable labor price variance may be unavoidable when experienced workers are in short supply.

Determine reasons for an unfavorable labor efficiency variance, including

Cause	Responsible entity
Improper supervision	Factory foremen
Deficient machinery	Maintenance
Poor-quality material	Purchasing
Inadequate material supply	Purchasing

Overhead Variances. The overhead variance consists of the controllable and volume variances. The necessary computations are

- Overhead control variance equals actual overhead versus standard overhead (standard hours times standard overhead rate)
- Controllable variance equals actual overhead versus budget adjusted to standard hours. Note: Budget adjusted to standard hours equals fixed overhead plus variable overhead (standard hours times standard variable overhead rate)
- Volume variance equals standard overhead versus budget adjusted to standard hours

EXAMPLE 3.18

The following information is provided by Company M:

Budgeted overhead (includes fixed overhead of $7,500 and variable overhead of $10,000)	$17,500
Budgeted hours	10,000
Actual overhead	$ 8,000
Actual units produced	800
Standard hours per unit of production	5

Preliminary calculations

Budgeted fixed overhead ($7,500/10,000 hr)	$0.75
Budgeted variable overhead ($10,000/10,000 hr)	1.00
Total budgeted overhead ($17,500/10,000 hr)	$1.75
Standard hours (800 units × 5 hr per unit)	4,000 hr

Overhead control variance

Actual overhead		$ 8,000
Standard overhead		
Standard hours	4,000 hr	
Standard overhead rate	$1.75	(7,000)
		$ 1,000 U

Controllable variance

Actual overhead		$ 8,000
Budget adjusted to standard hours		
Fixed overhead	$7,500	
Variable overhead (standard hours × standard variable overhead rate—4,000 × $1)	4,000	11,500
		3,500 F

Volume variance

Standard overhead	$ 7,000
Budget adjusted to standard hours	11,500
	$ 4,500 U

Factory foremen have responsibility for the controllable variance and thus influence actual overhead incurred. The volume variance looks at plant utilization and thus is controllable by management executives and production managers.

MANAGEMENT EXECUTIVES: Variable overhead variance data are useful in formulating output level and output mix decisions. They also help in appraising decisions regarding variable inputs. WARNING: Fixed overhead variance data do not generate useful information for operating decisions, but they do furnish information regarding decision-making astuteness when buying some combination of fixed plant size and variable production inputs.

A consistently unfavorable overhead volume variance may arise from purchasing the wrong size plant, deficient scheduling, insufficient orders, material shortages, equipment failure, long operating time, or poorly trained employees. Idle capacity may indicate long-run operating planning problems.

Raw Material Costs. Examine the variability in raw material costs. MANAGERIAL ACCOUNTANTS: Look at price instability as discussed in trade publications. HINT TO MANAGEMENT EXECUTIVES: Emphasize vertical integration to reduce the price and supply risk of raw materials.

Variances for Selling Expenses. Cost variances for the selling function may pertain to the territory, product, or personnel. MARKETING MANAGERS: Evaluate your sales force within a territory, including time spent and expenses incurred.

EXAMPLE 3.19

Company O provided the following sales data:

Standard cost	$240,000
Standard salesperson days	2,000
Standard rate per salesperson day	$ 120
Actual cost	$238,000
Actual salesperson days	1,700
Actual rate per salesperson day	$ 140
Total cost variance	
Actual cost	$238,000
Standard cost	240,000
	$ 2,000 F

Categorize the total favorable variance of $2,000 into salesperson days and salesperson costs.

Variance in salesperson days

Actual days versus standard days times
standard rate per day
(1,700 vs. 2,000 × $120) $36,000 F

Since less days than expected were required to handle the sales territory, the variance is favorable.

Variance in salesperson costs

Actual rate versus standard rate times
actual days ($140 vs. $120 × 1,700) $34,000 U

Because the actual rate per day exceeded the standard rate per day, the variance is unfavorable.

FINANCIAL AND ECONOMIC MEASURES

4

Break-even, Operating Leverage, and Discounting Analysis

Break-even analysis lies at the heart of your company's success. Whether you're a management executive, managerial accountant, financial manager, or financial analyst, understanding this technique is a must.

As its basis, break-even analysis draws upon contribution margin analysis, discussed in Section 3.2. Operating leverage (see Section 1.2.1) follows directly from break-even analysis. The third component, present and future value analysis, completes the spectrum of analytic techniques found in this chapter. Together, they will help you keep your company afloat and turn a profit.

4.1 BREAK-EVEN ANALYSIS

What is break-even analysis?

Break-even analysis, also known as cost–volume–profit analysis, is used to determine the sales volume at which a company is able to cover all its costs without making or losing money.

What are the uses of break-even analysis?

Use break-even analysis to organize your thinking on important broad features of your business. It is especially pertinent when beginning a new activity, such as starting a new business, expanding an already existing business, or introducing a new product or service.

Many managers within a company will find uses for break-even analysis. It answers these important questions:

- *Management executives:* Have the company's break-even possibilities been improving, or have they been deteriorating over time? What will be the impact of major labor negotiations?
- *Marketing managers:* Will a major marketing campaign generate sufficient sales to justify the cost of the campaign? Would introduction of a new product add or detract from the company's profitability?
- *Production managers:* Would modernization of production facilities pay for itself?

If you are an accountant, providing data for the break-even analysis will be your responsibility. If you are a financial analyst or investor, you might want to know about efforts a company makes to reduce its break-even point.

NOTE: Break-even analysis has its limitations. Refer to Section 4.3 for a discussion of them.

CHECKLIST OF USES
FOR BREAK-EVEN ANALYSIS

- Evaluating the start of a new business
- Evaluating the profitability of a new product line or service
- Evaluating the profitability of investing in a major capital expansion

What are the key factors in break-even analysis?

The break-even point depends on three factors:

- The product's selling price
- The variable costs of production, selling, and administration
- The fixed costs of production, selling, and administration

The stability of the selling price during a given income period depends on several factors, including the general market conditions and the behavior of the economy overall.

Break-even analysis, if used properly, will enable an in-depth evaluation of production and administrative activities. WHAT TO DO: You need to forecast production, selling, and administrative costs and then exclude those that are fixed or variable.

How do I determine the break-even point?

HERE'S WHAT TO DO: First, separate variable from fixed costs. Use this example as a guide:

EXAMPLE 4.1

Company A produces a single product that has very elastic demand. Assume a stable market price over the income period. The product sells for $100 per unit. The variable cost per unit is $20 (this includes variable production, marketing, and administrative costs). Fixed cost is $1,000,000. At normal capacity, 100,000 units can be produced during this income period using a single production shift.

The contribution margin income statement, assuming normal capacity, is given as follows:

	Amount	% of Sales
Sales (100,000 units × $100 per unit)	$10,000,000	100%
Less variable costs (100,000 units × $20 per unit)	(2,000,000)	(20)
Contribution margin	8,000,000	80
Less fixed costs	(1,000,000)	(10)
Operating income	$7,000,000	70

At 80% capacity, the income statement would appear as follows:

	Amount	% of Sales
Sales (0.80 × 100,000 units × $100 per unit)	$8,000,000	100
Less variable costs (0.80 × 100,000 units × $20 per unit)	(1,600,000)	(20)
Contribution margin	6,400,000	80
Less fixed costs	(1,000,000)	(12.5)
Operating income	$5,400,000	67.5

REMEMBER THIS: With fixed selling price and per-unit variable cost, as sales volume drops below normal capacity, variable costs to sales remain constant, as do contribution margins to sales. At break-even, sales equals variable costs plus fixed costs, and net income equals zero. Also, break-even contribution margin equals fixed cost:

$$S_b = VC_b + FC, \text{ and}$$
$$CM_b = FC$$

where

S_b = Sales volume at break-even
VC_b = Total variable cost at break-even

FC = Total fixed costs
CM_b = Contribution margin at break-even

Contribution margin, whether at break-even or otherwise, relates to sales as follows:

$$CM = a \times S$$

where

a = the constant ratio of contribution margin to sales.

Substituting for contribution margin in the above formulas, you can derive these:

$$a \times S_b = FC$$

$$S_b = \frac{FC}{a}$$

EXAMPLE 4.2

The break-even sales volume for Company A described in the preceding example is calculated as follows:

$$S_b = \frac{\$1,000,000}{0.80}$$

$$S_b = \$1,250,000$$

ANOTHER WAY: You can express these formulas in more conventional ways as follows:

$$a = \frac{CM}{S}$$

$$CM = S - VC$$

$$a = \frac{S - VC}{S}$$

$$S_b = \frac{FC}{\dfrac{S - VC}{S}}$$

How do I express break-even in physical units?

To express break-even in units rather than dollars, you need to relate dollar sales to volume. With a single-product company, this can be expressed as follows:

$$S = P \times Q$$

where

P = unit selling price
Q = sales volume in physical units

You also need to express total variable cost (VC) per unit or average variable cost (AVC). The relation between the two is expressed as follows:

$$VC = AVC \times Q$$

At break-even, this formula becomes

$$CM_b = (P \times Q_b) - (AVC \times Q_b)$$
where
Q_b = break-even sales in physical units.

The conventional formula for break-even sales volume in physical units is given as follows:

$$Q_b = \frac{FC}{P - AVC}$$

Again, using Company A from the previous examples, break-even sales volume in physical units is computed as follows:

$$Q_b = \frac{\$1,000,000}{\$100 - \$20}$$
$$Q_b = \frac{\$1,000,000}{\$80}$$
$$Q_b = 12,500 \text{ units}$$

Break-even sales volume in dollars relates to break-even sales volume in physical units as follows:

$$S_b = P \times Q_b$$
$$S_b = \$100 \times 12,500$$
$$S_b = \$1,250,000$$

CONCLUSION: If each unit sold provides a unit contribution margin of $80, then 12,500 units sold will be necessary to generate enough variable profits to cover fixed costs of $1,000,000.

Proof

	Average	Physical Units[a]	Total
Sales	$100	12,500	$1,250,000
Less variable costs	(20)	(12,500)	(250,000)
Contribution margin	80	12,500	$1,000,000
Less fixed costs	(80)	(12,500)	(1,000,000)
Operating income	0		$ 0

[a]Break-even sales volume.

Can I express break-even graphically?

Graphs are usually quite helpful in illustrating break-even. Here's an example:

EXAMPLE 4.3

Figure 4.1 shows break-even sales in dollars. To the left, sales volume is below break-even, shown as a loss. Above break-even, each sales volume shows a profit. REMEMBER: Profit divided by loss equals sales minus total costs.

Figure 4.1 shows four dollar amounts:

Amount	Significance
$1,000,000	Total fixed costs; dollar amount that contribution margin must achieve for break-even
$1,250,000	Break-even sales volume at which contribution margin will equal total fixed costs
$1,333,333	Dollar value of contribution margin when it covers both total fixed costs and total variable costs
$1,666,667	Dollar sales volume at which contribution margin covers total costs

FIGURE 4.1: BREAK-EVEN IN TERMS OF CONTRIBUTION MARGIN

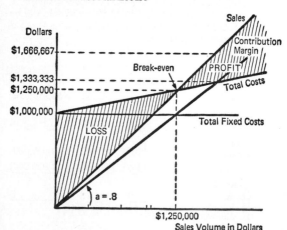

Here's how to calculate $1,666,667 and $1,333,333:
Remember,

$$S = \frac{FC}{a - b}$$

For this formula to be useful, a must be greater than b.
In the given analysis, $a = 80\%$ and $b = 20\%$. Thus, the
sales volume at which contribution margin just covers
costs is

$$S = \frac{\$1,000,000}{0.8 - 0.2} = \$1,666,667$$

To calculate contribution margin at this sales volume,

$$CM = 0.8 \times \$1,666,667 = \$1,333,333$$

CALCULATE FOR YOURSELF: When contribution margin is $1,333,333, then total costs also equal this figure.

Figure 4.2 shows break-even sales volume in physical
units. The dollar amounts are the same as for Figure 4.1.
One new amount, $250,000, represents the total variable
cost at break-even sales volume of 12,500 units. NOTE: At
break-even, sales of $1,250,000 less $250,000 of total variable costs equals the contribution margin, $1,000,000.

**FIGURE 4.2: BREAK-EVEN IN PHYSICAL UNITS
FOR THE SINGLE-PRODUCT FIRM**

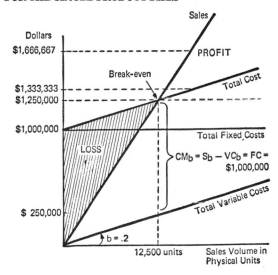

4.2 SENSITIVITY ANALYSIS: CHANGES IN BREAK-EVEN

How do changes in selling price affect break-even?

So far, break-even analysis has assumed a constant selling price. If it changes, then somewhat different formulas for break-even would be applied. Recall this formula from Section 4.1:

$$a = \frac{CM}{S} = \frac{P - AVC}{P}$$

You can see that a is dependent on the selling price and the unit variable cost. If the unit selling price changes, then a would change as follows:

$$\Delta a = \left(\frac{AVC}{P}\right) \times \left(\frac{\Delta P}{P + \Delta P}\right)$$

where

Δa = change in the ratio of contribution margin to sales

ΔP = change in the unit selling price

EXAMPLE 4.4

Using the same information for Company A given in Section 4.1, consider now a change in selling price from $100 to $80. The ratio of contribution margin to dollar sales is computed as follows:

$$a = \left(\frac{\$20}{\$100}\right) \times \left(\frac{-\$20}{(\$100 + [-\$20])}\right) = -0.05$$

CONCLUSION: The decreased selling price has reduced the ratio of contribution margin to dollar sales from 80% to 75%.

Proof

	Amount	% of Sales
Sales (100,000 units × $80 per unit)	$8,000,000	100.0
Less variable costs (100,000 units × $20 per unit)	(2,000,000)	(25.0)
Contribution margin	6,000,000	75.0
Less fixed costs	(1,000,000)	(12.5)
Operating income	$5,000,000	62.5

Now calculate the new break-even sales volume as follows:

$$S_b = \frac{\$1,000,000}{0.75} = \$1,333,333$$

$$Q_b = \frac{\$1,000,000}{\$80 - \$20} = 16,667 \text{ units}$$

NOTE: The new break-even sales volume in physical units (16,667) times the new unit selling price ($80) results in a new break-even dollar sales volume ($1,333,333). This agrees with the preceding calculations.

This is a form of sensitivity analysis; that is, the sensitivity of a company's break-even sales volume to changes in the selling price. In this example, the selling price dropped by 20 percent, which required an increase in break-even dollar sales volume from $1,250,000 to $1,333,333, or 6.67 percent. The required increase in break-even sales volume of physical units would be 4,167 units (12,500 to 16,667), or 33.3 percent.

How can a change in unit selling price affect the break-even sales volume?

Recall the discussion in Section 3.7 comparing standard and actual amounts. Now make a similar comparison between old and new actual amounts, referred to as *variations* (not variances). Three relevant variations are described as follows:

Price Variation. Price variation refers to the loss in sales revenue on the original physical break-even sales volume resulting from lower selling price. *Formula:* Price variation equals the new price minus the old price times the old physical break-even sales volume.

Quantity Variation. This refers to the gain in sales revenue resulting from the required increase in the physical break-even sales volume at the new unit selling price.

Cost Variation. Cost variation refers to the rise in total variable costs owing to the required increase in physical break-even sales volume. *Formula:* Cost variation equals new physical break-even sales volume minus old physical break-even sales volume times unit variable cost.

EXAMPLE 4.5

Using the preceding formulas, calculations for Company A are given as follows:

Price variation = ($80 − $100) × 12,500 = −$250,000
Quantity variation = (16,667 − 12,500) × $80 = $333,333
Cost variation = (16,667 − 12,500) × $20 = $83,333

Analysis combining the three is shown as follows:

	Amount	% of Old Break-even Sales
Favorable quantity variation	$333,333	26.67
Less unfavorable price variation	(250,000)	(20.00)
Net rise in break-even dollar sales	83,333	6.67
Less unfavorable cost variation	(83,333)	(6.67)
Break-even	$ 0	0

ª$333,333/$1,250,000 = 26.67
$250,000/$1,250,000 = 20%
$83,333/$1,250,000 = 6.67

How can a change in unit variable cost affect break-even?

To determine the change in unit variable cost, use this formula:

$$\Delta a = \frac{-(\Delta AVC)}{P}$$

where
ΔAVC = the change in the unit variable cost and P is assumed unchanged

EXAMPLE 4.6

For Company A, there has been a rise in unit variable cost from $20 to $30. Calculations for the change in a (or the ratio of CM to S) is shown as follows:

$$\Delta a = \frac{-\$10}{\$100} = -0.10$$

A decline in the value is demonstrated as follows:

	Amount	% of Sales
Sales (100,000 units × $100)	$10,000,000	100
Less variable costs (100,000 units × $30 per unit)	(3,000,000)	(30)
Contribution margin	7,000,000	70
Less fixed costs	(1,000,000)	(10)
Operating income	$ 6,000,000	60

The new break-even dollar sales volume can be calculated as follows:

$$S_b = \frac{\$1,000,000}{0.7} = \$1,428,571$$

The rise in unit variable costs will have a greater impact on the break-even sales volume. Why? Because the fall in the unit selling price changes only the value of a, whereas the rise in unit variable cost has a greater effect.

How do changes in total fixed costs affect break-even?

You can compute the impact of a change in total fixed costs on break-even by using the following formula:

$$\Delta S_b = \frac{\Delta FC}{a}$$

where
  ΔS_b = the change in dollar break-even sales volume
  ΔFC = the change in total fixed costs, and a is assumed unchanged

EXAMPLE 4.7

For Company A, total fixed costs rose from $1,000,000 to $1,500,000. The impact in terms of new break-even dollar sales is computed as follows:

$$\Delta S_b = \frac{\$500,000}{0.8} = \$625,000$$

As a result of the $500,000 increase in total fixed costs, the break-even dollar sales rises from $1,250,000 to $1,875,000.

How can I summarize these changes?

Remember these simple rules:

- A rise in the unit selling price will lower the break-even sales volume, whether in dollars or in physical units, and vice versa

- A rise in the unit variable cost will increase the break-even sales volume, and vice versa

- A rise in total fixed costs will increase the break-even sales volume, and vice versa

EXAMPLE 4.8

Changes between break-even dollar sales, unit selling price, unit variable cost, and total fixed costs are shown in the three tables on pages 102–104.

BREAK-EVEN DOLLAR SALES IN RELATION TO CHANGES IN UNIT SELLING PRICE

(1) Unit Selling Price (P)	(2) Unit Variable Cost (AVC)	(3) Unit Contribution Margin (P − AVC)	(4) Ratio of Unit Contribution Margin to Unit Selling Price $\left(\frac{P - AVC}{P}\right)$	(5) Total Fixed Costs (FC)	(6) Break-even Dollar Sales (S_b)
$ 20	$20	$ 0	0	$1,000,000	Undefined
40	20	20	0.50	1,000,000	$2,000,000
60	20	40	0.67	1,000,000	1,500,000
80	20	60	0.75	1,000,000	1,333,333
100	20	80	0.80	1,000,000	1,250,000
120	20	100	0.83	1,000,000	1,200,000

BREAK-EVEN DOLLAR SALES IN RELATION TO CHANGES IN AVERAGE VARIABLE COST

(1) Unit Selling Price (P)	(2) Unit Variable Cost (AVC)	(3) Unit Contribution Margin (P − AVC)	(4) Ratio of Unit Contribution Margin to Unit Selling Price $\left(\dfrac{P - AVC}{P}\right)$	(5) Total Fixed Costs (FC)	(6) Break-even Dollar Sales (S_b)
$100	$ 5	$95	0.95	$1,000,000	$1,052,632
100	10	90	0.90	1,000,000	1,111,111
100	15	85	0.85	1,000,000	1,176,471
100	20	80	0.80	1,000,000	1,250,000
100	25	75	0.75	1,000,000	1,333,333
100	30	70	0.70	1,000,000	1,428,571

BREAK-EVEN DOLLAR SALES IN RELATION TO CHANGES IN TOTAL FIXED COSTS

(1) Unit Selling Price (P)	(2) Unit Variable Cost (AVC)	(3) Unit Contribution Margin (P − AVC)	(4) Ratio of Unit Contribution Margin to Unit Selling Price $\left(\frac{P - AVC}{P}\right)$	(5) Total Fixed Costs (FC)	(6) Break-even Dollar Sales (S_b)
$100	$20	$80	0.80	$ 400,000	$ 500,000
100	20	80	0.80	600,000	750,000
100	20	80	0.80	800,000	1,000,000
100	20	80	0.80	1,000,000	1,250,000
100	20	80	0.80	1,200,000	1,500,000

You can make these observations:

- The lower the unit selling price (1), the lower the unit contribution margin (3)
- The ratio of unit contribution margin to unit selling price (4) falls as the unit selling price drops
- The break-even dollar sales (6) is a result of dividing the unit contribution margin ratio (4) into the total fixed costs (5)

Figure 4.3 shows an inverse linear relation between break-even dollar sales and different values of the unit selling price. The lower limit is equal to the total fixed costs, shown with broken lines in the figure. The lower the unit selling price, the lower the unit contribution margin ratio and the higher the break-even dollar sales volume. As the unit selling price falls and approaches the constant unit variable cost, the contribution margin ratio approaches zero and the break-even dollar sales volume will become impossibly high. There is no upper limit to break-even sales.

In Figure 4.4, there is a direct but nonlinear relation between break-even dollar sales and the different values of the unit variable cost. Figure 4.5 also shows a direct linear relation between the break-even dollar sales and the different values of total fixed costs.

FIGURE 4.3: BREAK-EVEN DOLLAR SALES IN RELATION TO CHANGES IN UNIT SELLING PRICE

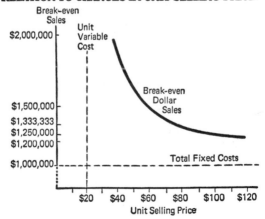

FIGURE 4.4: BREAK-EVEN DOLLAR SALES IN RELATION TO CHANGES IN AVERAGE VARIABLE COST

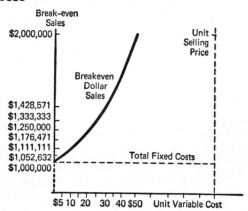

FIGURE 4.5: BREAK-EVEN DOLLAR SALES IN RELATION TO CHANGES IN TOTAL FIXED COSTS

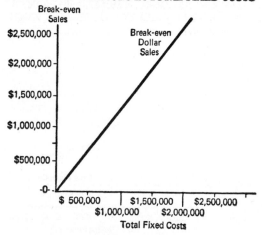

4.3 FROM BREAK-EVEN TO TARGET PROFITS

How can I determine desired profit levels?

The objective of your business is not simply to break even but to make a profit. Break-even analysis can be easily extended to focus on a target level of profits. A simple modification of the break-even formula will help you compute target profits:

$$S_d = \frac{FC + \pi_d}{\dfrac{S - VC}{S}}$$

where
S_d = the desired or target level of dollar sales, and
π_d = the desired or target level of profits

What is the relation between operating leverage and break-even?

The measure of operating leverage used with break-even analysis is called degree of operating leverage (DOL), defined as follows:

$$DOL = \frac{\text{percent change in operating income}}{\text{percent change in sales}}$$

The relationship between degree of operating leverage, and dollar sales volume, and break-even is stated as follows:

$$DOL = 1 + \frac{S_b}{S - S_b}$$

EXAMPLE 4.9

The relationship between degree of operating leverage and dollar sales volume as well as break-even dollar sales is shown in the following table, and also in Figure 4.6.

DEGREE OF OPERATING LEVERAGE RELATED TO DOLLAR SALES VOLUME FOR TWO LEVELS OF BREAK-EVEN DOLLAR SALES

Dollar Sales (S)	Break-Even Dollar Sales (S_b)	(DOL_1)	Break-Even Dollar Sales (S_b)	(DOL_2)
$ 0	$625,000	0	$1,250,000	0
500,000	625,000	4	1,250,000	-½
625,000	625,000	Undefined	1,250,000	-1
666,667	625,000	16	1,250,000	-1½
750,000	625,000	6	1,250,000	-1½
833,333	625,000	4	1,250,000	-2
1,000,000	625,000	2⅔	1,250,000	-4
1,250,000	625,000	2	1,250,000	Undefined

1,333,333	625,000	$1\frac{15}{17}$	1,250,000	16
1,500,000	625,000	$1\frac{5}{7}$	1,250,000	6
1,666,667	625,000	$1\frac{9}{10}$	1,250,000	4
2,000,000	625,000	$1\frac{5}{11}$	1,250,000	$2\frac{2}{3}$
2,500,000	625,000	$1\frac{1}{3}$	1,250,000	2
2,666,667	625,000	$1\frac{15}{49}$	1,250,000	$1\frac{15}{17}$
3,000,000	625,000	$1\frac{5}{19}$	1,250,000	$1\frac{5}{7}$
3,333,333	625,000	$1\frac{3}{13}$	1,250,000	$1\frac{9}{10}$
4,000,000	625,000	$1\frac{5}{27}$	1,250,000	$1\frac{5}{11}$
5,000,000	625,000	$1\frac{1}{7}$	1,250,000	$1\frac{1}{3}$
5,333,333	625,000	$1\frac{15}{113}$	1,250,000	$1\frac{15}{49}$
6,000,000	625,000	$1\frac{15}{129}$	1,250,000	$1\frac{5}{19}$
6,666,667	625,000	$1\frac{5}{87}$	1,250,000	$1\frac{3}{13}$
8,000,000	625,000	$1\frac{5}{59}$	1,250,000	$1\frac{5}{27}$
$10,000,000	625,000	$1\frac{1}{15}$	1,250,000	$1\frac{1}{7}$

FIGURE 4.6: DEGREE OF OPERATING LEVERAGE
RELATED TO DOLLAR SALES VOLUME FOR TWO
LEVELS OF BREAK-EVEN DOLLAR SALES

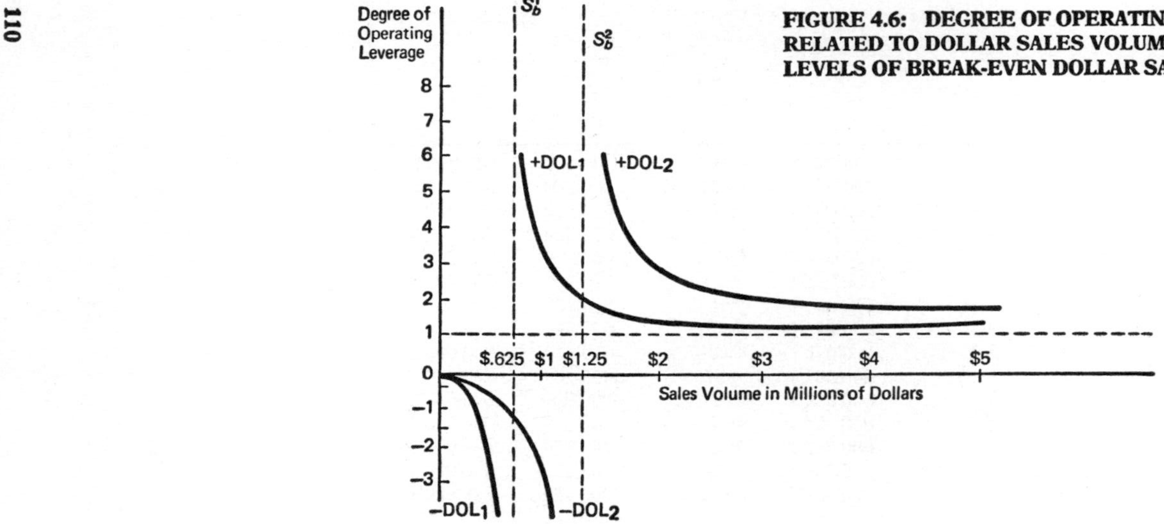

CONCLUSIONS: If you double the break-even dollar sales volume, you must double your actual dollar sale volume in order to maintain the same level of responsiveness of profits to changes in dollar sales volume.

The previous example assumes two different levels of break-even dollar sales. Another break-even dollar sales volume can result from a change in either the unit selling price, the unit variable cost, or the total fixed costs.

EXAMPLE 4.10

From the previous example, assume the break-even dollar sales volume of $625,000 is basically the result of a change in total fixed costs from $1,000,000 to $500,000. The responsiveness of profits in relation to operating income and to changes in dollar sales volume is shown on page 112.

Assumptions: $I = S - VC - FC$ and $VC = (0.2) \times S$; two levels of fixed costs (FC) = $500,000 and $1,000,000. As dollar sales rise from $750,000 to $833,333, operating income also rises from $100,000 to $166,667, assuming break-even dollar sales level equals $625,000. The percent change in operating income (66.67 percent) equals the ratio of the change in operating income ($66,667) to the old operating income ($110,000). The percent change in sales (11.11) equals the ratio of the increase in sales ($83,333) to the old level ($750,000). When break-even sales volume doubles to $1,250,000, the dollar sales volume also must double in order to yield the same percent changes in operating income and sales. The degree of operating leverage shows that the percent change in income is 6 times the percent change in sales when break-even dollar sales total $625,000 and actual sales increase from $750,000 to $833,333. If actual sales rise from $1,500,000 to $1,666,667, the same degree of operating leverage holds for break-even dollar sales ($1,250,000).

What happens when a fixed capacity exists that limits sales volume, and break-even sales increase because of declining selling prices or increasing unit variable cost? REMEMBER THIS: As the unit selling price or unit variable cost changes, break-even dollar sales and the degree of operating leverage will also vary. Example 4.11 shows the relation between DOL and break-even dollar sales (BE$S) for a given capacity sales volume.

CHANGES IN BREAK-EVEN DOLLAR SALES AND THE RESPONSIVENESS OF PROFITS TO CHANGES IN DOLLAR SALES VOLUME

Dollar Sales (S)	Break-Even Dollar Sales (S_b)	Operating Income (I)	Change in Operating Income (ΔI)	Percent Change in I	Percent Change in S	Degree of Operating Leverage (DOL)
$ 750,000	$ 625,000	$100,000				
833,333	625,000	166,667	66,667	66.67	11.11	6
1,500,000	1,250,000	200,000				
1,666,667	1,250,000	333,333	$133,333	66.67	11.11	6

EXAMPLE 4.11

DOL IN RELATION TO BE$S

Break-Even Sales (BE$S)	Capacity Sales	Profit-Generating Sales	Degree of Operating Leverage
$0.3	$6.0	$5.7	1.05
1.0	6.0	5.0	1.20
2.0	6.0	4.0	1.50
3.0	6.0	3.0	2.0
4.0	6.0	2.0	3.0
5.0	6.0	1.0	6.0
6.0	6.0	0.0	Undefined

OBSERVATIONS: Degree of operating leverage begins at a minimum value of 1.05 and increases as break-even sales increase. The relation, which is not linear, is shown in Figure 4.7. The increase in break-even sales or the responsiveness of profits to sales leads to an ever-larger increase in the degree of operating leverage. The given percent changes in sales lead to larger percent changes in profits at higher break-even levels. CONCLUSION: The responsiveness of profits to sales is a double-edged sword. Why? The higher break-even levels operate regardless of a rise or fall in sales.

FIGURE 4.7: OPERATING LEVERAGE AND CAPACITY

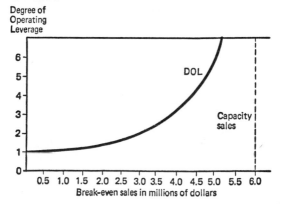

What are the limitations of break-even analysis?

In its simplest form, break-even analysis makes a number of assumptions about which you must be very clear. One such assumption treats the unit selling price as a constant. This, in turn, rests on two further assumptions: (1) the elasticity of demand must be very high for the unit selling price to remain constant as sales volume expands and (2) the selling price must remain relatively stable over the income period. In truth, neither is likely to hold in actual practice, and this makes forecasting the unit selling price much more difficult.

The second major assumption holds that unit variable costs are also constant and that fixed and variable costs have been properly separated, identified, and quantified. However, separating out variable from fixed costs is an ongoing problem.

Once you have determined the unit variable cost, make certain it remains constant over the income period. If it does not, then you must compute a series of breakdown calculations incorporating the most probable unit variable costs.

Likewise, examine the likelihood that total fixed costs will remain constant. Do this at every level of your analysis. If you find factors that will cause fixed costs to vary, then you must compute a series of break-even analyses using the most probable values of total fixed costs.

A RULE FOR MANAGEMENT EXECUTIVES: One of your major objectives should be to keep a tight grip on your company's break-even volume. This means constant efforts to keep break-even from increasing as a result of adverse conditions that lower unit selling price and raise unit variable costs and total fixed costs.

CHECKLIST OF QUESTIONS CONCERNING BREAK-EVEN ANALYSIS

- Is demand sufficiently elastic that rises in sales volume would have no appreciable effect on unit selling price?
- Is unit selling price expected to be relatively stable over the income period to which the break-even analysis applies?
- Have costs been measured properly? Have historical costs been adjusted appropriately to reflect future costs during the income period or income periods under study?
- Are total fixed costs expected to remain constant over the income period under study?

- Does the break-even analysis assume organizational slack, that is, are costs assumed to have been appropriately minimized?
- Is unit variable cost assumed to be constant?
- Is the probable range of break-even volumes estimated in terms of a particular future period or periods?
- Does the break-even analysis provide probability estimates as to whether or not break-even can be achieved?

4.4 PRESENT AND FUTURE VALUE: WHEN YOU RECEIVE THE MONEY

You will often find that today's and tomorrow's dollars are treated the same when, in fact, they are not. This section explores the relation between present and future values of money.

In this section you will learn present and future (also called compound) values in terms of loans, leases, and bonds. You will also find applications to such items as accumulation of a sinking fund, calculation of sales growth, and present value of a fund-raising campaign for a nonprofit organization.

What is the importance of present and compound value calculations?

If you are a management executive, planner, financial or investment analyst, or investor, present and compound value calculations lie at the very heart of your decisions.

Use present and compound value techniques when estimating the present values of items reported in a statement of financial condition. BE AWARE: Every statement is composed of present values of asset, liability, and ownership interest. In reality, accountants do not report most items appearing on the statement in terms of present values, but rather on historical costs or some modification thereof. The longer an item appears on a statement, the less likely it is that these cost values relate to present values. You must be aware of this limitation in order to use the statement properly.

Present and compound value techniques are essential for planning purposes, particularly when estimating

- Present values used in investment and capital budget decisions
- Effects of inflation on organizational activities

- Present values of loans, bonds, annual installments to a sinking fund, and so on

How do I calculate the relation between today's and tomorrow's values over one period?

Use this formula:

$$FV = (1 + i) \times PV$$

where

   FV = future value at the end of the period
   PV = present or today's value
   i = interest rate

The difference between PV and FV is calculated as follows:

$$IA = FV - PV$$

or

$$IA = i \times PV$$

where

   IA = the dollar interest amount earned on the loan by the lender

If you know the future value rather than the present value of the loan, then you can calculate the present value as follows:

$$PV = \left(\frac{FV}{1 + i} \right)$$

EXAMPLE 4.12

Company B borrows $500,000 for one year at 12% interest. The company is obligated to pay off its loan plus interest at the end of the one-year borrowing period. How much must the company pay? Use the formula to calculate the value of the loan at maturity:

$$FV = (1 + 0.12) \times \$500,000 = \$560,000$$

Calculate the dollar interest amount as follows:

$$IA = \$560,000 - \$500,000 = \$60,000$$

or

$$IA = 0.12 \times \$500,000 = \$60,000$$

If you know the future value of the loan plus interest and you know the interest rate is 12%, calculate the present value as follows:

$$PV = \frac{\$560,000}{1 + 0.12} = \$500,000$$

How do I calculate present and future value over more than one period?

Future or Compound Value. If tomorrow's value were two years in the future rather than one, the relation between compound value and present value would be

$$FV = PV \times (1 + i)^2$$

Generally, this relationship for any number of periods is expressed as

$$FV = PV \times (1 + i)^n$$
where
n = number of periods of time

This is the formula for compound value. It can be somewhat impractical when the number of periods is more than two or three. Fortunately, standard tables are available that make the computations much easier. Table 4.1 (pages 135–137) shows computations for $1 compounded at i over n periods.

The interest amount owed on the loan is expressed as follows:

$$IA = FV - PV$$
or
$$IA = PV \times ([1 + i]^n - 1)$$

EXAMPLE 4.13

Assume Company C borrows $500,000 for 20 years at 12% interest. Interest on the loan is to be compounded once a year for 20 years, and the company is not obligated to pay back the principal or any interest until the end of the 20-year period. How much would the company pay at the end of the 20-year period? The maturity value of the loan is shown as follows:

$$FV = PV \times (1 + i)^n$$
$$FV = (\$500,000) \times (1 + 0.12)^{20}$$

Using the table of compound values, you can determine the compound value of $1 at 12% interest for 20 periods as 9.646293. Thus, the future value of $500,000 is calculated as follows:

$$FV = (\$500,000) \times 9.646293 = \$4,823,146$$

The interest amount is $4,323,156 ($4,823,146 − $500,000), which can alternatively be calculated as follows:

$$IA = \$500,000 \times ([1 + 0.12]^{20} - 1)$$
$$= \$500,000 \times (9.646293 - 1)$$
$$= \$500,000 \times 8.646293 = \$4,323,146$$

The calculation of future values of $500,000 at the end of years one, two, three, and 20, as well as the interest amount as it accumulates on the loan for these years, is shown in Exhibit 4.1. NOTE: The compounding of interest takes place once a year at the end of each year.

EXHIBIT 4.1: CALCULATION OF THE FUTURE VALUE OF $500,000 AND CUMULATIVE INTEREST THEREON AT 12% PER YEAR FOR 20 YEARS

Present Value BOY1[a] (PV)	Future Value of 1 at 12%[b] (CV)	End of Period n	Future Value EOYn[c] (FV)	Cumulative Interest Amount (IA)
$500,000	1.120000	1	$ 560,000	$ 60,000
500,000	1.254400	2	627,200	127,200
500,000	1.404928	3	702,464	202,464
.	.	.	.	.
.	.	.	.	.
.	.	.	.	.
$500,000	9.646293	20	$4,823,146	$4,232,146

[a]BOY1: beginning of year 1.
[b]Compounded once a year as of the end of the year.
[c]EOYn: end of year n.

Present Value. Suppose you expect to receive $1 20 years from now. The present value of that dollar is not $1, but less. How much less depends on the interest rate used to reduce or discount tomorrow's value to its present value.

If you assume that future value is known along with the interest rate and number of periods, you can calculate present value as follows:

$$PV = \frac{FV}{(1 + i)^n}$$

As with compound values, this formula can be cumbersome to use. Standard tables are available that simplify the calculations, as least for certain typical values of interest rates and number of periods. Table 4.2 (pages 138–140) lists present values of $1 over n periods at i interest rate.

EXAMPLE 4.14

You expect to receive $1 in 20 years (periods) at a 12% discount rate. From Table 4.2, the present discounted value (PDV) is given as 0.103667. In other words, if $1 words, if $1 is discounted for 20 periods at a rate of 12%, then it is worth approximately 10.367 cents today.

A SHORTCUT: There is an inverse relationship between the compound value and the present discount value, as follows:

$$CV \times PDV = 1$$

You can get PDV by dividing the related CV into 1.

EXAMPLE 4.15

From Table 4.1, the future value of $1 compounded at 12% interest for 20 periods is 9.646293. To get the present discounted value of $1 at the same rate for the same number of periods, divide this number as follows:

$$PV = \frac{1}{9.646293} = 0.103667$$

Proof
$$CV \times PVD = 1$$
$$9.646293 \times 0.103667 = 1$$

EXAMPLE 4.16

In Example 4.13 we learned that the future value of $500,000 compounded at 12% for 20 years is $4,823,146. Reversing this, you can calculate the present value of this amount as follows:

$$PV = \frac{FV}{(1 + i)^n} = \frac{1}{(1 + i)^n} \times FV$$
$$PV = \frac{\$4,823,146}{(1 + 0.12)^{20}} = \frac{1}{(1 + 0.12)^{20}} \times \$4,823,146$$
$$PV = 0.103667 \times \$4,823,146 = \$500,001$$

Calculations of present values for several years are given in Exhibit 4.2.

How do I determine present and future value of an ordinary annuity?

Present Value. An annuity is a series of payments over time. When the payments are made at the end of each period, it is known as an ordinary annuity. Annuities with payments made at the beginning of the period are called annuities due or annuity in advance.

One approach to determining the present or future value of an annuity is to separate each payment, calculate the values, and aggregate them over the length of its life. If the annuity consists of equal payments made at equal time

EXHIBIT 4.2: ALTERNATIVE CALCULATION OF THE FUTURE VALUE OF $500,000 AT 12% PER YEAR FOR 20 YEARS

BOYn	Present Value BOYn[a] (PV)	Single Period Compounded at 12%	Future Value EOYn[b] (FV)
1	$ 500,000	1.12	$ 560,000
2	560,000	1.12	627,200
3	627,200	1.12	702,464
.	.	.	.
.	.	.	.
.	.	.	.
20	$4,306,380	1.12	$4,823,146

[a]BOYn: beginning of year n.
[b]EOYn: end of year n.

intervals, then the calculations can be simplified considerably.

The amount an investor would be willing to invest in an annuity (or lease) is shown as follows:

$$PV = \frac{R}{(1 + i)} + \frac{R}{(1 + i)^2} + \cdots + \frac{R}{(1 + i)^n}$$
$$PV = \frac{R}{i} - \frac{1}{(1 + i)^n} \times \frac{R}{i}$$

where

PV = present value of the annuity (or lease)
R = equal annuity payments (or rentals)
i   = interest rate (or rate of return desired by investor)

Notice that this formula really has two parts, each a present value calculation. The first part

$$PV = \frac{R}{i}$$

defines the formula for a perpetual annuity, that is, one whose payments continue indefinitely.

When an annuity is for a defined period of time, you need to subtract the present value of the annual payments for the years after the periods have expired. This is done with the following formula:

$$PV = \frac{1}{(1 + i)^n} \times \frac{R}{i}$$

From this you can see that the first formula equals the difference of the second and third formulas. In other words, if you subtract the present value at the end of the periods from its present value today, you will arrive at the present value of the annuity.

The calculations can be simplified by using a standard table, such as Table 4.3 (pages 141–143). This shows the present values of an ordinary annuity of $1 per period for a given number of periods at a given interest rate.

EXAMPLE 4.17

Company C leases a property that it owns. The lease provides an annual rental income of $25,000 per year for 20 years. The lessee covers all costs associated with the leased property under the terms of the lease, so that the $25,000 per year is pure income to the lessor. Simple multiplication tells you that the rent payment to be paid over 20 years is $500,000. Assume this amount is to be paid in a series of equal payments. How much would be paid to produce a cash flow of $25,000 per year over 20 years? In other words, what is the present value of the 20 payments of $25,000 each?

Using the preceding formula, the calculations are as follows:

$$PV = \frac{\$25,000}{0.12} - \frac{1}{(1 + 0.12)^{20}} \times \frac{\$25,000}{0.12}$$
$$PV = \$208,333 - (0.103667)(\$208,333)$$
$$PV = \$208,333 - \$21,597$$
$$PV = \$186,736$$

In the case of the lease, payments of $25,000 per year continue forever; that is, perpetually. The present value of the leased property to the owner at the time it is leased for 20 years at $25,000 per year with payments made at the end of each year and at a desired rate of return of 12% would be calculated as follows:*

$$PV = \frac{\$25,000}{0.12} = \$208,333$$

Over a defined 20-year period, however, the present value of the lease is calculated as follows:

$$PV = \frac{1}{(1 + 0.12)^{20}} \times \frac{\$25,000}{0.12}$$
$$PV = 0.103667 \times \$208,333 = \$21,597$$

*This assumes the property will not deteriorate but will provide the same quality of services indefinitely.

From Table 4.3, the present value of $1 lease for 20 periods at 12% interest is 7.469444. Therefore, the present value of this lease is $25,000 × 7.469444, or $186,736.

Present Value of an Annuity Due. With an annuity due, periodic payments take place at the beginning of the period. The formula for calculating the present value of an annuity due is

$$PV_{ad} = R + \frac{R}{(1+i)} + \frac{R}{(1+i)^2} + \cdots + \frac{R}{(1+i)^{n-1}}$$

$$PV_{ad} = \frac{R(1+i)}{i} - \frac{1}{(1+i)^n} \times \frac{R(1+i)}{i}$$

You can also use Table 4.3 to calculate the present value of an annuity due. To do so, find the present value of $1 for one period less than the life of the annuity. Then add 1 to this number.

EXAMPLE 4.18

Consider the preceding example to be an annuity due. Calculations for the present value are shown as follows:

$$PV = \frac{(\$25,000)(1+0.12)}{0.12} - \frac{1}{(1+0.12)^{20}}$$
$$\times \frac{(\$25,000)(1+0.12)}{0.12}$$

$$PV = \frac{\$28,000}{0.12} - 0.103667$$
$$\times \frac{\$28,000}{0.12}$$

$$PV = \$233,333 - 0.103667 \times \$233,333$$
$$PV = \$233,333 - \$24,189$$
$$PV = \$209,144$$

Table 4.3 gives the present value of $1 for 19 years as 7.365777. Thus,

$$PV = 8.365777 \times \$25,000 = \$209,144$$

The relationship between the present value of an annuity due to an ordinary annuity is shown as follows:

$$PV_{ad} = (1+i) \times PV_{oa}$$
where

PV_{ad} = present value of an annuity due

PV_{oa} = present value of an ordinary annuity

Using the preceding examples, this formula can be applied as follows:

$$PV_{ad} = (1 + 0.12) \times \$186,736 = \$209,144$$

Future Value of an Ordinary Annuity. The formula for calculating the future value of an ordinary annuity is

$$FV_{oa} = R(1 + i)^{n-1} + R(1 + i)^{n-2} + \ldots$$
$$+ R(1 + i)^2 + R(1 + i) + R$$
$$FV_{oa} = (1 + i)^n$$
$$\times \frac{R}{i} - \frac{R}{i}$$

Table 4.4 (pages 144–146) is a standard table for calculation of future values.

EXAMPLE 4.19

Assume Company D plans to pay into a municipal bond fund $25,000 per year, at the end of each year, for the next 20 years. The fund earns an interest of 12% compounded once a year. What accumulated amount would be expected at the end of 20 years, or what is the future value of this ordinary annuity?

Calculations are

$$FV_{oa} = (1 + 0.12)^{20} \times \frac{\$25,000}{0.12} - \frac{\$25,000}{0.12}$$
$$FV_{oa} = (9.646293) \times (\$208,333) - \$208,333$$
$$FV_{oa} = \$2,009,641 - \$208,333 = \$1,801,308$$

By using Table 4.4 to calculate the accumulated value of the municipal bond fund at the end of 10 years, you can check your work:

$$FV_{oa} = 72.052442 \times \$25,000 = \$1,801,308$$

Actually, the future value of an ordinary annuity uses two future values. Consider the first part of the formula, which takes the present value of an ordinary perpetual annuity and calculates its future value. In terms of the municipal bond fund example, the present value is calculated at $208,333. This is then multiplied by the future value of $1 for 20 periods at 12 percent interest per period, yielding $2,009,641, or the future value of an ordinary perpetual annuity after 20 years. However, if the fund is not perpetual, but terminates after 20 years, the present value must be calculated for 20 periods. By subtracting $208,333 from $2,009,641, you arrive at the future value of the 20-year municipal bond fund at the end of its 20-year life. NOTE: You can speak of the present value of a perpetual annuity, but future value of a perpetual annuity must be tied into a specific future year.

Future Value of an Annuity Due. The formula for calculating the future value of an annuity due is given as follows:

$$FV_{ad} = R(1 + i)^n + R(1 + i)^{n-1} + \ldots$$
$$+ R(1 + i)^2 + R(1 + i)$$
$$FV_{ad} = (1 + i) \times \left([1 + i]^n \times \frac{R}{i} - \frac{R}{i} \right)$$

You can also use Table 4.4 to calculate future value of an annuity.

EXAMPLE 4.20

Use the previous example of a 20-year municipal bond fund at 12% interest compounded once a year. This time, however, assume the annual payment is made at the beginning of the year. Of course, no payment will be made into the fund at the end of the twentieth year.

The accumulated value of the fund is calculated as follows:

$$FV_{ad} = (1 + 0.12) \times \left([1 + 0.12]^{20} \right.$$
$$\left. \times \left[\frac{\$25,000}{0.12} - \frac{\$25,000}{0.12} \right] \right)$$
$$FV_{ad} = 1.12 \times \$1,801,308 = \$2,017,465$$

Using Table 4.4, find the future value of $1 for 21 years (81.698736). Then subtract 1 from this to obtain 80.698736. This number is then used to calculate future value of the annuity due as follows:

$$FV_{ad} = 80.698736 \times \$25,000 = \$2,017,468$$

What are the uses of present and compound values?

Amortizing a Loan. The methods previously described can be used to calculate the payments required to amortize a loan when the loan possesses the appropriate characteristics. Use this formula to calculate the amount of equal payments required:

$$R = \frac{PV_{oa}}{IF_{poa}}$$

where

R = amount of the equal payment
PV_{oa} = present value of the ordinary annuity
IF_{poa} = interest factor of an ordinary annuity, obtained from Table 4.3

EXAMPLE 4.21

Company A borrows $500,000 for 20 years at an interest rate of 12% per year compounded once a year. The loan agreement requires the company to repay the loan, both interest and principal, in a series of 20 equal payments to be made at the end of each year. Such terms are in reality an ordinary annuity.

Calculations follow:

$$R = \frac{\$500,000}{7.469444} = \$66,939.99$$

The interest factor of 7.469444 is obtained from Table 4. The 20 equal installments of $66,939.39 will pay the $500,000 loan, both interest and principal, over the 20-year period. This is further demonstrated in Exhibit 4.3.

NOTE THIS: At the end of year one, the first installment of $66,939.39 is divided between interest and principal. Interest is calculated simply at 12% of $500,000, or $60,000. The balance of the payment, $6,939.39, is used to reduce the principal. As the balance of the loan is reduced, the amount of interest falls and the amount applied to the principal rises.

Market Value of a Bond. A long-term bond can be amortized in the same way as a loan. Present-value methods are appropriate here, too.

EXHIBIT 4.3: AMORTIZING A LOAN

End of Year	Balance of Loan	ANNUAL INSTALLMENTS		
		Interest	Principal	Total
0	$500,000.00			
1	493,060.61	$ 60,000.00	$ 6,939.39	$ 66,939.39
2	485,288.49	59,167.27	7,772.12	66,939.39
3	476,583.72	58,234.62	8,704.77	66,939.39
·	·	·	·	·
·	·	·	·	·
·	·	·	·	·
18	113,131.00	19,293.26	47,646.13	66,939.39
19	59,767.33	13,575.72	53,363.67	66,939.39
20	0.02	7,172.08	59,767.31	66,939.39
		$838,787.82	$499,999.98	$1,338,787.80

The formula for calculating the present value of a bond is

$$PV_b = \frac{1 - \dfrac{1}{(1 + i_m)^n}}{i_m} \times (i_c F) + \frac{1}{(1 + i_m)^n} \times M$$

where

PV_b = present value of the bond
i_m = market rate of interest
i_c = coupon rate of interest
F = face value of the bond used as the basis for calculating interest amount to be paid (IA)
M = maturity value or redemption value of the bond
n = number of years

This formula assumes annual compounding, since n has been defined by years. For semiannual compounding, use this slightly modified formula:

$$PV_b = \frac{1 - \dfrac{1}{\left(1 + \dfrac{i_m}{2}\right)^{2n}}}{\dfrac{i_m}{2}} \times \left(\frac{i_c}{2}\right)(F) + \frac{1}{\left(1 + \dfrac{i_m}{2}\right)^{2n}} \times M$$

NOTE: When the market rate of interest (annual or semiannual) is higher than the coupon rate, then the present value or market value of the bonds is lower than the face value of the bonds.

You can use standard tables, such as Table 4.5 (pages 147–148) for calculating future present value of bonds. Here, the present values at different market rates of interest are given for a $100 bond that pays a 10-percent coupon rate of interest per year, compounded semiannually. The table also shows different present values for a given rate of interest for various maturities. For example, looking at the table, you will find that a 20-year bond at 10-percent coupon and market interest rate will have a face value equal to its market value of $100. However, if the 10-percent bond is issued to yield 12 percent, then the present value of the $100 bond falls to $84.95.

EXAMPLE 4.22

Company F issues $500,000 of 20-year bonds, which pay an annual interest rate of 10% compounded twice a year. The bonds are issued at a market rate of interest to yield the investor 12% per year, compounded twice a year. The interest is payable semiannually, on January 1 and July 1. Principal is to be repaid at the end of 20 years. The present or market value of the bonds on the date of issue is determined as follows: The present value consists of two parts: (1) present value of the principal and (2) present value of 40 semiannual interest payments over 20 years. Since the interest is compounded semiannually, present-value calculations would use 40 periods of six months each with a coupon rate of 5% and a market rate of 6% for each six-month period. Using the formula, calculations are

$$PV_b = \frac{\dfrac{1}{\left(1 + \dfrac{0.12}{2}\right)^{(2)(20)}}}{\dfrac{0.12}{2}} \times \left(\dfrac{0.10}{2}\right)\left(\$500{,}000\right)$$

$$+ \frac{1}{\left(1 + \dfrac{0.12}{2}\right)^{(2)(20)}}\left(\$500{,}000\right)$$

$$PV_b = \frac{1 - \dfrac{1}{(1 + 0.06)^{40}}}{0.06}$$

$$\times (0.05)(\$500{,}000) + \frac{1}{(1 + 0.06)^{40}}\,(\$500{,}000)$$

$$PV_b = 15.046297 \times \$25{,}000$$
$$+ 0.097222 \times \$500{,}000$$
$$PV_b = \$376{,}157 + \$48{,}611 = \$424{,}768$$

Using Table 4.5, we find that the $500,000 bond issue is equivalent to 5,000 bonds of $100 face value each. The present or market value of $500,000 bonds issued at 12% interest is 5,000 × $84.95 = $424,750.

OBSERVATIONS: The present or market value of the bonds compounded semiannually is $424,768, whereas the face value is $500,000. Why? Because market interest rate is higher than the coupon rate. The reverse holds too: When market rate is below coupon rate, then market or present value is higher than face value.

Sinking Fund. A company would establish a sinking fund in order to accumulate financial resources for the purpose of paying off the maturity value of debt when due. You can use present or future value methods to calculate the company's annual contribution to the sinking fund. Use this formula:

$$R = \frac{M}{IF_{foa}}$$

where

    R = annual payment to the sinking fund
    M = maturity value of the bonds
    IF_{foa} = interest factor that represents the future value
              of an ordinary annuity of $1

EXAMPLE 4.23

From the preceding example, Company F needs to set up and maintain a sinking fund for the retirement of the bond principal at the end of 20 years. The company is required to make annual payments into the fund at the end of each year. The future value of the sinking fund at the end of 20 years will be equal to the maturity value of the bonds. Management expects to earn 8% interest compounded annually on the sinking fund investment. Using the formula and Table 4.4, you can calculate the annual contribution to the sinking fund as follows:

$$R = \frac{\$500,000}{45.76194} = \$10,926.10$$

The sinking fund will grow as a result of both the annual contribution and the interest earnings. From the calculations you can see the growth of the sinking fund at 8% interest earnings. By year 20, the company will have enough funds to repay its principal as indicated in Exhibit 4.4.

Sales Growth and Compound Growth. Compound growth calculations can be used to simplify the calculation of anticipated sales when such sales are expected to grow in some uniform manner. WHAT TO DO: In applying future or compound growth techniques to sales growth, treat "no-growth" sales as if they were an annuity. Then calculate the anticipated growth rate using the following formula:

$$\text{Anticipated growth rate} = \frac{\text{Anticipated sales of year } n - \text{Anticipated sales of year } n-1}{\text{Anticipated sales of year } n-1}$$

Use Example 4.24 on page 132 as a guide.

EXHIBIT 4.4: SCHEDULE OF SINKING FUND PAYMENTS AND ACCUMULATION

Year	Beginning Balance	Annual Payment	Interest Earned	Annual Accumulation	Ending Balance
1	$ 0	$ 10,926.10	$ 0	$ 10,926.10	$ 10,926.10
2	10,926.10	10,926.10	874.09	11,800.19	22,726.29
3	22,726.29	10,926.10	11,818.10	12,744.20	35,470.49
.	.	.	.	.	.
.	.	.	.	.	.
.	.	.	.	.	.
18	368,758.35	10,926.10	29,500.67	40,426.77	409,185.12
19	409,185.12	10,926.10	32,734.81	43,660.91	452,846.03
20	452,846.03	10,926.10	36,227.68	47,153.78	499,999.81
		$218,522.00	$281,477.81	$499,999.81	

EXHIBIT 4.5: ANTICIPATED SALES GROWTH USING A COMPOUND GROWTH APPROXIMATION

End of Month	Monthly Sales— No Growth	Growth Factor (1%)	Monthly Sales at 1% Growth Rate	CUMULATIVE		ANNUAL	
				Growth Factor	Sales	Sales	Growth Rate
1	$ 100,000	1.000000	$100,000	1.000000	$ 100,000		
2	100,000	1.010000	101,000	2.010000	201,000		
3	100,000	1.020100	102,010	3.030100	303,010		
.	.	.	.	.	.		
.	.	.	.	.	.		
.	.	.	.	.	.		
10	100,000	1.093685	109,369	10.462213	1,046,221		
11	100,000	1.104622	110,462	11.566835	1,156,683		
12	100,000	1.115668	111,567	12.682503	1,268,250	$1,268,250	12.68%
.	.	.	.	.	.		
.	.	.	.	.	.		

22	100,000	1.232392	123,239	24.471586	2,447,159	
23	100,000	1.244716	124,472	25.716302	2,571,630	
24	100,000	1.257163	125,716	26.973465	2,697,346	1,429,096 12.68%
·	·	·	·	·	·	
·	·	·	·	·	·	
·	·	·	·	·	·	
34	100,000	1.388690	138,869	40.257699	4,025,770	
35	100,000	1.402577	140,258	41.660276	4,166,028	
36	100,000	1.416603	141,660	43.076878	4,307,688	1,610,342 12.68%
·	·	·	·	·	·	
·	·	·	·	·	·	
·	·	·	·	·	·	
46	100,000	1.564811	156,481	58.045885	5,804,588	
47	100,000	1.580459	158,046	59.626344	5,962,634	
48	100,000	1.596263	159,626	61.222608	6,122,261	1,814,573 12.68%
Totals	$4,800,000					$6,122,261

131

EXAMPLE 4.24

Assume Company D anticipates sales growth of about 12% per year over the next four years, and expects this growth to be relatively uniform over the period. How would such a growth pattern look?

Assume anticipated sales will grow approximately 1% per month. The anticipated sales growth pattern is shown in Exhibit 4.5 on pages 130–131. Note that growth factors that are applied to the "no-growth" sales column in the Exhibit are simply compound interest factors taken from Table 4.1. Then note the cumulative growth factors applied to the no-growth sales. These are taken from Table 4.4, and are simply the future values of an ordinary annuity of $1 growing at 1% per period.

The calculations also show annual anticipated sales and their growth. If the monthly growth rate is 1%, the compound annual growth rate is 12.68% per year. Let us now look at the expected sales growth in Exhibit 4.5.

Proof
Using the preceding formula, anticipated growth rate is computed as follows:

$$\text{Anticipated growth rate} = \frac{\$1,286,250 - \$1,125,508}{\$1,125,508}$$
$$= 12.68\%$$

This assumes actual sales for the prior year also grew at 1% per month. In fact, you can easily reconstruct this using Exhibit 4.6.

WHAT TO DO NEXT: From Table 4.2, apply discount factors to no-growth sales at a rate of 1% per period. The cumulative discount factors are present values of an ordinary annuity of $1 (Table 4.3) that have been discounted at the rate of 1% per period.

What are the limitations of present and compound-value techniques?

What are some assumptions that underlie the present- and compound-value techniques? First, all the ingredients (or variables) used in the calculation of present or compound value (amounts being discounted or subject to growth, the interest rates used, and the discount or growth periods) are known with certainty. Second, the interest rate used for discounting or growth is constant over the given time period. Third, all amounts in a series are equal to each other. The second and third assumptions can be dropped, but doing so leads to an entirely new realm replete with

EXHIBIT 4.6: THE MOST RECENT YEAR'S ACTUAL SALES RECONSTRUCTED USING PRESENT VALUE

End of Month	Monthly Sales— No Growth	Discount Factor (1%)	Monthly Sales at 1% Discount Rate	CUMULATIVE Discount Factor	CUMULATIVE Sales
1	$100,000	0.990099	99,010	0.990099	99,010
2	100,000	0.980296	98,030	1.970395	197,040
3	100,000	0.970590	97,059	2.940985	294,099
.	.	.	.	.	.
.	.	.	.	.	.
.	.	.	.	.	.
10	100,000	0.905287	90,529	9.471305	947,130
11	100,000	0.896324	89,632	10.367628	1,036,763
12	100,000	0.887449	88,745	11.255077	1,125,508

difficulties. If the first assumption is dropped, then various statistical estimation techniques will be necessary, and present and compound values become subject to statistical estimation rather than arithmetic calculation.

In the real world, you are always confronted with uncertainty. This means that appropriate statistical techniques should be used to determine best estimates for each variable.

TABLE 4.1

$$IF_f = \text{future or compound value of } \$1 = (1 + i)^n$$

n^i	1%	2.5%	6%	8%	9%	10%	12%
1	0.010000	1.025000	1.060000	1.080000	1.090000	1.100000	1.120000
2	1.020100	1.050625	1.123600	1.166400	1.188100	1.210000	1.254400
3	1.030301	1.076891	1.191016	1.259712	1.295029	1.331000	1.404928
4	1.040604	1.103813	1.262477	1.360489	1.411582	1.464100	1.573519
5	1.051010	1.131408	1.338226	1.469328	1.538624	1.610510	1.762342
6	1.061520	1.159693	1.418519	1.586874	1.677100	1.771561	1.973823
7	1.072135	1.188686	1.503630	1.713824	1.828039	1.948717	2.210681
8	1.082857	1.218403	1.593848	1.850930	1.992563	2.143589	2.475963
9	1.093685	1.248863	1.689479	1.999005	2.171893	2.357948	2.773079
10	1.104622	1.280085	1.790848	2.158925	2.367364	2.593742	3.105848
11	1.115668	1.312087	1.898299	2.331639	2.580426	2.853117	3.478550
12	1.126825	1.344889	2.012196	2.518170	2.812665	3.138428	3.895976
13	1.138093	1.378511	2.132928	2.719624	3.065805	3.452271	4.363493
14	1.149474	1.412974	2.260904	2.937194	3.341727	3.797498	4.887112
15	1.160969	1.448298	2.396558	3.172169	3.642482	4.177248	5.473566
16	1.172579	1.484506	2.540352	3.425943	3.970306	4.594973	6.130394

TABLE 4.1 (cont.)

n^i	1%	2.5%	6%	8%	9%	10%	12%
17	1.184304	1.521618	2.692773	3.700018	4.327633	5.054470	6.866041
18	1.196147	1.559659	2.854339	3.996019	4.717120	5.559917	7.689966
19	1.208109	1.598650	3.025600	4.315701	5.141661	6.115909	8.612762
20	1.220190	1.633616	3.207135	4.660957	5.604411	6.727500	9.646293
21	1.232392	1.679582	3.399564	5.033834	6.108808	7.400250	10.803848
22	1.244716	1.721571	3.603537	5.436540	6.658600	8.140275	12.100310
23	1.257163	1.764611	3.819750	5.871464	7.257874	8.954302	13.552347
24	1.269735	1.808726	4.048935	6.341181	7.911083	9.849733	15.178629
25	1.282432	1.853944	4.291871	6.848475	8.623081	10.834706	17.000064
26	1.295256	1.900293	4.549383	7.396353	9.399158	11.918177	19.040072
27	1.308209	1.947800	4.822346	7.988061	10.245082	13.109994	21.324881
28	1.321291	1.996495	5.111687	8.627106	11.167140	14.420994	23.883866
29	1.334504	2.046407	5.418388	9.317275	12.172182	15.863093	26.749930
30	1.347849	2.097568	5.743491	10.062657	13.267678	17.449402	29.959922
31	1.361327	2.150007	6.088101	10.867669	14.461770	19.194342	33.555113
32	1.374941	2.203757	6.453387	11.737083	15.763329	21.113777	37.581726

33	1.388690	2.258851	6.840590	12.676050	17.182028	23.225154	42.091533
34	1.402577	2.315322	7.251025	13.690134	18.728411	25.547670	47.142517
35	1.416603	2.373205	7.686087	14.785344	20.413968	28.102437	52.799620
36	1.430769	2.432535	8.147252	15.968172	22.251225	30.912681	59.135574
37	1.445076	2.493349	8.636087	17.245626	24.253835	34.003949	66.231843
38	1.459527	2.555682	9.154252	18.625276	26.436680	37.404343	74.179664
39	1.474123	2.619574	9.703507	20.115298	28.815982	41.144778	83.081224
40	1.488864	2.685064	10.285718	21.724521	31.409420	45.259256	93.050970
41	1.503752	2.752190	10.902861	23.462483	34.236268	49.785181	104.217087
42	1.518790	2.820995	11.557033	25.339482	37.317532	54.763699	116.723137
43	1.533978	2.891520	12.250455	27.366640	40.676110	60.240069	130.729914
44	1.549318	2.963808	12.985482	29.555972	44.336960	66.264076	146.417503
45	1.564811	3.037903	13.764611	31.920449	48.327286	72.890484	163.987604
46	1.580459	3.113851	14.590487	34.474085	52.676742	80.179532	183.66116
47	1.596263	3.191697	15.465917	37.232012	57.417649	88.197485	205.706050
48	1.612226	3.271490	16.393872	40.210573	62.585237	97.017234	230.390776
49	1.628348	3.353277	17.377504	43.427419	68.217908	106.718957	258.037669
50	1.644632	3.437109	18.420154	46.901613	74.357520	117.390853	289.002190

TABLE 4.2

$$IF_p = \text{present value of \$1} = \frac{1}{(1+i)^n}$$

n^i	1%	2.5%	6%	8%	9%	10%	12%
1	0.990099	0.975610	0.943396	0.925926	0.917431	0.909091	0.892857
2	0.980296	0.951814	0.889996	0.857339	0.841680	0.826446	0.797194
3	0.970590	0.928599	0.839619	0.793832	0.772183	0.751315	0.711780
4	0.960980	0.905951	0.792094	0.735030	0.708425	0.683013	0.635518
5	0.951466	0.883854	0.747258	0.680583	0.649931	0.620921	0.567427
6	0.942045	0.862297	0.704961	0.630170	0.596267	0.564474	0.506631
7	0.932718	0.841265	0.665057	0.583490	0.547034	0.513158	0.452349
8	0.923483	0.820747	0.627412	0.540269	0.501866	0.466507	0.403883
9	0.914340	0.800728	0.591898	0.500249	0.460428	0.424098	0.360610
10	0.905287	0.781196	0.558395	0.463193	0.422411	0.385543	0.321973
11	0.896324	0.762145	0.526788	0.428883	0.387533	0.350494	0.287476
12	0.887449	0.743556	0.496969	0.397114	0.355535	0.318631	0.256675
13	0.878663	0.725420	0.468839	0.367698	0.326179	0.289664	0.229174
14	0.869963	0.707727	0.442301	0.340461	0.299246	0.263331	0.204620
15	0.861349	0.690466	0.417265	0.315242	0.274538	0.239392	0.182696

16	0.852821	0.673625	0.393646	0.291890	0.251870	0.217629	0.163122
17	0.844377	0.657195	0.371364	0.270269	0.231073	0.197845	0.145644
18	0.836017	0.641166	0.350344	0.250249	0.211994	0.179859	0.130040
19	0.827740	0.625528	0.330513	0.231712	0.194490	0.163508	0.116107
20	0.819544	0.610271	0.311805	0.214548	0.178431	0.148644	0.103667
21	0.811430	0.595386	0.294155	0.198656	0.163698	0.135131	0.092560
22	0.803396	0.580865	0.277505	0.183941	0.150182	0.122846	0.082643
23	0.795442	0.566697	0.261797	0.170315	0.137781	0.111678	0.073788
24	0.787566	0.552875	0.246979	0.157699	0.126405	0.101526	0.065882
25	0.779768	0.539391	0.232999	0.146018	0.115968	0.092296	0.058823
26	0.772048	0.526235	0.219810	0.135202	0.106393	0.083905	0.052521
27	0.764404	0.513400	0.207368	0.125187	0.097608	0.076278	0.046894
28	0.756836	0.500878	0.195630	0.115914	0.089548	0.069343	0.041869
29	0.749342	0.488661	0.184557	0.107328	0.082155	0.063039	0.037383
30	0.741923	0.476743	0.174110	0.099377	0.075371	0.057309	0.033378
31	0.734577	0.465115	0.164255	0.092016	0.069148	0.052099	0.029802
32	0.727304	0.453771	0.154957	0.085200	0.063438	0.047362	0.026609
33	0.720103	0.442703	0.146186	0.078889	0.058200	0.043057	0.023758
34	0.712973	0.431905	0.137912	0.073045	0.053395	0.039143	0.021212
35	0.705914	0.421371	0.130105	0.067635	0.048986	0.035584	0.018940
36	0.698925	0.411094	0.122741	0.062625	0.044941	0.032349	0.016910

TABLE 4.2 (cont.)

n^i	1%	2.5%	6%	8%	9%	10%	12%
37	0.692005	0.401067	0.115793	0.057986	0.041231	0.029408	0.015098
38	0.685153	0.391285	0.109239	0.053690	0.037826	0.026735	0.013481
39	0.678370	0.381741	0.103056	0.049713	0.034703	0.024304	0.012036
40	0.671653	0.372431	0.097222	0.046031	0.031838	0.022095	0.010747
41	0.665003	0.363347	0.091719	0.042621	0.029209	0.020086	0.009595
42	0.658419	0.354485	0.086527	0.039464	0.026797	0.018260	0.008567
43	0.651900	0.345839	0.081630	0.036541	0.024584	0.016600	0.007649
44	0.645445	0.337404	0.077009	0.033834	0.022555	0.015091	0.006830
45	0.639055	0.329174	0.072650	0.031328	0.020692	0.013719	0.006098
46	0.632728	0.321146	0.068538	0.029007	0.018984	0.012472	0.005445
47	0.626463	0.313313	0.064658	0.026859	0.017416	0.011338	0.004861
48	0.620260	0.305671	0.060998	0.024869	0.015978	0.010307	0.004340
49	0.614119	0.298216	0.057546	0.023027	0.014659	0.009370	0.003875
50	0.608039	0.290942	0.054288	0.021321	0.013449	0.008519	0.003460

TABLE 4.3

$$IF_{poa} = \text{present value of an ordinary annuity of \$1}$$

$$IF_{pca} = \frac{1 - \dfrac{1}{(1 + i)^n}}{i}$$

n^i	1%	2.5%	6%	8%	9%	10%	12%
1	0.990099	0.975610	0.943396	0.925926	0.917431	0.909091	0.892857
2	1.970395	1.927424	1.833393	1.783265	1.759111	1.735537	1.690051
3	2.940985	2.856024	2.673012	2.577097	2.531295	2.486852	2.401831
4	3.901966	3.761974	3.465106	3.312127	3.239720	3.169865	3.037349
5	4.853431	4.645829	4.212364	3.992710	3.889651	3.790787	3.604776
6	5.795476	5.508125	4.917324	4.622880	4.485919	4.355261	4.111407
7	6.728195	6.349391	5.582381	5.206370	5.032953	4.868419	4.563757
8	7.651678	7.170137	6.209794	5.746639	5.534819	5.334926	4.967640
9	8.566018	7.970866	6.801692	6.246888	5.995247	5.759024	5.328250
10	9.471305	8.752064	7.360087	6.710081	6.417658	6.144567	5.650223
11	10.367628	9.514209	7.886875	7.138964	6.805191	6.495061	5.937699
12	11.255077	10.257765	8.383844	7.536078	7.160725	6.813692	6.194374
13	12.133740	10.983185	8.852683	7.903776	7.486904	7.103356	6.423548

TABLE 4.3 (cont.)

n^i	1%	2.5%	6%	8%	9%	10%	12%
14	13.003703	11.690912	9.294984	8.244237	7.786150	7.366687	6.628168
15	13.865053	12.381378	9.712249	8.559479	8.060688	7.606080	6.810864
16	14.717874	13.055003	10.105895	8.851369	8.312558	7.823709	6.973986
17	15.562251	13.712198	10.477260	9.121638	8.543631	8.021553	7.119630
18	16.398269	14.353364	10.827603	9.371887	8.755625	8.201412	7.249670
19	17.226009	14.978891	11.158116	9.603599	8.950115	8.364920	7.365777
20	18.045553	15.589162	11.469921	9.818147	9.128546	8.513564	7.469444
21	18.856983	16.184549	11.764077	10.016803	9.292244	8.648694	7.562003
22	19.660379	16.765413	12.041582	10.200744	9.442425	8.771540	7.644646
23	20.455821	17.332110	12.303379	10.371059	9.580207	8.883218	7.718434
24	21.243387	17.884986	12.550358	10.528758	9.706612	8.984744	7.784316
25	22.023156	18.424376	12.783356	10.674776	9.822580	9.077040	7.843139
26	22.795204	18.950611	13.003166	10.809978	9.928972	9.160945	7.895660
27	23.559608	19.464011	13.210534	10.935165	10.026580	9.237223	7.942554
28	24.316443	19.964889	13.406164	11.051078	10.116128	9.306567	7.984423
29	25.065785	20.453550	13.590721	11.158406	10.198283	9.369606	8.021806
30	25.807708	20.930293	13.764831	11.257783	10.273654	9.426914	8.055184

31	26.542285	21.395407	13.929086	11.349799	10.342802	9.479013	8.084986
32	27.269589	21.849178	14.084043	11.434999	10.406240	9.526376	8.111594
33	27.989693	22.291881	14.230230	11.513888	10.464441	9.569432	8.135352
34	28.702666	22.723786	14.368141	11.586934	10.517835	9.608575	8.156564
35	29.408580	23.145157	14.498246	11.654568	10.566821	9.644159	8.175504
36	30.107505	23.556251	14.620987	11.717193	10.611763	9.676508	8.192414
37	30.799510	23.957318	14.736780	11.775179	10.652993	9.705917	8.207513
38	31.484663	24.348603	14.846019	11.828869	10.690820	9.732651	8.220993
39	32.163033	24.730344	14.949075	11.878582	10.725523	9.756956	8.233030
40	32.834686	25.102775	15.046297	11.924613	10.757360	9.779051	8.243777
41	33.499689	25.466122	15.138016	11.967235	10.786569	9.799137	8.253372
42	34.158108	25.820607	15.224543	12.006699	10.813366	9.817397	8.261939
43	34.810008	26.166446	15.306173	12.043240	10.837950	9.833998	8.269589
44	35.455454	26.503849	15.383182	12.077074	10.860505	9.849089	8.276418
45	36.094508	26.833024	15.455832	12.108402	10.881197	9.862808	8.282516
46	36.727236	27.154170	15.524370	12.137409	10.900181	9.875280	8.287961
47	37.353699	27.467483	15.589028	12.164267	10.917597	9.886618	8.292822
48	37.973959	27.773154	15.650027	12.189136	10.933575	9.896926	8.297163
49	38.588079	28.071369	15.707572	12.212163	10.948234	9.906296	8.301038
50	39.196118	28.362312	15.761861	12.233485	10.961683	9.914814	8.304498

TABLE 4.4

$$IF_{foa} = \text{future value of an ordinary annuity of \$1}$$
$$IF_{foa} = \frac{(1 + i)^n - 1}{i}$$

n^i	1%	2.5%	6%	8%	9%	10%	12%
1	1.000000	1.000000	1.000000	1.000000	1.000000	1.000000	1.000000
2	2.010000	2.025000	2.060000	2.080000	2.090000	2.100000	2.120000
3	3.030100	3.075625	3.183600	3.246400	3.278100	3.310000	3.374400
4	4.060401	4.152516	4.374616	4.506112	4.573129	4.641000	4.779328
5	5.101005	5.256329	5.637093	5.866601	5.984711	6.105100	6.352847
6	6.152015	6.387737	6.975319	7.335929	7.523335	7.715610	8.115189
7	7.213535	7.547430	8.393838	8.922803	9.200435	9.487171	10.089012
8	8.285671	8.736116	9.897468	10.636628	11.028474	11.435888	12.299693
9	9.368527	9.954519	11.491316	12.487558	13.021036	13.579477	14.775656
10	10.462213	11.203382	13.180795	14.486562	15.192930	15.937425	17.548735
11	11.566835	12.483466	14.971643	16.645487	17.560293	18.531167	20.654583
12	12.682503	13.795553	16.869941	18.977126	20.140720	21.384284	24.133133
13	13.809328	15.140442	18.882138	21.495297	22.953385	24.522712	28.029109
14	14.947421	16.518953	21.015066	24.214920	26.019189	27.974983	32.392602

15	16.096896	17.931927	23.275970	27.152114	29.360916	31.772482	37.279715
16	17.257864	19.380225	25.672528	30.324283	33.003399	35.949730	42.753280
17	18.430443	20.864730	28.212880	33.750226	36.973705	40.544703	48.883674
18	19.614748	22.386349	30.905653	37.450244	41.301338	45.599173	55.749715
19	20.810895	23.946007	33.759992	41.446263	46.018458	51.159090	63.439681
20	22.019004	25.544658	36.785591	45.761964	51.160120	57.274999	72.052442
21	23.239194	27.183274	39.992727	50.422921	56.764530	64.002499	81.698736
22	24.471586	28.862856	43.392290	55.456755	62.873338	71.402749	92.502584
23	25.716302	30.584427	46.995828	60.893296	69.531939	79.543024	104.602894
24	26.973465	32.349038	50.815577	66.764759	76.789813	88.497327	118.155241
25	28.243200	34.157764	54.864512	73.105940	84.700896	98.347059	133.333870
26	29.525632	36.011708	59.156383	79.954415	93.323977	109.181765	150.333934
27	30.820888	37.912001	63.705766	87.350768	102.723135	121.099942	169.374007
28	32.129097	39.859801	68.528112	95.338830	112.968217	134.209936	190.698887
29	33.450388	41.856296	73.629798	103.965936	124.135356	148.630930	214.582754
30	34.784892	43.902703	79.058186	113.283211	136.307539	164.494023	241.332684
31	36.132740	46.000271	84.801677	123.345868	149.575217	181.943425	271.292606
32	37.494068	48.150278	90.889778	134.213537	164.036987	201.137767	304.847719
33	38.869009	50.354034	97.343165	145.950620	179.800315	222.251544	342.429446
34	40.257699	52.612885	104.183755	158.626670	196.982344	245.476699	384.520979
35	41.660276	54.928207	111.434780	172.316804	215.710755	271.024368	431.663496

TABLE 4.4 (cont.)

n^i	1%	2.5%	6%	8%	9%	10%	12%
36	43.076878	57.301413	119.120867	187.102148	236.124723	299.126805	484.463116
37	44.507647	59.733948	127.268119	203.070320	258.375948	330.039486	543.598690
38	45.952724	62.227297	135.904206	220.315945	282.629783	364.043434	609.830533
39	47.412251	64.782979	145.058458	238.941221	309.066463	401.447778	684.010197
40	48.886373	67.402554	154.761966	259.056519	337.882445	442.592556	767.091420
41	50.375237	70.087617	165.047684	280.781040	369.291865	487.851811	860.142391
42	51.878989	72.839808	175.950545	304.243523	403.528133	537.636992	964.359478
43	53.397779	75.660803	187.507577	329.583005	440.845665	592.400692	1081.082615
44	54.931757	78.552323	199.758032	356.949646	481.521775	652.640761	1211.812529
45	56.481075	81.516131	212.743514	386.505617	525.858734	718.904837	1358.230032
46	58.045885	84.554034	226.508125	418.426067	574.186021	791.795321	1522.217636
47	59.626344	87.667885	241.098612	452.900152	626.862762	871.974853	1705.883752
48	61.222608	90.859582	256.564529	490.132164	684.280411	960.172338	1911.589803
49	62.834834	94.131072	272.958401	530.342737	746.865648	1057.189572	2141.980579
50	64.463182	97.484349	290.335905	573.770156	815.083556	1163.908529	2400.018249

146

TABLE 4.5 PRESENT BOND VALUESᵃ

Annual Yield (%)	Years to Maturity					
	1	5	10	15	20	30
7.0	102.85	112.47	121.32	127.59	132.03	137.42
7.5	102.37	110.27	117.37	122.29	125.69	129.67
8.0	101.89	108.11	113.59	117.29	119.79	122.62
8.5	101.41	106.01	109.97	112.58	114.31	116.19
9.0	100.94	103.96	106.50	108.14	109.20	110.32
9.5	100.47	101.95	103.18	103.96	104.44	104.94
10.0	100.00	100.00	100.00	100.00	100.00	100.00
10.5	99.54	98.09	96.95	96.26	95.85	95.46
11.0	99.08	96.23	94.02	92.73	91.98	91.28
11.5	98.62	94.41	91.22	89.39	88.35	87.41
12.0	98.17	92.64	88.53	86.24	84.95	83.84
12.5	97.72	90.91	85.95	83.24	81.77	80.53
13.0	97.27	89.22	83.47	80.41	78.78	77.45
13.5	96.82	87.57	81.09	77.73	75.98	74.59
14.0	96.38	85.95	78.81	75.18	73.34	71.92
14.5	95.95	84.38	76.62	72.77	70.85	69.43

TABLE 4.5 (cont.)

Annual Yield (%)	Years to Maturity					
	1	5	10	15	20	30
15.0 . . .	95.51	82.84	74.51	70.47	68.51	67.10
15.5 . . .	95.08	81.34	72.49	68.30	66.31	64.92
16.0 . . .	94.65	79.87	70.55	66.23	64.23	62.87
16.5 . . .	94.22	78.44	68.68	64.26	62.26	60.94
17.0 . . .	93.80	77.04	66.88	62.39	60.40	59.13
17.5 . . .	93.38	75.67	65.15	60.80	58.64	57.42
18.0 . . .	92.96	74.33	63.49	58.91	56.97	55.81
18.5 . . .	92.55	73.02	61.89	57.29	55.39	54.28
19.0 . . .	92.14	71.75	60.34	55.74	53.89	52.84
19.5 . . .	91.73	70.50	58.86	54.27	52.46	51.47
20.0 . . .	91.32	69.28	57.43	52.87	51.10	50.16

•Bonds have a coupon rate of 10%, semiannual compounding, and semiannual interest payments.

148

5

Capital Budgeting Techniques and Risk–Return Trade-Off

Capital budgeting involves planning for the best selections and financing of long-term investments. In this chapter, the following four techniques are described to help you select the best long-term investment proposals:

- Net present value
- Internal rate of return
- Payback
- Profitability index

Your selection will necessarily involve judgments about future events about which you have no direct knowledge. Your task will be to minimize your chances of being wrong. The risk–return trade-off method shown in this chapter is one way to help you come to grips with uncertainty.

5.1 CAPITAL BUDGETING: FOUR TECHNIQUES FOR EVALUATING AN INVESTMENT PROPOSAL

What is capital budgeting?

Capital budgeting is a selection technique used to evaluate long-term investment proposals. It can be done in a number of ways, four of which are described in this chapter. Understanding these techniques is important for managerial accountants and management executives in both for-profit and nonprofit industries. Mid-level managers should also be familiar with capital budgeting, because they are also concerned with investment and management of resources to a degree.

What are the uses of capital budgeting?

Whenever you are faced with a decision of how to invest major chunks of resources, you have a capital budgeting problem. Ask yourself these questions:

- Should I replace certain equipment?
- Should I expand facilities by renting additional space, buying an existing building, or constructing a new building?
- Do I have an opportunity to refinance an outstanding debt issue? Should I do it?
- I've been contemplating a merger. Should I go ahead with it?
- I've been thinking about adding a new product to our line. Should I?
- I'm considering a new major advertising campaign. Should I hold off?

How do I use the present value method?

The present value method compares present value of future cash flows expected from an investment project to the initial cash outflow attributable directly to the investment. Net cash inflows are defined as the difference between expected cash inflow received as a result of the investment and expected cash outflow of the investment.

Net present value (NPV) is defined as follows:

$$NPV = PV - CI$$

where

CI = cash outflow resulting from the cost of the investment

$$PV = \frac{R_1}{(1+i)} + \frac{R_2}{(1+i)^2} + \ldots + \frac{R_n}{(1+i)^n}$$
$$= \text{present value}$$

where

R_n = expected cash flow of the nth period.

RULE OF THUMB: If the net present value is positive (NPV > 0), then the proposal would be a good candidate for investment by your company.

EXAMPLE 5.1

Company A is replacing some of its machinery in order to reduce costs and gain certain other savings. The cost savings will result in expected cash inflows over the six-year life of the replacement machinery as follows:

Year	Net Cash Inflows	Year	Net Cash Inflows
1	$10,000	4	$30,000
2	20,000	5	40,000
3	30,000	6	50,000

Initial cash outflow as a result of the investment consisted of the following elements:

Purchase price paid for new machinery	$86,000
Installation costs paid	3,000
Cash realized (net of taxes) from disposal of old machinery	1,000
Total initial cash outflow	$90,000

In addition, it is expected that, at the end of its useful life, the new machinery will result in a cash inflow (net of taxes) of $1,000. The incremental cost of capital to the company (also called its required rate of return) is assumed to be 12%.

Using the formula, calculations of present value and net present value are

$$PV = \frac{\$10,000}{(1 + 0.12)} + \frac{\$20,000}{(1 + 0.12)^2} + \cdots$$
$$+ \frac{\$50,000}{(1 + 0.12)^6}$$
$$NPV = \frac{\$10,000}{(1 + 0.12)} + \frac{\$20,000}{(1 + 0.12)^2} + \cdots$$
$$+ \frac{\$50,000}{(1 + 0.12)^6} - \$90,000$$

In tabular format, calculations are presented in Exhibit 5.1. (See page 152.) (NOTE: The interest factors are present values of $1 at 12% taken from Table 4.2.)

CONCLUSIONS: The investment in the replacement machinery is expected to result in a net present value of $23,828. If the company has no other investment opportunities, then this positive value indicates the investment should be made.

EXHIBIT 5.1: NET PRESENT VALUE OF EXPECTED NET CASH INFLOWS FROM REPLACEMENT OF MACHINERY

End of Year	Cash Outflow	Net Cash Inflows	IF_p at ICC[a]	PRESENT VALUES Inflows	PRESENT VALUES Outflows	Net Present Value	Cash Inflows Impact on NPV
0	-$90,000		1.000000		-$90,000	-$90,000	-$90,000
1		$10,000	0.892857	$ 8,929		8,929	- 81,071
2		20,000	0.797194	15,944		15,944	- 65,127
3		30,000	0.711780	21,353		21,353	- 43,774
4		30,000	0.635518	19,066		19,066	- 24,708
5		40,000	0.567427	22,697		22,697	- 2,011
6		50,000	0.506631	25,332		25,332	23,321
6		1,000	0.506631	507		507	23,828
				$113,828	-$90,000	$23,828	

[a]ICC: incremental cost of capital.

What if I have two investment opportunities?

If you have two opportunities that cannot be undertaken simultaneously, then select the project with the highest positive present value. This assumes no other projects are more attractive. If both projects can be undertaken together, and your company has the financial capacity to do it, then select both projects. Also, you must know whether the projects can actually be handled at the same time. Example 5.2 is a case in point.

EXAMPLE 5.2

Company A has two choices for replacement machinery. The first, Project A, has been described in Example 5.1. The second, Project B, is expected to generate the following cost savings, also over a six-year period:

Year	Net Cash Inflows	Year	Net Cash Inflows
1	$50,000	4	$30,000
2	40,000	5	20,000
3	30,000	6	10,000

At the end of its life, the replacement machinery of Project B is expected to have a salvage value that will generate a cash inflow (net of taxes) of $1,000. Assume costs generate an initial cash outflow of $120,000. Calculations of NPV for Project B are presented in Exhibit 5.2 on page 154.

DISCUSSION: Project B also shows a positive NPV. If the projects can be undertaken at the same time, then both investments would be selected. However, since both projects replace the same machinery, then the more profitable one (Project A) would be the right choice.

What is the internal rate of return method?

The internal rate of return (IRR) refers to the yield or interest rate that equates present value of expected cash flows from an investment project to the cost of the investment project. IRR is determined by setting NPV equal to zero, as shown in this formula:

$$NPV = 0$$
$$\left(\frac{R_1}{(1 + IRR)} + \frac{R_2}{(1 + IRR)^2} + \cdots + \frac{R_n}{(1 + IRR)^n} \right) - CI = 0$$

In calculating NPV, the number of periods involved (n), cash flows for each period (R), timing of cash flows, discount

EXHIBIT 5.2: NET PRESENT VALUE OF EXPECTED NET CASH INFLOWS FROM REPLACEMENT OF MACHINERY

End of Year	Cash Outflow	Net Cash Inflows	IF_p at ICC	PRESENT VALUES Inflows	PRESENT VALUES Outflows	Net Present Value	Cash Inflows Impact on NPV
0	-$120,000		1.000000		-$120,000	-$120,000	-$120,000
1		$50,000	0.892857	44,643		44,643	— 75,357
2		40,000	0.797194	31,888		31,888	— 43,469
3		30,000	0.711780	21,353		21,353	— 22,116
4		30,000	0.635518	19,066		19,066	— 3,050
5		20,000	0.567427	11,349		11,349	8,299
6		10,000	0.506631	5,066		5,066	13,365
6		1,000	0.506631	507		507	13,872
				$133,872	-$120,000	$13,872	

interest rate (i), and cost of the investment (CI) are presumed known. In calculating IRR, NPV is no longer treated as unknown, but is set equal to zero. On the other hand, interest rate is now unknown. Generally speaking, calculation of IRR is a trial-and-error process.

With this method, IRR must be greater than or equal to the incremental cost of capital (ICC) in order for the project to be a good candidate for investment. Thus,

$$IRR \geqq ICC$$

EXAMPLE 5.3

Consider Project A from Example 5.1. Exhibit 5.3 (page 156) shows a simple trial-and-error process used to calculate the discount interest rate that approximates IRR. When the discount interest rate is set equal to 19%, NPV is just $9, which is sufficiently close to zero. Exhibit 5.4 (page 157) analyzes the result of setting this rate approximately equal to IRR.

DISCUSSION: The IRR of Project A is approximately 19%. In the initial calculations, the incremental cost of capital (ICC) was assumed to be 12%. At 19%, IRR is greater than ICC; therefore, Project A is a good candidate for use of capital funds.

EXAMPLE 5.4

Now consider Project B from Example 5.2. As shown in Exhibit 5.5, IRR would be approximately 17%.

DISCUSSION: Once again, IRR (17%) is greater than ICC (12%). Project A has a greater NPV and IRR than Project B. Thus, under either NPV or IRR methods, Project A should be selected over Project B if both cannot be undertaken at the same time.

How do I use the payback method?

The payback method focuses on the payback period (PB), which is defined as the amount of time a company expects to take before it recovers its initial investment. When the annual cash flows are constant and of equal amounts, then PB can be calculated by this simple formula:

$$PB = \frac{CI}{R}$$

NOTE: When periodic cash flows are not equal, then calculation of PB is more complex.

EXHIBIT 5.3: CALCULATION OF THE IRR

End of Year	Cash Flows	IF_p at 16%	NPV	IF_p at 22%	NPV	IF_p at 19%	NPV
0	-$90,000	1.000000	-$90,000	1.000000	-$90,000	1.000000	-$90,000
1	10,000	0.862069	8,621	0.819672	8,197	0.840336	8,403
2	20,000	0.743163	14,863	0.671862	13,437	0.706165	14,123
3	30,000	0.640658	19,220	0.550707	16,521	0.593416	17,802
4	30,000	0.552291	16,569	0.451399	13,542	0.498669	14,960
5	40,000	0.476113	19,045	0.369999	14,800	0.419049	16,762
6	50,000	0.410442	20,522	0.303278	15,164	0.352142	17,607
6	1,000	0.410442	410	0.303278	303	0.352142	352
			9,250		-5,036		9

EXHIBIT 5.4: SETTING THE YIELD OR DISCOUNT RATE OF INTEREST APPROXIMATELY EQUAL TO THE IRR—INVESTMENT PROJECT A

End of Year	Cash Outflow	Net Cash Inflows	IF_p appx.^a at IRR^b = 19%	PV AT IRR Inflows	PV AT IRR Outflows	NPV at IRR	Cash Inflows Impact on NPV at IRR
0	−$90,000		1.000000		−$90,000	−$90,000	−$90,000
1		$10,000	0.840336	$ 8,403		8,403	− 81,597
2		20,000	0.706165	14,123		14,123	− 67,474
3		30,000	0.593416	17,802		17,802	− 49,672
4		30,000	0.498669	14,960		14,960	− 34,712
5		40,000	0.419049	16,762		16,762	− 17,950
6		50,000	0.352142	17,607		17,607	− 343
6		1,000	0.352142	352		352	9
				$90,009	−$90,000	9	9

^a appx.: approximately.

^b IRR: discount rate of interest approximately equal to IRR.

EXHIBIT 5.5: SETTING THE YIELD OR DISCOUNT RATE OF INTEREST APPROXIMATELY EQUAL TO THE IRR—INVESTMENT PROJECT B

End of Year	Cash Outflow	Net Cash Inflows	IF_p appx. at IRR = 17%	PV AT IRR Inflows	PV AT IRR Outflows	NPV at IRR	Cash Inflows Impact on NPV at IRR
0	-$120,000		1.000000		-$120,000	-$120,000	-$120,000
1		$50,000	0.854701	$ 42,735		42,735	77,265
2		40,000	0.730514	29,221		29,221	48,044
3		30,000	0.624371	18,731		18,731	29,313
4		30,000	0.533650	16,010		16,010	13,303
5		20,000	0.456111	9,122		9,122	4,181
6		10,000	0.389839	3,898		3,898	283
6		1,000	0.389839	390		390	107
				$120,107	-$120,000	$ 107	

EXAMPLE 5.5

For Projects A and B, as discussed in the previous examples, calculation of the payback periods is shown in Exhibit 5.6.

PB for Project A is four years, but only three years for Project B. Under this method, if the company cannot undertake both projects, then Project B with the shorter payback period would be chosen over Project A. CAUTION: This method works with undiscounted amounts, so it ignores entirely the time value of money. NOTICE THIS: Whereas NPV and IRR methods show a preference for Project A, this method concludes just the opposite!

How does the profitability index work?

The profitability index uses the same variables as NPV but combines them differently. Profitability index (PI) is defined as follows:

$$PI = \frac{PV}{CI}$$

If PI is greater than 1, then the project is a good candidate for investment.

Normally, when comparing more than one project, the one with the higher PI is the more profitable. CAUTION: A higher PI does not always coincide with the project with the highest NPV.

EXAMPLE 5.6

The calculations of PI for Projects A and B as defined in the previous examples are shown as follows:

$$PIA = \frac{\$113,828}{\$90,000} = 1.26$$
$$PIB = \frac{\$133,872}{\$120,000} = 1.12$$

CONCLUSIONS: Project A is preferred over Project B. This agrees with the results of NPV and IRR methods.

EXAMPLE 5.7

Assume two projects X and Y. Project X has a PV of $1,000,000 and a CI of $500,000. Project Y has a PV of $225,000 and a CI of $100,000. According to NPV, both projects are candidates for investment. If only one can be undertaken, then Project X is preferable, because its

EXHIBIT 5.6: CALCULATION OF PAYBACK PERIODS

| End of Year | INVESTMENT PROJECT A | | INVESTMENT PROJECT B | |
	Cash Flows	Undiscounted Investment Balance to Be Recovered	Cash Flows	Undiscounted Investment Balance to Be Recovered
0	-$90,000	-$90,000	-$120,000	-$120,000
1	10,000	- 80,000	50,000	- 70,000
2	20,000	- 60,000	40,000	- 30,000
3	30,000	- 30,000	30,000	0
4	30,000	0		

NPV is greater. Now calculate PI for both projects as follows:

$$PIX = \frac{\$1,000,000}{\$500,000} = 2$$

$$PIY = \frac{\$225,000}{\$100,000} = 2.25$$

DISCUSSION: Since PI is greater than 1 for both projects, either is a potential candidate for investment. If only one can be undertaken, then Project Y would be preferred. However, it is clear that Project X has a significantly greater NPV and is, in fact, more economically attractive. CAUTION: This shows that the PI method does not really provide an unambiguous guide for ranking most profitable investment projects.

5.2 COMPARING AND SELECTING THE BEST PROPOSAL

How do the projects relate to each other?

Investment projects are either independent or mutually exclusive. They are *independent* if both can be undertaken simultaneously. When this occurs, there's no need to rank one project over another. Projects are *mutually exclusive* when only one project can be carried out. Then it is necessary to rank the projects to determine which is most attractive.

What methods are best for ranking projects?

NPV, IRR, and PI methods are considered equally effective in selecting economically viable independent investment projects. The payback method, however, is considered inadequate because it does not take the time value of money into account. For mutually exclusive projects, NPV, IRR, and PI methods are not always able to rank projects in the same order. That is, it is quite possible to end up with different rankings under each method. The payback method is also unsatisfactory for the same reason.

WHAT TO DO: You need to compare the techniques in greater depth. Then your decisions will be better informed.

How do I compare NPV with IRR?

This question is best answered with the following example.

EXAMPLE 5.8

Company A is considering three investment projects. Projects A and B were described in Section 5.1. Project C has identical cash flows to Project B, but its CI = $102,700. The calculation of NPV for Project C and the result of applying the IRR are shown in Exhibit 5.7.

You can see that Project C has the highest NPV and IRR of the three projects. However, in order to compare the two methods, let's calculate NPV for the three projects with differing discount interest rates. This is shown in Exhibit 5.8.

OBSERVATIONS: The NPVs of the three projects vary, as do the discount interest rates. In previous examples, the incremental cost of capital (ICC) was assumed to be 12%. However, ICC can change over time. Note the following observations:

- As ICC rises, NPV falls. This is an inverse relation.

- NPV for Project A is consistently higher than for Project B at each discount interest rate. The same is true for Project C compared with Project B. However, comparing Projects A and C, a consistent relationship cannot be observed. Below 6% interest, NPV is higher for Project A, but the relation is reversed when the rate rises above 6%.

- IRR of Project C is higher than for Project A, but NPVs are not always higher at every level of discount interest rate. This means you would choose Project A for certain interest rates and Project C for others. Yet, Project C has the higher IRR.

Figure 5.1 shows the NPV for each project at differing rates of interest (ICC). From it, you can see that the NPV for Project A is higher than Project B for interest rates below 6%, while the reverse is true for rates above 6%.

Which is the preferable project if NPV and IRR do not give consistent signals?

In order to resolve this conflict, you need to know the interest rate or rates at which the company will be able to reinvest net cash inflows from the projects as these funds are generated. In other words, you need to forecast future or compound values of the net cash inflows as of the end of the expected life of the projects.

EXHIBIT 5.7: NPV AND IRR FOR INVESTMENT PROJECT C

End of Year	Cash Flows	IF_p at ICC = 12%	Net Present Value	Cash Inflows Impact on NPV	IF_p appx. at IRR = 25%	NPV at IRR	Cash Inflows Impact on NPV at IRR
0	-$102,700	1.000000	-$102,700	-$102,700	1.000000	-$102,700	-$102,700
1	50,000	0.892857	44,643	58,057	0.800000	40,000	62,700
2	40,000	0.797194	31,888	26,169	0.640000	25,600	37,100
3	30,000	0.711780	21,353	4,816	0.512000	15,360	21,740
4	30,000	0.635518	19,066	14,250	0.409600	12,288	9,452
5	20,000	0.567427	11,349	25,597	0.327680	6,554	2,898
6	10,000	0.506631	5,066	30,665	0.262144	2,621	277
6	1,000	0.506631	507	31,172	0.262144	262	15
			$ 31,172			-$ 15	

163

EXHIBIT 5.8: BEHAVIOR OF NPV FOR INVESTMENT PROJECTS A, B, AND C

End of Year	CASH FLOWS—INVESTMENT PROJECTS		NET PRESENT VALUES AT ALTERNATIVE DISCOUNT INTEREST RATES						
	A	B	0%	6%	10%	12%	17%	19%	25%
0	-$90,000		-$90,000	-$90,000	-$90,000	-$90,000	-$90,000	-$90,000	-$90,000
1	10,000		10,000	9,434	9,091	8,929	8,547	8,403	8,000
2	20,000		20,000	17,800	16,529	15,944	14,610	14,123	12,800
3	30,000		30,000	25,189	22,539	21,353	18,731	17,802	15,360
4	30,000		30,000	23,763	20,490	19,066	16,010	14,960	12,288
5	40,000		40,000	29,890	24,837	22,697	18,244	16,762	13,107
6	50,000		50,000	35,248	28,224	25,332	19,492	17,607	13,107
6	1,000		1,000	705	564	507	390	352	262
NPVs—investment project A			$91,000	$52,029	$32,274	$23,828	$ 6,024	$ 9	-$15,076

0	-$120,000	-$120,000	-$120,000	-$120,000	-$120,000	-$120,000	-$120,000
1	50,000	47,170	45,455	44,643	42,735	42,017	40,000
2	40,000	35,600	33,058	31,888	29,221	28,247	25,600
3	30,000	25,189	22,539	21,353	18,731	17,802	15,360
4	30,000	23,763	20,490	19,066	16,010	14,960	12,288
5	20,000	14,945	12,418	11,349	9,122	8,381	6,554
6	10,000	7,050	5,645	5,066	3,898	3,521	2,621
6	1,000	705	564	507	390	352	262
NPVs—investment project B	$ 61,000	$ 34,422	$ 20,169	$ 13,872	$ 107	-$ 4,720	-$ 17,315

Adjust cost of investment
project B to that of
investment project C:

Cost of project B $120,000
Cost of project C   102,700

	17,300	17,300	17,300	17,300	17,300	17,300	17,300
NPVs—investment project C	$ 78,300	$ 51,722	$ 37,469	$ 31,172	$ 17,407	$ 12,580	-$ 15

FIGURE 5.1: NPV IN RELATION TO DIFFERING DISCOUNT RATES OF INTEREST

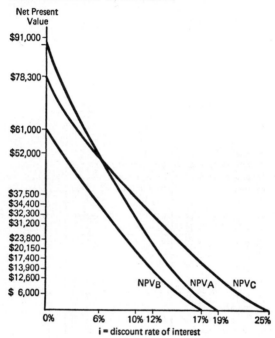

How do I calculate the future values of investment projects?

The calculation of the future values of investment projects is similar to that of an ordinary annuity where annual installments are equal to each other. However, while your investment projects generate an "annuity" of net cash inflows, the "installments" are not equal to each other. Recall this formula for future or compound value of an ordinary annuity:

$$FV_{on} = R_1(1 + i)^{n-1} + R_2(1 + i)^{n-2} + \ldots + R_{n-1}(1 + i) + R$$

Future values of investment projects can be calculated as follows:

$$FV_I = FV_R - FV_C$$
where

FV_I = future value of an investment project
FV_R = future value of net cash inflows as of the end of periods $1, 2, \ldots n$
FV_C = future value of the net cash outflow due to the original cost of the project

Note that $FV_C = CI(1 + i)^n$. Thus

$$FV_I = R_1(1 + i)^{n-1} + R_2(1 + i)^{n-2} + \ldots + R_{n-1}(1 + i) + R_n - CI(1 + i)^n$$

EXAMPLE 5.9

For this example, use Projects A and C from the previous examples. Assume two companies, X and Y, are interested in both projects. Company X is assumed to have an ICC of 4%. Company Y has an ICC of 12%. Both companies can reinvest cash inflows generated from the projects at reinvestment rates (RR) equal to their respective ICCs.

Calculations for the two projects are shown in Exhibit 5.9.

DISCUSSION: You can see that the future value of Project A is greater than that of Project C for Company X (RR = 4%). On the other hand, the reverse is true for Company Y (RR = 12%). At RR less than 6%, both present and future values of Project A exceed those of Project C. At RR above 6%, the reverse holds.

The IRR can be interpreted as the potential RR for each project. For both Projects A and C, IRR is above 6%, and NPV of Project C is continually higher than that of Project A. Thus, NPV for Project A will become zero at a lower discount interest rate than will Project C. CONCLUSION: Only when RR is above 6% will IRR and NPV give consistent signals.

What do these calculations prove?

From these calculations of future values, you can see that the NPV method generally gives more reliable signals. By following this method and using your best estimates of reinvestment rates, you will select the projects expected to be most advantageous.

What is capital rationing?

Capital rationing occurs whenever a company cannot or will not undertake all investment projects with NPV greater than or equal to zero. Usually the company has set an upper limit to its capital budget, thereby preventing it from undertaking all projects.

EXHIBIT 5.9: FUTURE OR COMPOUND VALUES OF INVESTMENT PROJECTS A AND C AT ALTERNATIVE REINVESTMENT RATES

| End of Year | Cash Flows—Investment Projects | | IF_p at $ICC=4\%$ | IF_p at $ICC=12\%$ | FUTURE OR COMPOUND VALUES OF INVESTMENT PROJECTS AT REINVESTMENT RATES (RR) | | | | Differential Compound Values—Investment Project A less Investment Project C | |
| | | | | | Company X | | Company Y | | | |
	A	C			A RR=4%	C RR=4%	A RR=12%	C RR=12%	RR=4%	RR=12%
0	−$90,000	−$102,700	1.265319	1.973823	−$113,879	−$129,948	−$177,644	−$202,712	$16,069	$25,068
1	10,000	50,000	1.216653	1.762342	12,167	60,833	17,623	88,117	− 48,666	− 70,494
2	20,000	40,000	1.169859	1.573519	23,397	46,794	31,470	62,941	− 23,397	− 31,471
3	30,000	30,000	1.124864	1.404928	33,746	33,746	42,148	42,148	0	0
4	30,000	30,000	1.081600	1.254400	32,448	32,448	37,632	37,632	0	0
5	40,000	20,000	1.040000	1.120000	41,600	20,800	44,800	22,400	20,800	22,400
6	50,000	10,000	1.000000	1.000000	50,000	10,000	50,000	10,000	40,000	40,000
6	1,000	1,000	1.000000	1.000000	1,000	1,000	1,000	1,000	0	0
					$ 80,479	$ 75,673	$ 47,029	$ 61,526	4,806	−$14,497

EXAMPLE 5.10

Use Projects A, B, and C as described earlier. Assume
there are three companies, X, Y, and Z, with capital
budgets for the current year of $100,000, $150,000, and
$200,000 respectively. Each company has ICC at 12%.
Using the NPV method, the projects are ranked as follows:

Investment project	CI	NPV	Rank
A	$ 90,000	$23,828	2
B	120,000	13,872	3
C	102,700	31,173	1
	$312,700		

The investment projects to be financed by the capital
budgets of Companies X, Y, and Z are summarized below.

CAPITAL BUDGETS AND SELECTION
OF CAPITAL PROJECTS

	Projects	Rank	X	Y	Z
				Companies	
	C	1	—	$102,700	$102,700
	A	2	$90,000	—	90,000
	B	3	—	—	—
Projects financed			$90,000	$102,700	$192,700
Unutilized capital budget			10,000	47,300	7,300
Total capital budget			$100,000	$150,000	$200,000

NOTE: With capital rationing, the project with the highest ranking index and not the highest NPV will be selected for investment. Company X does not choose Project
C but Project A instead. Company Y selects Project C
only. Company Z selects Projects C and A but not Project
B.

5.3 EVALUATING THE RISK–RETURN TRADE-OFF

5.3.1 One-Year Life Projects

As a manager, you are continually confronted with the risk of making wrong decisions. At the heart of the risk lies your uncertainty about future events that will bear upon the success of the project. The risk–return trade-off analysis is one way of trying to estimate the amount of risk associated with a particular project or set of projects. In this first part, let's consider the simplest case, an investment project with a one-year life.

What is the expected value of future cash flows?

Since you have no direct knowledge about future cash flows, you must rely on forecasts. These estimates take the form of probabilities that specific cash flows will be realized for the coming year. This is expressed in the following formula:

$$E(R) = \sum_{m=1}^{M} R_m P_m$$

where

$E(R)$ = expected value of R during a particular fiscal period (in this case, assumed to be the end of the fiscal period)

R_m = the mth value of R (cash flow) associated with P_m

P_m = probability of occurrence of R_m

m = *number of occurrences of R* and associated number of probabilities P, where $m = a, 2, \ldots M$

Σ = summation sign

EXAMPLE 5.11

Investment Project D is estimated to have cash flows for the coming fiscal year as follows:

Cash flows	Probability of occurrence
$ 8,000	.1
9,000	.2
10,000	.4
11,000	.2
$12,000	.1

The cash flows take place at the end of the year. Applying the above formula, calculations for the expected value of cash flows for the coming year are as follows:

$$E(R) = (.1)(\$8,000) + (.2)(\$9,000) + (.4)(\$10,000)$$
$$+ (.2)(\$11,000) + (.1)(\$12,000)$$
$$= \$800 + \$1,800 + \$4,000 + \$2,200 + \$1,200$$
$$= \$10,000$$

The expected value of cash flows is simply a weighted average of the cash flows, where the weights equal the probabilities of occurrence. Another notation for expected value would be

$$E(R) = \overline{R}$$
where
$\overline{R}$ = average of the expected cash flows (also called R bar)

If certain circumstances prevail, then the expected value of cash flows for the coming year would be the most probable value that you can expect to occur. MOST CRITICAL: Correct estimation of the probabilities and their associated cash flows will ensure your success. However, anyone with experience in forecasting knows how perilous any attempts to make useful guesses about the future can be.

How can I estimate risk associated with cash flow estimates?

Standard deviation measures the average dispersion of the individual cash flows, R_m, around the expected value of the cash flows, $E(R)$. First, the dispersion of cash flows, known as variance, is defined as follows:

$$\text{var}(R) = \sum_{m=1}^{M} (R_m - \overline{R})^2 P_m$$

or

$$\text{var}(R) = \delta^2_R$$

The standard deviation of the cash flows is given as follows:

$$\delta_R = \sqrt{\delta^2_R}$$

or

$$\delta_R = \sqrt{\sum_{m=1}^{M} (R_m - \overline{R})^2 P_m}$$

EXAMPLE 5.12

Consider Project D from the previous example. The calculation of expected value, variance, and standard deviation are given in Exhibit 5.10.

NOTE: Standard deviation is considered a measure of absolute risk. The higher the standard deviation, the greater the risk.

How do these measures affect net present value?

When comparing investments, you do not really compare their cash flows but their net present values or yields. You need to understand how variability of future cash flows affect these figures. The expected value of NPV is given by the following formula:

$$E(\text{NPV}) = \sum_{m=1}^{M} \text{NPV}_m P_m$$

The standard deviation of NPV is given in Exhibit 5.10.

EXHIBIT 5.10: CALCULATION OF EXPECTED VALUE, VARIANCE, AND STANDARD DEVIATION OF EXPECTED CASH FLOWS

m	R_m	P_m	$R_m P_m$	$(R_m - \overline{R})$	$(R_m - \overline{R})^2$	$(R_m - \overline{R})^2 P_m$
1	$ 8,000	.1	$ 800	$ 8,000 − $10,000	$ 4,000,000	$ 400,000
2	9,000	.2	1,800	9,000 − 10,000	1,000,000	200,000
3	10,000	.4	4,000	10,000 − 10,000	0	0
4	11,000	.2	2,200	11,000 − 10,000	1,000,000	200,000
5	12,000	.1	1,200	12,000 − 10,000	4,000,000	400,000
		1.0	$10,000		$10,000,000	$1,200,000

$E(R) = \overline{R} = \$10,000$
$\text{var}(R) = \$1,200,000$
$\sigma_R = \$1,095$

EXAMPLE 5.13

Begin again with Project D, but note some additional information. The cost of the project is $8,000, and the company estimates an incremental cost of capital of 12%. Assume the investment cost is incurred at the beginning of next year and cash flows occur at the end of next year.

The calculations of NPV for expected cash flows, as well as their variance and standard deviation, are shown in Exhibits 5.11 and 5.12.

EXHIBIT 5.11: CALCULATION OF NPV

m	R_m	IF_p at $ICC = 12\%$	$PV(R_m)$	CI	NPV_m
1	$ 8,000	0.892857	$ 7,143	$8,000	−$857
2	9,000	0.892857	8,036	8,000	36
3	10,000	0.892857	8,929	8,000	929
4	11,000	0.892857	9,821	8,000	1,821
5	12,000	0.892857	10,714	8,000	2,714

Recall that NPV depends on R, as shown in Section 5.1. Since this example considers just one future year, the following expected net present value, $E(\text{NPV})$, can be computed as follows:

$$E(\text{NPV}) = \frac{E(R)}{(1 + i)} - CI$$

$$E(\text{NPV}) = \frac{\$10,000}{(1 + 0.12)} - \$8,000$$

$$E(\text{NPV}) = \$8,929 - \$8,000 = \$929$$

NOTE: In the previous example, both CI and i are assumed to be known with certainty. If they are not, then these variables must also be treated in terms of expected values. WHAT TO DO: Treat all variables in terms of expected values. For illustrative purposes in this chapter, however, only future cash flows are considered in terms of net present value.

What is the relation between standard deviation of future cash flows and standard deviation of net present value?

The relation between standard deviation of NPV and standard deviation of R is given by the following formula:

$$\delta_{NPV} = \sqrt{\sum_{m=1}^{M} (NPV_m - \overline{NPV})^2 P_m}$$

EXHIBIT 5.12: CALCULATION OF E(NPV), var (NPV), AND σ_{NPV}

m	NPV_m	P_m	E(NPV)	$NPV_m - \overline{NPV}$	$(NPV_m - \overline{NPV})^2$	var(NPV)
1	-$ 857	.1	-$ 85.7	-1,786	$3,189,796	$318,980
2	36	.2	7.2	- 893	797,449	159,490
3	929	.4	371.6	0	0	0
4	1,821	.2	364.2	892	795,664	159,133
5	2,714	.1	271.4	1,785	3,186,225	318,623
			$928.7			$956,226

E(NPV) = $\overline{NPV}$ = $ 929
var (NPV) = $956,226
σ_{NPV} = $ 978

With the previous example, this formula yields a standard deviation of NPV and R as follows:

$$\delta_{NPV} = \frac{\$1,095}{(1 + 0.12)} = \$978$$

5.3.2 Two-Year Life Projects

This section continues where the last left off. Here, expected value and standard deviation of future cash flows will be considered for a two-year investment project.

How do I compute expected value and standard deviation of the second year's cash flows?

The formulas for the calculation of expected value, variance, and standard deviation of the expected cash flows of the second year of a project parallel those of the first year:

$$E(R_2) = \sum_{m=1}^{M} R_{2m}P_{2m}$$

$$\text{var}(R_2) = \sum_{m=1}^{M} (R_{2m} - \overline{R}_2)^2 P_{2m}$$

$$\delta_{R2} = \sqrt{\sum_{m=1}^{M} (R_{2m} - \overline{R}_{2m}) P_{2m}}$$

EXAMPLE 5.14

Investment Project E is estimated to have cash flows and probabilities of occurrence as follows:

YEAR 1		YEAR 2	
Cash Flows	Probability of Occurrence	Cash Flows	Probability of Occurrence
$ 8,000	.1	$16,000	.1
9,000	.2	18,000	.2
10,000	.4	20,000	.4
11,000	.2	22,000	.2
$12,000	.1	$24,000	.1

All cash flows are assumed to take place at the end of each of the two future years. Calculations for the expected value, variance, and standard deviation of the expected cash flows for the first year are given in Example 5.12. For the second year, calculations are given in Exhibit 5.13.

EXHIBIT 5.13: CALCULATION OF EXPECTED VALUE, VARIANCE, AND STANDARD DEVIATION OF EXPECTED CASH FLOWS FOR THE SECOND YEAR OF INVESTMENT PROJECT E

m	R_{2m}	P_{2m}	$R_{2m}P_{2m}$	$R_{2m} - \bar{R}_2$	$(R_{2m} - \bar{R}_2)^2$	$(R_{2m} - \bar{R}_2)^2 P_{2m}$
1	$16,000	.1	$ 1,600	$16,000 − $20,000	$16,000,000	$1,600,000
2	18,000	.2	3,600	18,000 − 20,000	4,000,000	800,000
3	20,000	.4	8,000	20,000 − 20,000	0	0
4	22,000	.2	4,400	22,000 − 20,000	4,000,000	800,000
5	24,000	.1	2,400	24,000 − 20,000	16,000,000	1,600,000
		1.0	$20,000		$40,000,000	$4,800,000

R_{2m} = the mth value of R_2 (the second year's cash flow) associated with P_{2m}

P_{2m} = the second year's probability of occurrence of R_{2m}

$\bar{R}_2 = E(R_2)$ = expected value of R during the second year; assumed in the present case to take place at the end of the second year

$\bar{R}_2$ = $20,000

$\text{var}(R_2)$ = $4,800,000

σR_2 = $2,191

How do I compute expected value of net present value?

Formulas for the calculation of the expected value and standard deviation for net present value are as follows:

$$E(NPV) = \frac{E(R_1)}{(1+i)} + \frac{E(R_2)}{(1+i)^2} - CI$$

$$E(NPV) = \frac{\sum_{m=1}^{M} R_{1m}P_{1m}}{1+i} + \frac{\sum_{m=1}^{M} R_{2m}P_{2m}}{(1+i)^2} - CI$$

Note the similarity between these formulas and those for a one-year project. Once again, these assume that CI and i are known with certainty.

For present purposes, let's assume the probabilities that certain cash flows would materialize at the end of each year are the same. That is,

$$Pn,m = Pn+1,m \text{ for } n = 1, 2, \ldots, n$$

where

Pn,m = the probability of year n that the mth cash flow will be realized

EXAMPLE 5.15

Use Project E as described previously. Assume the cost of investment (CI) equals $20,800 and the incremental cost of capital (i) is 12%.

The calculation of the expected values of the future cash flows of the first and second future years, $E(R_1)$ and $E(R_2)$, are shown in Exhibit 5.14.

EXHIBIT 5.14: CALCULATION OF THE EXPECTED VALUES OF THE FUTURE CASH FLOWS OF INVESTMENT PROJECT E

m	R_{1m}	P_{1m}	$R_{1m}P_{1m}$	R_{2m}	P_{2m}	$R_{2m}P_{2m}$
1	$ 8,000	.1	$ 800	$16,000	.1	$ 1,600
2	9,000	.2	1,800	18,000	.2	3,600
3	10,000	.4	4,000	20,000	.4	8,000
4	11,000	.2	2,200	22,000	.2	4,400
5	12,000	.1	1,200	24,000	.1	2,400
			$10,000			$20,000

$E(R_1) = \$10,000$

$E(R_2) = \$20,000$

From the formula for E(NPV) given in Section 5.3, you can calculate E(NPV) for Project E as follows:

$$E(\text{NPV}) = \frac{\$10,000}{(1 + 0.12)} + \frac{\$20,000}{(1 + 0.12)^2} - \$20,800$$

$$E(\text{NPV}) = (0.892857)(\$10,000) + (0.797194)(\$20,000) - \$20,800$$

$$E(\text{NPV}) = \$8,929 + \$15,944 - \$20,800$$

$$E(\text{NPV}) = \$4,073$$

How do I compute standard deviation of net present value?

The variance of net present value, var(NPV), is equal to the variance of the present value, var(PV), or

$$\text{var(NPV)} = \text{var(PV)}$$

where

$$\text{var(CI)} = 0$$

This assumes that the cost of the project, CI, is known with certainty and is a given constant.

Assume also that variations in the expected cash flows of the first future year are independent of those of the second year. This leads to the following formula:

$$\text{var(PV)} = \sum_{m=1}^{M} (PV_{1m} - E[PV_1])^2 P_{1m} \\ + \sum_{m=1}^{M} (PV_{2m} - E[PV_2])^2 P_{2m}$$

$$\text{var(PV)} = \text{var}(PV_1) + \text{var}(PV_2)$$

where

$$\text{cov}(PV_1, PV_2) = 0$$

The covariance, cov(PV1, PV2), is a measure of whether the variations in the expected cash flows of future year one are associated with those of future year two. Since these variations are assumed to be independent of each other, $\text{cov}(PV_1, PV_2) = 0$.

EXAMPLE 5.16

The present values of the probable cash flows for the first and second years for Project E are given in Exhibit 5.15. With these calculations completed, the variances of the present values of future cash flows can be shown as in Exhibit 5.16.

**EXHIBIT 5.15: CALCULATION OF THE
PRESENT VALUES AND EXPECTED VALUES
OF PROBABLE FUTURE CASH FLOWS OF
INVESTMENT PROJECT E**

m	R_{1m}	One-Year Discount ICC = 12%	$PV(R_{1m})$	P_{1m}	$PV(R_{1m})$ $\times P_{1m}$
1	$ 8,000	.892857	$ 7,142.86	.1	$ 714.29
2	9,000	.892857	8,035.71	.2	1,607.14
3	10,000	.892857	8,928.57	.4	3,571.43
4	11,000	.892857	9,821.43	.2	1,964.29
5	12,000	.892857	10,714.28	.1	1,071.43
					$ 8,928.58

m	R_{2m}	Two-Year Discount ICC = 12%	$PV(R_{2m})$	P_{1m}	$PV(R_{1m})$ $\times P_{1m}$
1	$16,000	.797194	$12,755.10	.1	$ 1,275.51
2	18,000	.797194	14,349.49	.2	2,869.90
3	20,000	.797194	15,943.88	.4	6,377.55
4	22,000	.797194	17,538.27	.2	3,507.65
5	24,000	.797194	19,132.66	.1	1,913.27
					$15,943.88

$E(PV_1) = \$8,928.57$
$E(PV_2) = \$15,943.88$

The overall variance of Project E would then be

$$\text{var(PV)} = \$956,632 + \$3,050,496 = \$4,007,128$$

Remember, cash flows of future years one and two are independent of each other.

Having calculated var(PV), then the standard deviation of the present value would be given by this formula:

$$\delta_{PV} = \sqrt{\text{var(PV)}}$$

For Project E, then,

$$\delta_{PV} = \sqrt{\$4,007,128} = \$2,002$$

NOTE: The standard deviation of the present value, δ_{PV}, is also the standard deviation of the net present value

$$\delta_{NPV} = \delta_{PV} = \$2,002.$$

EXHIBIT 5.16: CALCULATION OF THE VARIANCES OF THE PRESENT VALUES OF INVESTMENT PROJECT E

m	$PV_{1m} - E(PV_1)$		$(PV_{1m} - E[PV_1])^2$	P_{1m}	$(PV_{1m} - E[PV_{1m}])^2 P_{1m}$
1	\$ 7,142.86 − \$ 8,928.57	\$ −1,785.71	\$ 3,188,760	.1	\$ 318,876
2	8,035.71 − 8,928.57	−892.86	797,199	.2	159,440
3	8,928.57 − 8,928.57	0	0	.4	0
4	9,821.43 − 8,928.57	+892.86	797,199	.2	159,440
5	10,714.23 − 8,928.57	+1,785.71	3,188,760	.1	318,876
					\$ 956,632

EXHIBIT 5.16 (cont.)

m	$PV_{2m} - E(PV_2)$		$(PV_{2m} - E[PV_2])^2$	P_{2m}	$(PV_{2m} - E[PV_2])^2 P_{2m}$
1	$12,755.10 - \$15,943.88$	$\$-3,188.78$	$\$10,168,318$	.1	$\$1,016,832$
2	$14,349.49 - 15,943.88$	$-1,594.39$	$2,542,079$	.2	$508,416$
3	$15,943.88 - 15,943.88$	0	0	.4	0
4	$17,538.27 - 15,943.88$	$+1,594.39$	$2,542,079$	.2	$508,416$
5	$19,132.66 - 15,943.88$	$+3,188.78$	$10,168,318$	.1	$1,016,832$
					$\$3,050,496$

$\text{var}(PV_1) = \$956,632$

$\text{var}(PV_2) = \$3,050,496$

What is the relation between standard deviation of net present value and standard deviation of future cash flows?

In order to derive a relation between the standard deviation of the present value and net present value to those of future cash flows, use the following formulas:

$$var(PV_1) = \frac{var(R_1)}{(1 + i)^2}$$

and

$$var(PV_2) = \frac{var(R_2)}{(1 + i)^4}$$

By substitution, you can obtain the following relation:

$$var(NPV) = \frac{var(R_1)}{(1 + i)^2} + \frac{var(R_2)}{(1 + i)^4}$$

where

$$cov(R_1, R_2) = 0$$

Thus, the relationship for the standard variations would be expressed as follows:

$$\delta_{NPV} = \sqrt{\frac{var(R_1)}{(1 + i)^2} + \frac{var(R_2)}{(1 + i)^4}}$$

where

$$cov(R_1, R_2) = 0$$

5.3.3 Multiyear Life Projects

How do I compute expected value of future cash flows and net present value?

In Section 5.3, determination of net present value (NPV) was based on the assumption that future cash flows are known with certainty. When you consider the notion of probable future cash flows, then you must calculate the expected value of NPV, $E(NPV)$, according to the following formula:

$$E(NPV) = \frac{E(R_1)}{1 + i} + \frac{E(R_2)}{(1 + i)^2} + \ldots + \frac{E(R_N)}{(1 + i)^N} - CI$$

where

$$E(R_n) = \sum_{m=1}^{M} R_{nm}P_{nm} \quad \text{for} \quad n = 1, 2, \ldots, N$$

The formula can also be written as follows:

$$E(NPV) = \left(\frac{\sum\limits_{m=1}^{M} R_{1m}P_{1m}}{(1+i)} + \frac{\sum\limits_{m=1}^{M} R_{2m}P_{2m}}{(1+i)^2} + \ldots \frac{\sum\limits_{m=1}^{M} R_{Nm}P_{Nm}}{(1+i)^n} \right) - CI$$

EXAMPLE 5.17

The cost of investment project F is \$68,928. The incremental cost of capital is 12%. Project F is assumed to have a five-year horizon as well as five probable levels of future cash flows, given as follows:

PROBABLE FUTURE CASH FLOWS FOR PROJECT F

| | m (probable future cash flow) | | | | |
n (year)	1	2	3	4	5
1	\$ 8,000	\$ 9,000	\$10,000	\$11,000	\$12,000
2	16,000	18,000	20,000	22,000	24,000
3	24,000	27,000	30,000	33,000	36,000
4	32,000	36,000	40,000	44,000	48,000
5	40,000	45,000	50,000	55,000	60,000

Also, assume the probabilities of occurrence do not change. As a result, the probability of occurrence for the mth cash flows is .1 for $m=1$, .2 for $m=2$, .4 for $m=3$, and .1 for $m=5$.

WHAT TO DO: First, calculate the expected values of the future cash flows for each five years. For years 1 and 2, these values are shown in Example 5.16 above. Calculations for years 3, 4, and 5 are shown below in Exhibit 5.17.

The calculation of the expected value of PV and NPV are given in Exhibit 5.18.

How do I measure variance and standard deviation of future cash flows?

You would measure variance and standard deviation of the probable cash flows of subsequent years as you would for years 1 and 2.

EXHIBIT 5.17: CALCULATION OF THE EXPECTED VALUES OF THE FUTURE CASH FLOWS OF INVESTMENT PROJECT F FOR YEARS 3, 4, AND 5

m	R_{3m}	P_{3m}	$R_{3m}P_{3m}$	R_{4m}	P_{4m}	$R_{4m}P_{4m}$	R_{5m}	P_{5m}	$R_{5m}P_{5m}$
1	$24,000	.1	$ 2,400	$32,000	.1	$ 3,200	$40,000	.1	$ 4,000
2	27,000	.2	5,400	36,000	.2	7,200	45,000	.2	9,000
3	30,000	.4	12,000	40,000	.4	16,000	50,000	.4	20,000
4	33,000	.2	6,600	44,000	.2	8,800	55,000	.2	11,000
5	36,000	.1	3,600	48,000	.1	4,800	60,000	.1	6,000
			$30,000			$40,000			$50,000

$E(R_3) = \$30,000$

$E(R_4) = \$40,000$

$E(R_5) = \$50,000$

EXAMPLE 5.18

For Project F, variance and standard deviation of future
cash flows for years 1 and 2 are shown.

EXHIBIT 5.18: CALCULATION OF THE EXPECTED VALUE OF THE PRESENT VALUE AND NET PRESENT VALUE OF THE FUTURE CASH FLOWS OF INVESTMENT PROJECT F

End of Year n	$E(R_n)$	IF_p at $ICC = 12\%$	EV of Present Value
1	$10,000	0.892857	$ 8,929
2	20,000	0.797194	15,944
3	30,000	0.711780	21,353
4	40,000	0.635518	25,421
5	50,000	0.567427	28,371
			$100,018

$E(NPV) = E(PV) - CI$

$E(NPV) = \$100,018 - \$68,928$

$E(NPV) = \$31,090$

EXHIBIT 5.19: CALCULATION OF THE VARIANCES AND STANDARD DEVIATIONS OF THE FUTURE CASH FLOWS OF INVESTMENT PROJECT F FOR YEARS 3, 4, AND 5

m	$R_{3m} - \bar{R}_3$	$(R_{3m} - \bar{R}_3)^2$	P_{3m}	$(R_{3m} - \bar{R}_3)^2 P_{3m}$
1	$24,000 - $30,000	$ 36,000,000	.1	$3,600,000
2	27,000 - 30,000	9,000,000	.2	1,800,000
3	30,000 - 30,000	0	.4	0
4	33,000 - 30,000	9,000,000	.2	1,800,000
5	36,000 - 30,000	36,000,000	.1	3,600,000
				$10,800,000

m	$R_{4m} - \bar{R}_4$	$(R_{4m} - \bar{R}_4)^2$	P_{4m}	$(R_{4m} - R_4)^2 P_{4m}$
1	$32,000 - $40,000	$ 64,000,000	.1	$ 6,400,000
2	36,000 - 40,000	16,000,000	.2	3,200,000
3	40,000 - 40,000	0	.4	0
4	44,000 - 40,000	16,000,000	.2	3,200,000
5	48,000 - 40,000	64,000,000	.1	6,400,000
				$ 19,200,000

EXHIBIT 5.19 (cont.)

m	$R_{Sm} - \overline{R}_S$	$(R_{Sm} - \overline{R}_S)^2$	P_{Sm}	$(R_{Sm} - \overline{R})^2 P_{Sm}$
1	\$40,000 − \$50,000	\$100,000,000	.1	\$10,000,000
2	45,000 − 50,000	25,000,000	.2	5,000,000
3	50,000 − 50,000	0	.4	0
4	55,000 − 50,000	25,000,000	.2	5,000,000
5	60,000 − 50,000	100,000,000	.1	10,000,000
				\$30,000,000

$\text{var}(R_3) = \$10,800,000;\quad \sigma R_3 = \$3,286$
$\text{var}(R_4) = \$19,200,000;\quad \sigma R_4 = \$4,382$
$\text{var}(R_5) = \$30,000,000;\quad \sigma R_5 = \$5,477$

For years 3, 4, and 5, these values are computed as shown in Exhibit 5.19.

How do I compute variance and standard deviation of net present value?

The formula for the calculation of the variance of the net present value, var(NPV) of an investment project with independent probable cash flows for any number of future years, would be as follows:

$$\text{var(NPV)} = \left(\frac{\text{var}[R_1]}{[1 + i]^2} + \frac{\text{var}[R_2]}{[1 + i]^4} + \cdots \right.$$
$$\left. + \frac{\text{var}[R_n]}{[1 + i]^{2n}} \right) - \text{CI}$$
$$\text{var(NPV)} = \sum_{n=1}^{N} \frac{\text{var}(R_n)}{(1 + i)^{2n}}$$

where

$$\text{var}(R_n, R_n + 1) = 0 \text{ for } n = 1, 2, \ldots, N$$

The formula for the calculation of the standard deviation of the net present value would be as follows:

$$\delta_{NPV} = \sqrt{\sum_{n=1}^{N} \frac{\text{var}(R_n)}{(1 + i)^{2n}}}$$

where the $\text{cov}(R_n, R_{n+1}) = 0$ for $n = 1, 2, \ldots, N$

EXAMPLE 5.19

Use the data from Project F for this example. The calculation of the var(NPV) and the δ(NPV) is shown in Exhibit 5.20.

EXHIBIT 5.20:   CALCULATION OF THE VAR(NPV) AND σ_{NPV} OF INVESTMENT PROJECT F

n	$var(R_n)$	$\dfrac{1}{(1+i)^{2n}}$	$var(R_n) \cdot \left[\dfrac{1}{(1+i)^{2n}}\right]$
1	$ 1,200,000	.797194	$ 956,633
2	4,800,000	.635518	3,050,486
3	10,800,000	.506631	5,471,615
4	19,200,000	.403883	7,754,554
5	30,000,000	.321973	9,659,190
			$26,892,478

var(NPV) = $26,892,478

σ_{NPV} = $5,186

What is relative risk and how is it measured?

Relative risk, also called the coefficient of variation (CV), is defined as the ratio of the standard variation of the net present value to the net present value of the investment. The formula is stated as follows:

$$CV_{NPV} = \frac{\delta_{NPV}}{E(NPV)}$$

EXAMPLE 5.20

For Projects D, E, and F from the previous examples, see the calculations of CV as follows:

Investment Project	σ_{NPV}	$E(NPV)$	CV_{NPV}
D	978	$ 929	1.05
E	2.002	4,073	0.49
F	5,186	31,090	0.17

CONCLUSIONS: Project F has the lowest level of risk compared with the others. Notice that as the level of absolute risk (as measured by δ_{NPV}) rises, the level of return (as measured by $E([NPV])$) rises even more. THE RESULT: Relative risk falls.

What is the trade-off between risk and return?

Typically you want to minimize the risk to which your investments are exposed. In order to consider bearing a greater risk, you would require a higher return. The desired trade-off between risk and return is shown in Figure 5.3. This graph, called an indifference curve, assumes the return will have to be increased at an increasing rate as the level of risk rises. Because the curve shows only the level of return required to compensate for the burden of additional risk, the investor is indifferent among the investments found on the curve. The curve also shows the minimal level of return desired by an investor even when risk is absent (zero level of risk).

What are the limitations of capital budgeting techniques?

Now that you have reviewed the techniques of capital budgeting, you should be aware of their limitations. First, such techniques require that certain types of data be forecast, and this holds special perils that must not be neglected.

The net present value method basically assumes you can forecast future cash flows with some degree of usefulness. It also assumes the incremental cost of capital will be constant over the future forecast periods. In order to use this method, you must know or be able to reasonably

FIGURE 5.2: THE DESIRED TRADE-OFF BETWEEN RISK AND RETURN

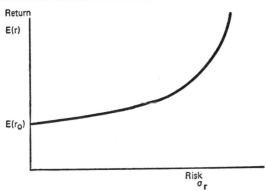

$E(r) =$ the expected value of return (normally measured in percent)

$\sigma_r =$ the standard deviation of return

$E(r_0) =$ the expected value of return on an investment that an investor desires in the absence of risk

forecast the cost of the investment project. When uncertain, and this is the usual state of affairs, you must be able to forecast not only the amount and timing of future cash flows but also the probabilities of their occurrence.

Capital budgeting techniques also require evaluation of not only the returns expected to be generated by the investment projects but also an evaluation of the risk perceived to be associated with the returns. The calculation of standard deviation of the NPV is itself dependent on the calculation of the NPV.

6

Assets Management and Financing Techniques

In this chapter you will learn how to manage your company's assets and liabilities in order to generate the highest return at the lowest possible risk. Whether you are a financial manager, managerial accountant, or investment analyst, you should be concerned with

- Determining the proper mixture of assets in the total asset structure
- Receiving cash promptly while delaying its payment
- Selling to the right customers
- Formulating a sound investment strategy

This chapter also helps you develop techniques for obtaining financing. If you're a financial manager, you'll learn how to go about raising funds on a short-, intermediate-, and long-term basis. Or, if you're a management executive, the following factors will be very much your concern:

- The cost of capital for examining financing alternatives
- The appropriateness of your company's dividend policy
- The effects of inflation
- The effects of the business cycle

ECONOMISTS AND FINANCIAL MANAGERS: You'll learn how to use economic indicators of performance for purposes of evaluating your own company's financial health. All these techniques will help you cope with situations as they arise every day.

6.1   MANAGING WORKING CAPITAL

What is working capital?

Working capital equals current assets less current liabilities. It is a measure of liquidity. CAUTION TO FINANCIAL MANAGERS: A higher balance in total current assets means greater ability to meet your debt. But it also means less return earned on total assets. Remember: Fixed assets generate a higher rate of return than current assets.

What is the risk–return trade-off in current versus fixed assets?

Fixed assets comprise the basic structure of a business, representing plant and manufacturing equipment. Assuming a viable business, you would expect a higher return on machinery than marketable securities which, in fact, usually come to less than the overall cost of capital. You can see a risk–return trade-off here, since current assets represent less risk but lower return. Similarly, financing with current liabilities rather than long-term debt typically involves lower cost but greater liquidity risk. The greater the debt maturity, the more uncertainty and hence generally the greater the cost.

What approach should I use for financing assets?

FOR MANAGEMENT EXECUTIVES: It's probably best to use a hedging approach whereby assets are financed by liabilities of similar maturity. This will ensure that adequate funds are available to meet the debt when due.

6.2   MAXIMIZING YOUR RETURN ON CASH

What is necessary for good cash management?

If you're a financial manager or management executive, cash management is important to you. If you are holding on to cash unnecessarily, you are losing a return that could be earned by investing. The cash balance held should depend on forecasted cash flows, probability of running out of cash, maturity of debt, and ability to borrow. You'll need forecasting information to determine (1) the best time to incur and pay back debt and (2) the amount to transfer daily between accounts. Use such techniques as accounting budgets, zero base budgeting (see Section 3.6) and quantitative models like time series and probabilities (see Section 7.3).

MANAGEMENT EXECUTIVES USE THIS RULE: Required cash balance equals transaction balances (required for normal business activity) plus precautionary balances (needed for emergencies) plus compensating balances (needed for financing commitments).

How can I accelerate cash receipts?

Use the following techniques.

CHECKLIST OF WAYS
TO ACCELERATE CASH RECEIPTS

- Lockbox. This is a location where customer payments are mailed, usually a strategic post office box. Payments are then picked up several times during the day by the bank.
- Concentration banking. Funds are collected in local banks and transferred to a main concentration account.
- Immediate transfer of funds between banks. Transfers would be accomplished through depository transfer checks or via wire.
- Cash discounts for early payment.
- Accelerated billing practices.
- Personal collection efforts.
- Cash-on-delivery.
- Postdated customer checks.
- Depositing checks promptly.
- Obtaining cash tied up unnecessarily in other accounts (for example, loans to company officers).

WHAT TO DO: Compare the return earned from the newly acquired cash to the cost of implementing an accelerated cash management system. Lockbox services are primarily good for collecting large dollar, low-volume receipts. Because of its high per-item cost, a lockbox does not always provide net savings.

EXAMPLE 6.1

Akel Corporation is considering a lockbox arrangement costing $350,000 per year. Daily collections average $1,000,000. Mailing and processing time will be reduced by four days with the arrangement. The rate of return is 10%. The cost–benefit analysis is shown as follows:

Annual return on freed cash

10% × 4 × $1,000,000	$400,000
Annual cost	350,000
Savings	$ 50,000

CONCLUSION: The lockbox arrangement is profitable.

EXAMPLE 6.2

Loft Corporation presently has a lockbox with Colt Bank. The bank handles $1.5 million per day for $300,000 compensating balance. Loft is considering canceling this arrangement and instead dividing its western region through arrangements with two other banks. Most Bank will handle $1 million a day, with a compensating balance of $225,000, and Davis Bank will handle $500,000 a day, with a compensating balance of $200,000. In both instances, collections will improve by one half-day. The rate of return is 11%. A cost–benefit analysis shows the following:

Accelerated cash receipts of $1.5 million per day × ½ day	$750,000
Increased compensating balance	125,000
Increased cash flow	$625,000
Return rate	× 11%
Net annual savings	$ 68,750

CONCLUSION: The new arrangement is financially feasible.

How can I delay cash payments?

Try these techniques:

CHECKLIST OF WAYS TO DELAY CASH PAYMENTS

- Centralize the payable operation. This enables you to meet obligations at the most profitable time. It also enhances your ability to predict disbursement float in the system.
- Use drafts. A draft is given to the bank for collection, which in turn goes to the issuer for acceptance. After that, the funds are deposited to pay the draft.
- Use a computer terminal to transfer funds between various bank accounts at opportune times.
- Draw checks on remote banks, for example, a New York company could use a California bank.
- Mail checks from post offices with limited services or where mail must go through several handling points.
- Use probability analysis to determine the expected time for checks to clear. For example, funds deposited on payday may not equal the entire payroll since not all checks will be cashed on that day.
- Make partial payments.

SUGGESTION FOR MANAGEMENT EXECUTIVES: Consider "payment float," that is, the difference between the checkbook balance and the bank balance. When float is used effectively, a company can hold a higher bank balance even though a lower cash balance appears on the books.

EXAMPLE 6.3

Company X writes checks averaging $50,000 per day; each check takes three days to clear. The company will have a checkbook balance $150,000 less than the bank's records.

How much cash do I need on hand?

You can predict the optimum amount of transaction cash needed under conditions of certainty. First, compute the sum of the fixed cost applicable to transactions and the opportunity cost of holding cash balances as follows:

$$\frac{F(T)}{C} + \frac{i(C)}{2}$$

where
   C = given cash balance
   F = fixed cost of transaction
   T = total cash required for time period
   i = interest rate on marketable securities

The following formula was developed by W. Baumol to compute the optimal cash level (K):

$$K = \sqrt{\frac{2FT}{i}}$$

Average cash balance equals

$$\frac{K}{2}$$

and the number of required transactions equals

$$\frac{\text{transaction cash}}{K}$$

EXAMPLE 6.4

Company B expects a cash need of $4,000,000 over a one-month period, to be paid out at a constant rate. The opportunity interest rate is 0.5% for one month. The cost for each transaction is $100. The optimal transaction size is computed as follows:

$$K = \sqrt{\frac{2FT}{i}} = \sqrt{\frac{2(100)(4,000,000)}{0.005}} = \$400,000$$

The average cash balance equals:

$$\frac{K}{2} = \frac{\$400,000}{2} = \$200,000$$

The number of transactions required equals:

$$\frac{\$4,000,000}{400,000} = 10$$

SUGGESTION FOR FINANCIAL MANAGERS: You can use a stochastic model for cash management when major uncertainty regarding cash payments exists. The Miller–Orr model places an upper ceiling (referred to as d dollars) and lower limit ("zero" dollars) for cash balances. When the upper limit is reached, a transfer takes place from securities to cash. The transaction will not occur as long as the cash balance falls within the limits of the model.

You should take the following factors into account when using the Miller–Orr model:

- Fixed costs of a securities transaction (F)
- The daily interest rate on marketable securities (i)
- The deviation in daily net cash flows (σ^2)

Your objective is to meet cash requirements at the lowest possible cost. When the cash balance reaches d, this amount less the cost of securities bought (z) reduces the balance to z dollars. When the cash balance equals zero, z dollars are sold and the new balance again reaches z. NOTE TO MANAGEMENT EXECUTIVES: The minimum cash balance is established at an amount greater than zero to act as a safety buffer as, for example, delays in transfer.

Use these formulas for optimal and average cash balance:

Optimal cash balance $(z) = \sqrt[3]{\frac{3F\sigma^2}{4i}}$

Optimal upper limit $(d) = 3z$

Average cash balance $= \frac{(z + d)}{3}$

EXAMPLE 6.5

Company J wishes to use the Miller–Orr model. The following data are given:

Fixed cost of a securities transaction	$10
Deviation in daily net cash flows	$50

Daily interest rate on securities (10%/360)   0.0003

The optimal cash balance, the upper limit of cash needed, and the average cash balance are computed as follows:

$$z = \sqrt[3]{\frac{3(10)(50)}{4(0.0003)}} = \sqrt[3]{\frac{3(10)(50)}{0.0012}} = \sqrt[3]{\frac{1500}{0.0012}}$$

$$= \sqrt[3]{1,250,000} = \$102$$

The optimal cash balance (z) = \$102
The upper limit (d) = $3 \times \$102 = \$306$
The average cash balance = $\dfrac{\$102 + \$106}{3} = \$136$

DISCUSSION: When the upper limit (\$306) is reached, \$204 of securities (\$306 − \$102) will be purchased, thereby obtaining the optimal cash balance of \$102. When the lower limit of \$0 dollars is reached, \$102 of securities will be sold, again bringing the optimal cash balance to \$102.

6.3 MANAGING ACCOUNTS RECEIVABLE

What can I do to manage receivables properly?

Whether you're a financial manager, managerial accountant, or management executive, you'll want to manage receivables in order to maximize return and minimize risk. Here are some of the many things you can do:

CHECKLIST OF APPROACHES TO THE
MANAGEMENT OF ACCOUNTS RECEIVABLE

- Age accounts receivable for overdue balances and compare them to industry and competitive norms as well as your own prior years.
- Periodically revise credit limits based on your customers' changing financial health.
- When there might be a problem with collection, obtain collateral at least equal in amount to the account balance.
- Use collection agencies when warranted.
- Factor (sell) accounts receivable when net savings occur.
- Bill large sales immediately.
- Employ cycle billing for uniformity in the billing process.
- Mail customer statements within one day of the period end.
- Offer delayed payment terms to stimulate demand.

- Carefully evaluate customers' financial health before giving credit.
- Obtain credit insurance to guard against abnormal losses from bad debt.
- Avoid typically high-risk receivables, for example, customers in a financially troubled industry or country.

Should I consider cash discounts?

MANAGEMENT EXECUTIVES: You must decide whether cash discounts should be given for early payment. WHAT TO DO: Implement discount policy provided the return on funds obtained from early collection is greater than the cost of the discount.

EXAMPLE 6.6

Blake Company provides the following data:

Current annual credit sales	$8,000,000
Collection period	2 months
Terms	net/30
Minimum rate of return	15%

The financial manager is considering whether to offer a 2/10 net/30 discount. He anticipates that 25% of the customers will take advantage of it. The collection period should decline to 1.5 months.

The advantage of the policy is shown as follows:

Return

Average accounts receivable balance prior to change in policy:

$$\frac{\text{credit sales}}{\text{accounts receivable turnover}} = \frac{\$8,000,000}{6}$$

	$1,333,333

Average accounts receivable balance subsequent to change in policy:

$$\frac{\$8,000,000}{8}$$

	1,000,000
Decrease in average accounts receivable	$ 333,333
Rate of return	× 15%
Return	$ 50,000

Discount

Cost of discount 0.02 × 0.25 × $8,000,000	$ 40,000
Net advantage of discount policy	$ 10,000

When should I give credit to marginal customers?

MANAGEMENT EXECUTIVES: You are often faced with a decision of whether to give credit to somewhat marginal customers. WHAT TO DO: Give credit when the profitability of the additional sales is greater than the additional cost associated with the discount. When idle capacity exists, this additional profitability equals the contribution margin (sales minus variable cost). But, remember to add these costs, too: higher bad debts, opportunity cost of putting funds in receivables for a longer period of time, and increased clerical costs for servicing an additional customer base.

EXAMPLE 6.7

Long Corporation provides the following data:

Selling price per unit	$5
Variable cost per unit	$2
Fixed cost per unit	$2
Annual credit sales	600,000 units
Collection period	1 month
Minimum return	24%

The financial manager is considering a proposal to liberalize credit. He expects sales to increase by 20%. The collection period on total accounts will be two months. Bad debts will increase by $90,000.

The following calculations show that the policy should be implemented:

Additional profit on increased sales

Additional units (600,000 × 20%)		120,000
Contribution margin per unit		
Selling price	$5	
Less variable cost	$2	× $3
Additional profitability		$360,000

Bad debts

Higher bad debts	$90,000

Opportunity cost of increased balance in accounts receivable

Current average investment in accounts receivable:

Average accounts receivable

$$\times \frac{cost}{selling\ price}$$

$$\frac{credit\ sales}{accounts\ receivable\ turnover} \times \frac{cost}{selling\ price}$$

$$\frac{\$3,000,000^a}{12} \times \frac{\$4}{\$5} \qquad \underline{\$200,000}$$

Average investment in accounts receivable after change in credit policy:

$$\frac{\$3,600,000^b}{6} \times \frac{\$3.67^c}{\$5} \qquad \$440,400$$

Increased average investment in accounts receivable	$240,400
Minimum rate	×0.24
Opportunity cost	$ 57,696

Net advantage to policy

Additional profitability		$360,000
Additional cost		
Bad debts	$90,000	
Opportunity cost	57,696	(147,696)
Savings		$212,304

Calculations

a) $5 × 600,000 units = $3,000,000
b) $3,000,000 + 0.20 ($3,000,000) = $3,600,000
c) New average unit cost:

	Units	× Unit Cost =	Total Cost
Current volume	600,000	$4	$2,400,000
Additional volume	120,000	2	240,000
After proposal	720,000		$2,640,000

New average unit cost = $2,640,000/720,000 units = $3.67
The new average unit cost went down from $4 to $3.67 because the fixed cost is spread over more units.

How much credit should I give?

MANAGEMENT EXECUTIVES: Sometimes you must decide whether to give full credit to presently limited- or no-credit customers. REMEMBER THIS: Use full credit only when it will lead to a net profit.

EXAMPLE 6.8

Company D classifies its customers by risk ratings:

Category	Uncollectible Account (%)	Collection Period	Credit Policy	Increase in Annual Sales if Credit Restrictions Are Relaxed
A	1	20 days	Unlimited	$ 50,000
B	4	40	Restricted	500,000
C	18	70	No credit	700,000

Gross profit averages 20% of sales. The minimum rate of return is 14%. Of course, Category A receives unlimited credit. However, full credit should be extended only to Category B, and not Category C, as indicated in the table on page 202.

	Category B	Category C
Gross profit		
$500{,}000 \times 0.2$	$100,000	
$700{,}000 \times 0.2$		$140,000
Less bad debts addition		
$500{,}000 \times 0.04$	(20,000)	
$700{,}000 \times 0.18$		(126,000)
Incremental average investment in accounts receivable		
$\dfrac{40}{360} \times (80\% \times 500{,}000)$ $44,444		
$\dfrac{70}{360} \times (80\% \times 700{,}000)$		$108,889
Opportunity cost $\times .14$	(6,222)	$\times 0.14$ (15,244)
Net earnings	$73,778	($1,244)

202

6.4 FORMULATING THE BEST INVESTMENT STRATEGY

What factors should I consider when selecting an investment portfolio?

When you are selecting an investment portfolio, look at these factors:

- Financial
- Risk versus return
- Tax implications

A company's present financial picture governs the magnitude and type of risk you can undertake. For example, if liquidity is strong, you might choose long-term securities. Or, if you want to maintain needed liquidity, short-term bills (e.g., market certificates, treasury bills) might be better. REMEMBER THIS: With greater liquidity there is less return, because short-term securities yield less.

What are the various types of investments?

CHECKLIST OF INVESTMENT TYPES

- Direct *equity* claims
    Common stock
    Options
    Warrants
- Indirect *equity* claims
    Mutual funds
- *Creditor* claims
    Savings accounts
    Money market certificates
    Money market funds
    Treasury securities
    Commercial paper
    Bonds
- Preferred stock

How should I manage the investment portfolio?

FINANCIAL MANAGERS: Stagger the maturity dates of the securities. For example, if all the securities mature on a single date, your reinvestment may be subject to low returns if interest rates are low at that time.

MANAGEMENT EXECUTIVES: Examine the risk. Look at the degree of diversification and stability of the portfolio.

INVESTMENT ANALYSTS: Consider securities with negative correlations to each other. BE ON GUARD: Declines in portfolio market values may not be entirely reflected in the accounts. Use the ratio of revenue (dividend income, interest income, etc.) to the carrying value as a clue. Also, examine the footnotes for subsequent event disclosure regarding any unrealized losses that have taken place in the portfolio. FINANCIAL MANAGERS: You may want to adjust downward the extent to which an investment account can be realized in the case of such declines. You should also appraise the riskiness of the portfolio by computing the standard deviation of its rate of return.

EXAMPLE 6.9

Winston Company reports the following data for year-ends 19X1 and 19X2:

	19X1	19X2
Investments	$30,000	$33,000
Income from investments (dividends and interest)	4,000	3,200

The 19X2 annual report has a footnote titled "Subsequent Events," which indicates a $5,000 decline in the portfolio as of March 2, 19X3. The ratio of investment income to total investments went from 0.133 in 19X1 to 0.097 in 19X2, indicating a higher realization risk in the portfolio. Additionally, the post balance sheet disclosure of a $5,000 decline in value should prompt you to adjust downward the amount to which the year-end portfolio can be realized.

What kinds of risks are involved in investing?

CHECKLIST OF INVESTING RISKS

- *Business risk*. This relates to factors such as financial condition and product demand.
- *Liquidity risk*. This applies to the possibility that an investment may not be sold on short notice for its market value. A security sold at a high discount may have high liquidity risk.
- *Default risk*. This refers to the borrower's inability to make interest payments or principal repayments on debt. A bond issued by a company with significant financial problems might be a default risk.
- *Market risk*. This relates to changes in the stock price caused by changes in the market itself.
- *Purchasing power risk*. This applies to the likelihood of decreased purchasing power. Bonds are a good

example of this because the issuer pays back in cheaper dollars.

- *Interest rate risk.* This refers to the variability in the value of an investment as interest rates, money market, or capital market conditions change. This factor applies to fixed-income securities such as bonds. As interest rates increase, bond prices decrease.
- *Concentration risk.* This reflects a lack of diversification in the portfolio.

What should I know about taxes?

FINANCIAL MANAGERS: When formulating an optimal investment strategy, tax aspects must be considered. For example, interest income on bonds is fully taxable, whereas dividend income has an 85 percent tax exclusion (only 15 percent of dividends are subject to tax). When securities held for more than six months are sold at a gain, only 40 percent of the profit is taxable. Thus, you have an advantage in holding appreciated securities for longer than six months. REMEMBER THIS: Income from U.S. government securities are taxable for federal purposes but are exempt from local taxes. Income from municipals are exempt from both federal and local taxes.

What is a technical analysis?

A technical analysis looks at the direction and magnitude of the market in determining when or what to buy or sell. Technical analysts believe stock prices of individual companies tend to move with the market as they react to various supply and demand forces. Charts and graphs of internal market data, including prices and volume, are also helpful.

What are the key indicators of stock market performance?

A discussion of six major indicators of market performance follows.

Trading volume. This points to the health and trend of the market. Market volume of stocks depends on supply and demand relationships, which in turn point to market strength or weakness. For instance, you can expect higher prices when demand increases. An *upside–downside index* illustrates the difference between stock volume advancing and decreasing, typically based on a ten-day or thirty-day moving average. The index assists in identifying expected market turning points.

Market breadth. This relates to the dispersion of general price fluctuation and may be useful as an advance indicator of major price declines or advances. The *breadth index* involves computing daily the net advancing or declining issues of a broad range of securities from the New York Stock Exchange. The index is determined by dividing net advances (number of securities with price increases less declines) by the number of securities traded. This index differs from a limited stock market average (like the Dow Jones Industrial Average of 30 Stocks) by virtue of the greater spread between the number advances and declines.

EXAMPLE 6.10

Assume net declines equal 40, securities traded equals 1,100, and the breadth index equals −3.6.

This figure can be related to a base year or combined in a 150-day moving average. The figures obtained are then related to the Dow Jones Industrial Average. When *both* indexes are increasing, this indicates market strength.

You can also determine the market breadth for individual securities by computing net volume (up-ticks less down-ticks).

EXAMPLE 6.11

Bette Corporation trades 90,000 shares for the day with 60,000 on the upside, 20,000 on the downside, and 10,000 at no change. The net volume difference at day's end is 40,000 traded on up-ticks.

FINANCIAL MANAGERS: Look for any sign of divergence between the price trend and net volume. If one occurs, you can anticipate a reversal in the price trend.

The Barron's Confidence index. This is useful when evaluating the trading patterns of bond investors and helps determine when to buy and sell. The index assumes bond traders are more knowledgeable than stock traders and that they identify trends more quickly. The index equals

$$\frac{\text{Yield on Barron's 10 top-grade corporate bonds}}{\text{Yield on Dow Jones 40 bond average}}$$

The numerator reflects a lower yield than the denominator because it uses higher-quality bonds. For example, if the Dow Jones yield is 14 percent and the Barron's yield is 11.5 percent, the confidence index is 0.821. RULE OF THUMB: When bond investors are bullish, yield differences between high-grade and low-grade bonds will be small.

Odd-lot trading. This refers to transactions of 100 shares or less and is used as a reflection of popular opinion. THE RULE OF CONTRARY OPINION: The investment analyst determines what small traders are doing and then does the opposite. An *odd-lot index* consists of the ratio of odd-lot purchases to odd-lot sales.

Charts. These are used to appraise market conditions and price behavior of individual securities. By looking at past trends, you can possibly predict the future.

Relative strength analysis. This relates to predicting individual stock prices and consists of computing a ratio of monthly average stock prices to a monthly average "market index" or "industry group index." Or, you can compute the ratios of specific industry group indexes to the total market index. OBSERVATION: If a stock or industry group outperforms the market, you may view this as a positive sign.

6.5 HOW TO BEST FINANCE YOUR BUSINESS

What financing alternatives are available?

As a financial manager or executive, you should be familiar with three alternative sources of financing: short-term (less than one year), intermediate-term (one to five years) and long-term (longer than five years). To plan the best financing strategy, evaluate the risks and costs applicable to each alternative. Consider these factors:

- Your company's financial position (cash flow, debt position, etc.)
- Cost of alternative funding sources
- Availability of future financing
- Risk
- Inflation rate
- Expected money market trends
- Tax rate
- Stability of operations
- Overall management objectives

What type of financing should I select?

Here are some sources of short- and intermediate-term financing:

Trade credit. Trade credit is easy to get, has no or minimal cost, and requires no collateral. Creditors tend to be more lenient when payment problems occur, too.

Bank. To obtain a bank loan, you must have a good financial position with sufficient stockholders' equity. Loans may be secured (collateralized) or unsecured. In a secured loan, you have to pledge an asset to back the security. Or, you can obtain a line of credit that promises loans up to a maximum amount.

Finance company. If a bank loan is unavailable, a finance company may be necessary. There will be a higher interest rate and required collateral.

Commercial paper. This is a short-term, unsecured note issued by the highest-quality companies. Their interest rate is less than the prime rate charged by banks.

Receivable financing. Accounts receivable may be sold outright (factored) or assigned to a bank or finance company in return for immediate cash. There's a high financing cost involved here.

Inventory financing. This typically occurs when receivable financing has been used up. Inventory must be marketable.

Leasing. By leasing property, only a minor cash outlay may be required. Usually, a purchase option accompanies the agreement.

Here are some sources of long-term financing:

Mortgages. These are notes payable to banks that are secured by real property. Mortgages have favorable interest rates, fewer financing restrictions, long payment schedules, and ready availability.

Bonds. These are long-term debt issued to the public. Bonds offer some advantages over stocks. For instance, interest from bonds are tax deductible, whereas stock dividends are not; the payback is in cheaper dollars because of inflation; and equity interests (i.e., voting rights) remain intact. Also, call provisions enable you to buy back the bonds before maturity. On the other hand, you must accept certain risks, including the inability to meet debt payments as well as indenture restrictions. Indenture refers to the agreement between the bond issuer and the bond investor.

Equity securities (preferred and common stock). Common stock refers to residual equity ownership in the business. Common stockholders have voting power but come after preferred stockholders in receiving dividends and in liquidation. Equity securities do not involve fixed charges, maturity dates, or sinking fund requirements. You need not pay dividends during periods of financial distress. However, dividend payments are not tax deductible and therefore will incur higher costs to the company. And since they also hold greatest risk to common stockholders, the cost of funds will be greater. Common stocks dilute ownership and voting rights as well.

What is the cost of raising funds?

VITAL FOR FINANCIAL MANAGERS: The cost of capital is calculated from a weighted average of debt and equity security costs. Compare these averages under various alternative financing strategies. Your input will bear heavily when deciding the best source of financing in a given situation. REMEMBER THIS: The alternative with the least overall cost of capital is best.

What is the cost of short-term debt?

The cost of short-term debt applies to the interest rate on bank or finance company loans. Remember this: Interest is a tax-deductible expense.

$$\text{Cost of short-term debt} = \frac{\text{Interest}}{\text{Proceeds received}}$$

If a bank discounts a loan, interest is deducted from the face of the loan to get the proceeds. When a compensating balance is required (that is, a percent of the face loan is held by the bank as collateral), proceeds are also reduced. In either case, the effective or real interest rate on the loan is higher than the face interest rate owing to the proceeds received from the loan being less than the amount (face) of the loan.

EXAMPLE 6.12

Company A takes a $150,000, one-year, 13% loan. The loan is discounted, and a 10% compensating balance is required. The effective interest rate is computed as follows:

$$\frac{13\% \times \$150,000}{\$115,500^a} = \frac{\$19,500}{\$115,500} = 16.89\%$$

[a] Proceeds received =	
Face of loan	$150,000
Less interest	(19,500)
Compensating balance (10% × $150,000)	(15,000)
Proceeds	$115,500

Notice how the effective cost of the loan is significantly greater than the stated interest rate.

What is the cost of long-term debt?

The real cost of bonds is obtained by computing two types of yield: simple (face) yield and yield to maturity (effective interest rate). The first involves an easy approximation, but the second is much more accurate.

WHAT YOU SHOULD KNOW: The nominal interest

rate equals the interest paid on the face (maturity value) of the bond and is always stated on a per-annum basis. Bonds are always issued in $1,000 denominations and may be sold above face value (at a premium) or below (at a discount). A bond is sold at a discount when the interest rate is below the going market rate. In this case, the yield will be higher than the nominal interest rate. The opposite holds for bonds issued at a premium.

$$\text{Simple yield} = \frac{\text{nominal interest}}{\text{present value of bond}}$$

$$\text{Yield to maturity} = \frac{\text{nominal interest} + \dfrac{\text{discount}}{\text{Years}}\left(\dfrac{\text{or-premium}}{\text{years}}\right)}{\dfrac{\text{present value} + \text{maturity value}}{2}}$$

EXAMPLE 6.13

Prentice Corporation issues a $400,000, 12%, 10-year bond for 97% of face value. Yield computations follow:

Nominal annual payment	$= 12\% \times \$400,000$
	$= \$48,000$
Bond proceeds	$= 97\% \times \$400,000$
	$= \$388,000$
Bond discount	$= 3\% \times \$400,000$
	$= \$12,000 \text{ or}$
	$\$400,000 - \$388,000$
	$= \$12,000$

$$\text{Simple yield} = \frac{12\% \times \$400,000}{97\% \times \$400,000} = \frac{\$\,48,000}{\$388,000} = 12.4\%$$

$$\text{Yield to maturity} = \frac{\$48,000 + \dfrac{\$12,000}{10}}{\dfrac{\$388,000 + \$400,000}{2}}$$

$$= \frac{\$48,000 + \$1,200}{\$369,000}$$

$$= \frac{\$\,49,200}{\$394,000} = 12.5\%$$

NOTE: Because the bonds were sold at a discount, the yield exceeds the nominal interest rate (12%).

What is the cost of equity securities?

The cost of equity securities comes in the form of dividends, which are not tax deductible.

$$\text{The cost of common stock} = \frac{\text{dividends per share for current year}}{\text{net proceeds per share}} + \text{growth rate in dividends}$$

where

net proceeds per share = market price per share − flotation costs (that is, cost of issuing securities, such as brokerage fees and, printing costs). The cost of preferred stock is stated in the dividend rate. If this is not given, the cost of preferred stock would be computed as for common stock.

EXAMPLE 6.14

ABC Company's dividend per share is $10, net proceeds per share are $70, and the dividend growth rate is 5%.

$$\text{The cost of the stock} = \frac{\$10}{\$70} + 0.05 = 19.3\%$$

How do I compute the weighted average cost of capital?

When computing the weighted average cost of capital, consider the percent of the total and after-tax cost of each financing alternative.

EXAMPLE 6.15

Bloated Company provides the following from its financial statements:

Bonds payable (16%)	$ 4 million
Preferred stock (dividend rate = 13%)	1 million
Common stock	5 million
Total	$10 million

Dividends per share on common stock are $11; net proceeds per share are $80; growth rate on dividends is 4%, and tax rate is 40%.

The weighted average cost of capital is computed as follows:

	Percent	After-Tax Cost	Weighted Average Cost
Bonds payable	0.40	0.096[a]	0.038
Preferred stock	0.10	0.130	0.013
Common stock	0.50	0.178[b]	0.089
	1.00		0.140

[a]Cost of bonds payable: 16% × 60% = 0.096

[b] Cost of bonds payable $\dfrac{\text{dividends per share}}{\text{net proceeds per share}}$ + growth rate in dividends

$$\frac{\$11}{\$80} + 0.04 = 0.178$$

What is the cost of not taking a discount on accounts payable?

If you do not take a discount on accounts payable by paying earlier, you have lost an opportunity cost or the return foregone from an alternative use of funds or time. TAKE NOTICE: Financial managers who do not take the discount typically show a lack of financial astuteness. Why? The cost of paying is usually higher than the cost of borrowing money.

You can compute the opportunity cost with this formula:

$$\frac{\text{discount foregone}}{\text{use of proceeds}} \times \frac{360}{\text{days use of money}}$$

EXAMPLE 6.16

XYZ Company purchases $500,000 of merchandise on credit terms of 2/10, net/30. The company does not pay within 10 days and thus loses the discount.

$$\text{Opportunity cost} = \frac{0.02 \times \$500{,}000}{0.98 \times \$500{,}000} \times \frac{360}{20}$$
$$= \frac{\$10{,}000}{\$490{,}000} \times 180 = 36.7\%$$

Surely management would have been better off to take advantage of the discount by borrowing $490,000 at the prime interest rate.

How do I evaluate a dividend policy?

FOR FINANCIAL MANAGERS: A dividend policy must be attractive to the investing public by satisfying current stockholders and prompting new investment. Psychologically, investors like to receive stable dividends. If you cut dividends, stockholders may become worried and sell. The result: Your stock price declines.

On the other hand, from a purely financial perspective, earnings should be retained by the business rather than distributed to stockholders. Why? First, the company typically earns a greater return than the individual stockholder does, and this will result in appreciation in the market price of the stock. Second, there is a tax advantage to the investor. When stock held for more than six months is sold, only 40 percent of the gain is taxable. On the other hand, dividends will only provide a $100 exclusion to the investor.

MANAGEMENT EXECUTIVES: If financial problems exist within your company, the distribution will seriously impair the company's health. By distributing earnings, you'll have to refinance, and cost of capital will be very high. YOUR DILEMMA: It's generally best to retain funds rather than distribute them in the form of dividends to the company or individual investor. But, since stockholders are basically unsophisticated in financial analysis, they will demand dividends.

WHAT TO DO: To satisfy stockholders while retaining as much as possible, you have two options. You can establish a *minimum* dividend base and give a bonus dividend during very good times, or you can create the impression of a growth company that typically retains earnings for expansion purposes.

FINANCIAL MANAGERS: Look at the trends in these dividend-related ratios:

$$\text{Dividend payout} = \frac{\text{dividends per share}}{\text{earnings per share}}$$

$$\text{Dividend yield} = \frac{\text{dividends per share}}{\text{market price per share}}$$

Investors generally favor increasing trends.

How does the business cycle affect a company?

One company or industry cannot control fundamental economic conditions. To the extent that you can insulate yourself from the effects of a broader economy, your corporate stability will be greater. HINT: Look for stability in operations because it enhances predictability and planning.

Companies having product lines with inelastic demand (such as food and medicine) are affected less by the business cycle. Companies with product lines or services correlated positively to changes in real gross national product (such as the airlines) have greater earnings instability.

QUANTITATIVE METHODS AND COMPUTER APPLICATIONS

PART III

QUANTITATIVE
METHODS
AND COMPUTER
APPLICATIONS

7

Decision Making with Statistics and Forecasting

As a decision maker, you'll find yourself in many situations in which large volumes of data need to be analyzed. These data could be sales figures, income, or a multitude of other possibilities. And they could be used for a variety of purposes, including risk analysis, figuring return on investments, or other financial decisions. Effective use of statistics and forecasting techniques will prove necessary as your company grows.

7.1 HOW TO USE BASIC STATISTICS

The most commonly used statistics that describe characteristics of data are the mean and the standard deviation.

What is a mean and how is it used?

The mean gives an average (or central) value of your data. Three such means are common. They are

- Arithmetic mean
- Weighted mean
- Geometric mean

What is an arithmetic mean?

The arithmetic mean is a simple average. To find it, sum the values of your data and divide by the number of data entries or observations:

$$\bar{x} = \frac{\Sigma x}{n}$$

where
  $\bar{x}$ = the arithmetic mean (called x-bar)
  x = the data values
  n = number of observations

EXAMPLE 7.1

John Jay Lamp Company has a revolving credit agreement with a local bank. Last year, the loan showed the following month-end balances:

January	$18,500
February	21,000
March	17,600
April	23,200
May	18,600
June	24,500
July	60,000
August	40,000
September	25,850
October	33,100
November	41,000
December	28,400

The mean monthly balance is computed as follows;

$$\bar{x} = \frac{\begin{array}{c} \$18,500 + \$21,000 + \$17,600 + \$23,200 \\ + \$18,600 + \$24,500 + \$60,000 + \$40,000 \\ + \$25,850 + \$33,100 + \$41,000 + \$28,400 \end{array}}{12}$$

$$= \frac{\$351,750}{12} = \$29,312.50$$

What is a weighted mean?

When your observations have different degrees of importance or frequency, a weighted mean enables you to account for this. The formula for a weighted mean is

  Weighted mean = $\Sigma(w)(x)$

where

  w = weight assigned to each observation, expressed as a percentage or relative frequency

EXAMPLE 7.2

Company J uses three grades of labor to produce a finished product as follows:

Grade of Labor	Labor Hours per Unit of Labor	Hourly Wages (x)
Skilled	6	$10.00
Semiskilled	3	8.00
Unskilled	1	6.00

The arithmetic mean (average cost) of labor per hour for this product can be computed as follows:

$$\text{Arithmetic mean} = \frac{\$10.00 + \$8.00 + \$6.00}{3}$$
$$= \$8.00 \text{ per hour}$$

However, this implies that each grade of labor was used in equal amounts, and this is not the case. To calculate the average cost of labor per hour correctly, the weighted average should be computed as follows:

$$\text{Weighted mean} = \$10.00(6/10) + \$8.00(3/10)$$
$$+ \$6.00(1/10) = \$9.00 \text{ per hour}$$

NOTE: The weights equal the proportion of the total labor required to produce the product.

What is a geometric mean?

Sometimes quantities change over a period of time; for example, the rate of return on investment or rate of growth in earnings over a period of years. In such cases, you need to know the geometric mean, which uses the average rate or percentage of change. Use this formula:

Geometric mean
$$= \sqrt[n]{(1 + x_1)(1 + x_2) + \ldots + (1 + x_n)} - 1$$
where
x = the rate of change (in percent)
n = number of periods

EXAMPLE 7.3

A stock doubles during one period and then depreciates back to the original price, as shown in the following table:

	Time Periods		
	$t = 0$	$t = 1$	$t = 2$
Price (end of period)	$80	$160	$80
Rate of return	—	100%	−50%

The rate of return for periods 1 and 2 are computed as follows:

$$\text{Period 1 } (t=1) = \frac{\$160 - \$80}{\$80} = \frac{\$80}{\$80} = 100\%$$

$$\text{Period 2 } (t=2) = \frac{\$80 - \$160}{\$160} = \frac{-\$80}{\$160} = -50\%$$

The arithmetic mean return over the two periods equals the average of 100% and −50%, or 25%, as shown:

$$x = \frac{100\% + (-50\%)}{2} = 25\%$$

Clearly, you can see that the stock purchased for $80 and sold for the same price two periods later does not return 25%, but zero. Here's proof:

$$\begin{aligned}
\text{Geometric mean return} &= {}^2\sqrt{(1 + 1)(1 - 0.5)} - 1 \\
&= {}^2\sqrt{(2)(0.5)} - 1 \\
&= {}^2\sqrt{1} - 1 = 0\%
\end{aligned}$$

where

$n = 2$
$x_1 = 100\%$ or 1
$x_2 = -50\%$ or −0.5

What is standard deviation?

The standard deviation measures the extent to which data spread out or disperse. MANAGERS: You can make important inferences from past data with this statistic, for example, when measuring the risk of purchasing a financial asset. Standard deviation, denoted σ, is defined as follows:

$$\sigma = \sqrt{\frac{\Sigma(x - \bar{x})^2}{n - 1}}$$

where

$\bar{x}$ = the arithmetic mean

WHAT TO DO: Calculate the standard deviation using these five steps:

- Subtract the mean from each observation value
- Square each difference obtained in Step 1
- Sum all the squared differences
- Divide the sum of all the squared differences by the number of observations minus one
- Take the square root of the quotient

EXAMPLE 7.4

United Motors stock lists six consecutive quarterly returns as follows:

Time Period	x	$(x - \bar{x})$	$(x - \bar{x})^2$
1	10%	0	0
2	15	5	25
3	20	10	100
4	5	−5	25
5	−10	−20	400
6	20	10	100
	60		700

The mean return and standard deviation over this period are computed as follows:

$$\bar{x} = 60/6 = 10\%$$

$$6 = \sqrt{\frac{\Sigma (x - \bar{x})^2}{n - 1}} = \sqrt{\frac{702}{6 - 1}} = \sqrt{140} = 11.83\%$$

CONCLUSION: United Motors stock has returned on average 10% over the last six periods, and the variability about its mean return is 11.83%. This high standard deviation relative to the average return indicates this stock is very risky.

7.2 USING FORECASTING TECHNIQUES

7.2.1 Moving Averages

How do I use moving averages?

With a moving average, simply take the most recent observations (n) to calculate an average. Then, use this as the forecast for the next period. Moving averages are updated continually as new data are received. NOTE: You can choose the number of periods to use on the basis of the relative importance you attach to old versus current data.

EXAMPLE 7.5

The marketing manager has the following sales data:

Date	Actual Sales (y_t) (in Thousands of Dollars)
Jan. 1	46
2	54
3	53
4	46
5	58
6	49
7	54

In order for the marketing manager to predict sales for the seventh and eighth days of January, he must pick the number of observations to be averaged. He used two possibilities, a six-day and a three-day period:

1. $y_7 = \dfrac{46 + 54 + 53 + 46 + 58 + 49}{6} = 51$

$y_8 = \dfrac{54 + 53 + 46 + 58 + 49 + 54}{6} = 52.3$

2. $y_7 = \dfrac{46 + 58 + 49}{3} = 51$

$y_8 = \dfrac{58 + 49 + 54}{3} = 53.6$

		PREDICTED SALES $(\hat{y}_t)$	
Date	Actual Sales (y_t)	Case 1	Case 2
Jan. 1	46		
2	54		
3	53		
4	46		
5	58		
6	49		
7	54	51	51
8		52.3	53.6

In terms of the relative importance of new versus old data, in Case 1, the old data received a weight of ⅚ and current data ⅙. In Case 2, the old data received a weight of ⅔, whereas current observation received ⅓ weight.

7.2.2 Exponential Smoothing

What is the basis of exponential smoothing?

Exponential smoothing is a popular technique for short-run forecasting. It uses a weighted average of past data as the basis of the forecast. The procedure assumes the future is most dependent upon the recent past and thus gives heaviest weight to more recent data and smaller weights to those of the more distant past. WHEN TO USE IT: The method is most effective when there are random demand and no seasonal fluctuations. CAUTION: The method does not include industrial or economic factors such as market conditions, prices, or competitive actions.

What is the model?

Here is the formula for exponential smoothing:

$$\hat{y}_{t+1} = \alpha y_t + (1 - \alpha)\hat{y}_t$$

or

$$\hat{y}_{new} = \alpha y_{old} + (1 - \alpha)\hat{y}_{old}$$

where

$\hat{y}_{new}$ = Exponentially smoothed average to be used as the forecast
$\hat{y}_{old}$ = Most recent smoothed forecast
α = Smoothing constant

REMEMBER THIS: The higher the α, the greater the weight given to most recent data.

EXAMPLE 7.6

Company Y provides the following sales data:

Time Period (t)	Actual Sales (y_t) (in Thousands of Dollars)
1	$60.0
2	64.0
3	58.0
4	66.0
5	70.0
6	60.0
7	70.0

Time Period (t)	Actual Sales (y_t) (in Thousands of Dollars)
8	74.0
9	62.0
10	74.0
11	68.0
12	66.0
13	60.0
14	66.0
15	62.0

The manager decides to use a six-period average as the initial forecast ($\hat{y}_7$) with a smoothing constant = 0.40.

$$\hat{y}_7 = \frac{60 + 64 + 58 + 66 + 70 + 60}{6} = 63$$

Note that $y_7 = 70$. Then $\hat{y}_8$ is computed as follows:

$$\hat{y}_8 = \alpha y_7 + (1 - \alpha)\hat{y}_7$$
$$= (0.40)(70) + (0.60)(63)$$
$$= 28.00 + 37.80 = 65.80$$

Similarly,

$$\hat{y}_9 = \alpha y_8 + (1 - \alpha)\hat{y}_8$$
$$= (0.40)(74) + (0.60)(65.80)$$
$$= 29.60 + 39.48 = 69.08$$

and

$$\hat{y}_{10} = \alpha y_9 + (1 - \alpha)\hat{y}_9$$
$$= (0.40)(62) + (0.60)(69.08)$$
$$= 24.80 + 41.45 = 66.25$$

By using the same procedures, the values of $\hat{y}_{11}$ through $\hat{y}_{15}$ can be calculated. The following shows a comparison between actual and predicted sales by the exponential smoothing method:

Time Period (t)	Actual Sales (y_t)	Predicted Sales ($\hat{y}_t$)	Difference ($y_t - \hat{y}_t$)	Difference Squared ($y_t - \hat{y}_t)^2$
1	60.0			
2	64.0			
3	58.0			
4	66.0			

Time Period (t)	Actual Sales (y_t)	Predicted Sales ($\hat{y}_t$)	Difference ($y_t - \hat{y}_t$)	Difference Squared ($y_t - \hat{y}_t)^2$
5	70.0			
6	60.0			
7	70.0	63.00	7.00	49.00
8	74.0	65.80	8.20	67.24
9	62.0	69.08	−7.08	50.13
10	74.0	66.25	7.75	60.06
11	68.0	69.35	−1.35	1.82
12	66.0	68.81	−2.81	7.90
13	60.0	67.69	−7.69	59.14
14	66.0	64.61	1.39	1.93
15	62.0	65.17	−3.17	10.05
				307.27

How do I determine the best smoothing constant?

You can use a higher or lower smoothing constant in order to adjust your prediction to large fluctuations in the data series. For example, if the forecast is slow in reacting to increased sales (if the difference is negative), then you might want to try a higher α value. For practical purposes, the optimal α may be picked by minimizing the mean square error (MSE), which is the average sum of the variations between the historical data and forecast values for the corresponding periods. MSE is computed as follows:

$$MSE = \frac{\sum_{t-1}^{n} (y_t - \hat{y}_t)^2}{n - i}$$

where

    i = the number of observations used to determine the initial forecast

In the previous example, $i = 6$ and

$$MSE = \frac{307.27}{15 - 6} = \frac{307.25}{9} = 34.14$$

WHAT TO DO: Try to select the α that minimizes MSE.

Can a computer help?

As a manager, you will be confronted with complex problems requiring large sample data. You will also need to try different values of α for exponential smoothing. A computer can assist you here. To demonstrate, consider the following sales data.

Time Period	Actual Sales (in Thousands of Dollars)
1	117
2	120
3	132
4	141
5	140
6	156
7	169
8	171
9	174
10	182

Figure 7.1 is a printout of an exponential smoothing program. The input data entry is straightforward.

The best α for this particular example is 0.9, because it gives the least mean square error (MSE).

FIGURE 7.1 EXPONENTIAL SMOOTHING PROGRAM

PLEASE ENTER THE NUMBER OF OBSERVATIONS.
?10
ENTER YOUR DATA NOW.
THE DATA SHOULD BE SEPARATED BY COMMAS.
?117,120,132,141,140,156,169,171,174,182
ENTER THE NUMBER OF PERIODS OVER WHICH YOU COMPUTE THE AVERAGE TO BE USED AS THE FIRST FORECAST VALUE.
?1

**********EXPONENTIAL SMOOTHING PROGRAM–SINGLE SMOOTHING*********

JAE K. SHIM

PERIOD	ACTUAL VALUE	ESTIMATED VALUE	ERROR
1	117.00	.00	
2	120.00	117.00	

THE VALUE OF THE EXPONENTIAL SMOOTHER IS .1

3	132.00	117.30	14.70
4	141.00	118.77	22.23

FIGURE 7.1 (cont.)

5	140.00	120.99	19.01
6	156.00	122.89	33.11
7	169.00	126.20	42.80
8	171.00	130.48	40.52
9	174.00	134.54	39.46
10	182.00	138.48	43.52

THE TOTAL ABSOLUTE ERROR IN ESTIMATE IS 255.34
THE MEAN SQUARED ERROR IS 1136.48

THE VALUE OF THE EXPONENTIAL SMOOTHER IS .2

3	132.00	117.60	14.40
4	141.00	120.48	20.52
5	140.00	124.58	15.42
6	156.00	127.67	28.33
7	169.00	133.33	35.67
8	171.00	140.47	30.53
9	174.00	146.57	27.43
10	182.00	152.06	29.94

THE TOTAL ABSOLUTE ERROR IN ESTIMATE IS 202.24
THE MEAN SQUARED ERROR IS 690.23

THE VALUE OF THE EXPONENTIAL SMOOTHER IS .3

3	132.00	117.90	14.10
4	141.00	122.13	18.87
5	140.00	127.79	12.21
6	156.00	131.45	24.55
7	169.00	138.82	30.18
8	171.00	147.87	23.13
9	174.00	154.81	19.19
10	182.00	160.57	21.43

THE TOTAL ABSOLUTE ERROR IN ESTIMATE IS 163.66
THE MEAN SQUARED ERROR IS 447.49

THE VALUE OF THE EXPONENTIAL SMOOTHER IS .4

3	132.00	118.20	13.80
4	141.00	123.72	17.28
5	140.00	130.63	9.37
6	156.00	134.38	21.62
7	169.00	143.03	25.97

FIGURE 7.1 (cont.)

8	171.00	153.42	17.58
9	174.00	160.45	13.55
10	182.00	165.87	16.13

THE TOTAL ABSOLUTE ERROR IN ESTIMATE IS 135.31

THE MEAN SQUARED ERROR IS 308.97

THE VALUE OF THE EXPONENTIAL SMOOTHER IS .5

3	132.00	118.50	13.50
4	141.00	125.25	15.75
5	140.00	133.12	6.88
6	156.00	136.56	19.44
7	169.00	146.28	22.72
8	171.00	157.64	13.36
9	174.00	164.32	9.68
10	182.00	169.16	12.84

THE TOTAL ABSOLUTE ERROR IN ESTIMATE IS 114.16

THE MEAN SQUARED ERROR IS 226.07

THE VALUE OF THE EXPONENTIAL SMOOTHER IS .6

3	132.00	118.80	13.20
4	141.00	126.72	14.28
5	140.00	135.29	4.71
6	156.00	138.12	17.88
7	169.00	148.85	20.15
8	171.00	160.94	10.06
9	174.00	166.98	7.02
10	182.00	171.19	10.81

THE TOTAL ABSOLUTE ERROR IN ESTIMATE IS 98.13

THE MEAN SQUARED ERROR IS 174.23

THE VALUE OF THE EXPONENTIAL SMOOTHER IS .7

3	132.00	119.10	12.90
4	141.00	128.13	12.87
5	140.00	137.14	2.86
6	156.00	139.14	16.86
7	169.00	150.94	18.06
8	171.00	163.58	7.42
9	174.00	168.77	5.23
10	182.00	172.43	9.57

FIGURE 7.1 (*cont.*)

THE TOTAL ABSOLUTE ERROR IN ESTIMATE IS
85.76
THE MEAN SQUARED ERROR IS 140.55

THE VALUE OF THE EXPONENTIAL SMOOTHER
IS .8

3	132.00	119.40	12.60
4	141.00	129.48	11.52
5	140.00	138.70	1.30
6	156.00	139.74	16.26
7	169.00	152.75	16.25
8	171.00	165.75	5.25
9	174.00	169.95	4.05
10	182.00	173.19	8.81

THE TOTAL ABSOLUTE ERROR IN ESTIMATE IS
76.05
THE MEAN SQUARED ERROR IS 117.91

THE VALUE OF THE EXPONENTIAL SMOOTHER
IS .9

3	132.00	119.70	12.30
4	141.00	130.77	10.23
5	140.00	139.98	.02
6	156.00	142.25	3.75
7	169.00	154.40	14.60
8	171.00	167.54	3.46
9	174.00	170.65	3.35
10	182.00	173.67	8.33

THE TOTAL ABSOLUTE ERROR IN ESTIMATE IS
68.30
THE MEAN SQUARED ERROR IS 102.23

FIGURE 7.1 (cont.)
SUMMARY RESULTS

THE EXPONENTIAL SMOOTHER	.1	WITH A MEAN SQUARED ERROR OF	1136.48
THE EXPONENTIAL SMOOTHER	.2	WITH A MEAN SQUARED ERROR OF	690.23
THE EXPONENTIAL SMOOTHER	.3	WITH A MEAN SQUARED ERROR OF	447.49
THE EXPONENTIAL SMOOTHER	.4	WITH A MEAN SQUARED ERROR OF	308.97
THE EXPONENTIAL SMOOTHER	.5	WITH A MEAN SQUARED ERROR OF	226.07
THE EXPONENTIAL SMOOTHER	.6	WITH A MEAN SQUARED ERROR OF	174.23
THE EXPONENTIAL SMOOTHER	.7	WITH A MEAN SQUARED ERROR OF	140.55
THE EXPONENTIAL SMOOTHER	.8	WITH A MEAN SQUARED ERROR OF	117.91
THE EXPONENTIAL SMOOTHER	.9	WITH A MEAN SQUARED ERROR OF	102.23

7.3 REGRESSION ANALYSIS
FOR SALES AND EARNINGS PROJECTIONS

What is regression analysis?

Regression analysis is a statistical procedure for estimating mathematically the average relationship between a
dependent variable and an independent variable or variables. Simple regression involves one independent variable,
and multiple regression involves two or more. First, we will
discuss simple linear regression, defined by the following
formula:

$$y = a + bx$$

where
  y = dependent variable
  x = independent variable
  a = a constant or y intercept of regression line
  b = the slope of the regression line

How do I use the method of least squares?

The method of least squares attempts to find a line of
best fit for the graph of a regression equation. To better
explain this, let's define error, or u, as the difference between the observed and estimated values of sales or earnings. Symbolically,

$$u = y - \hat{y}$$

where
  y = observed value
  $\hat{y}$ = estimated value based on $\hat{y} = a + bx$

The least-squares method requires that the sum of the
squares of the errors be the smallest possible value, that is,

$$\text{Min}\Sigma u^2 = \Sigma(y - \hat{y})^2 \ (= \text{sum of the errors squared})$$

The typical line of best fit from the observed data points
is shown in Figure 7.2.

How do I compute the coefficients?

From differential calculus, the formula for b is as follows:

$$b = \frac{\text{cov}(x,y)}{\sigma^2 x}$$

where
  $\text{cov}(x,y)$ = covariance of x and y

FIGURE 7.2: ACTUAL VERSUS ESTIMATED

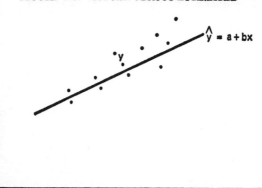

Use these simplified formulas for a and b:

$$b = \frac{n\Sigma xy - (\Sigma x)(\Sigma y)}{n\Sigma x^2 - (\Sigma x^2)}$$
$$a = \bar{y} - b\bar{x}$$

where
$$\bar{y} = \Sigma y/n$$
$$\bar{x} = \Sigma x/n$$

HINT: The formula for a is a shortcut, but it requires the computation of b first. If the data are too voluminous to fit into a calculator, b can be computed by the following formula:

$$b = \frac{\Sigma(x - \bar{x})(y - \bar{y})}{\Sigma(x - \bar{x})^2}$$
$$a = \bar{y} - b\bar{x}$$

EXAMPLE 7.7

Company M provides the following data of sales and advertising expenses:

Advertising (in Hundreds of Dollars)	Sales (in Thousands of Dollars)	xy	x²	y²
$ 9	$15	135	81	225
19	20	380	361	400
11	14	154	121	196
14	16	224	196	256

Advertising (in Hundreds of Dollars)	Sales (in Thousands of Dollars)	xy	x^2	y^2
23	25	575	529	625
12	20	240	144	400
12	20	240	144	400
22	23	506	484	529
7	14	98	49	196
13	22	286	169	484
15	18	270	225	324
17	18	306	289	324
$174	$225	$3,414	$2,792	$4,359

From this table:

$\Sigma x = 174$
$\Sigma y = 225$
$\Sigma xy = 3,414$
$\Sigma x^2 = 2,792$
$\bar{x} = \Sigma x/n = 174/12 = 14.5$
$\bar{y} = \Sigma y/n = 225/12 = 18.75$

You can calculate the values of a and b as follows:

$$b = \frac{(12)(3,414) - (174)(225)}{(12)(2,792) - (174)2} = \frac{1,818}{3,228} = 0.5632$$

$a = 18.75 - (0.5632)(14.5) = 18.75 - 8.1664$
$\quad = 10.5836$

Assume $10 in advertising will be expensed for the next year. Sales projections would be computed as follows:

$\hat{y} = \$10.5836 + \$0.5632x$
$\quad = \$10.5836 + \$0.5632(\$10)$
$\quad = \$10.5836 + \$5.632$
$\quad = \$16.2156$

If you wish to use the alternative formula for calculating b, you should develop a new table utilizing $(x - \bar{x})$ and $(y - \bar{y})$, shown as follows:

x	y	$(x-\bar{x})$	$(y-\bar{y})$	$(x-\bar{x})(y-\bar{y})$	$(x-\bar{x})^2$
$ 9	$ 15	-5.5	-3.75	20.625	30.25
19	20	4.5	1.25	5.625	20.25
11	14	-3.5	-4.75	16.625	12.25
14	16	-0.5	-2.75	1.375	0.25

x	y	$(x-\bar{x})$	$(y-\bar{y})$	$(x-\bar{x})(y-\bar{y})$	$(x-\bar{x})^2$
23	25	8.5	6.25	53.125	72.25
12	20	-2.5	1.25	-3.125	6.25
12	20	-2.5	1.25	-3.125	6.25
22	23	7.5	4.25	31.875	56.25
7	14	-7.5	-4.75	35.625	56.25
13	22	-1.5	3.25	-4.875	2.25
15	18	0.5	-0.75	-0.375	0.25
17	18	2.5	-0.75	-1.875	6.25
$174	$225			$151.5	$269.00

From this,

$$\Sigma(x - \bar{x})(y - \bar{y}) = 151.5$$
$$\Sigma(x - \bar{x})^2 = 269$$

Thus,

b = 151.5/269 = 0.5632
a = 10.5836 (same as above)

The final regression equation is

$$\hat{y} = \$10.5836 + \$0.5632x$$

where
   $\hat{y}$ = estimated sales
   x = advertising expense

How can I use trend analysis?

Trend analysis is a special type of regression analysis often used by financial executives for forecasting sales or earnings. This method involves a regression whereby a trend line is fitted to a time series of data according to the following equation:

$$y = a + bx$$

A time series refers to the relationship of variables over a period of time.

The formulas for the coefficients a and b are essentially the same as those used for simple regression. Each time period is assigned a number so that $\Sigma x = 0$. With an odd number of periods, the middle period is assigned zero value. If there are an even number of periods, then -1 and +1 are assigned to the two middle periods. Thus, in both cases, $\Sigma x = 0$.

EXAMPLE 7.8

Case 1	*19X1*	*19X2*	*19X3*	*19X4*	*19X5*	*19X6*
x =	−2	−1	0	+1	+2	
Case 2						
x =	−3	−2	−1	+1	+2	+3

In each case, $\Sigma x = 0$

The formulas for b and a thus reduce to the following:

$$b = \frac{n\ \Sigma xy}{n\ \Sigma x^2}$$
$$a = \Sigma\ y/n$$

EXAMPLE 7.9

TDK Company reports its historical earnings per share (EPS) as follows:

Year	EPS
19X1	$1.00
19X2	1.20
19X3	1.30
19X4	1.60
19X5	1.70

Since there is an odd number of years, the middle year is assigned zero value. Thus:

Year	x	EPS(y)	xy	x^2	y^2
19X1	−2	$1.00	−2.00	4	1.00
19X2	−1	1.20	−1.20	1	1.44
19X3	0	1.30	0	0	1.69
19X4	+1	1.60	1.60	1	2.56
19X5	+2	1.70	3.40	4	2.89
	0	$6.80	1.80	10	9.58

$$b = \frac{(5)(\$1.80)}{(5)(10)} = \frac{\$9}{50} = \$.18$$
$$a = \frac{\$6.80}{5} = \$1.36$$

The estimated trend equation is

$$\hat{y} = \$1.36 + \$0.18x$$

where

$\hat{y}$ = estimated EPS

x = year index value

To project sales for 19X6, assign $+3$ to the value of x. Thus

$$\hat{y} = \$1.36 + \$0.18(+3)$$
$$= \$1.36 + \$0.54 = \$1.90$$

A summary of the five forecasting methods described in this chapter is provided in Figure 7.3. Use it as a guide for determining which method is best for your specific circumstance.

7.4 WHAT STATISTICS TO LOOK FOR IN REGRESSION ANALYSIS

7.4.1 Simple Regression

A variety of statistics can be used to tell you about the accuracy and reliability of the regression result. We described three in this section:

- Correlation coefficient (r) and coefficient of determination (r^2)
- Standard error of the estimate (s_e)
- Standard error of the regression coefficient (s_b) and t statistic.

How can I measure the appropriateness of the regression equation?

The correlation coefficient (r) measures the degree of correlation between y and x. It takes a range of values between -1 and $+1$. The coefficient of determination (r^2) is more widely used, however. Simply put, r^2 tells how well the estimated equation fits the data, or, the "goodness of fit" in the regression. RULE OF THUMB: The higher the r^2, the more confidence you can have in your equation.

The coefficient of determination represents the proportion of the total variation in y that is explained by the regression equation. Its value ranges between 0 and 1. For example, the statement "Sales is a function of advertising with $r^2 = 0.70$" can be interpreted as, 70 percent of the total variation of sales is explained by the regression equation (or the change in advertising), and 30 percent is explained by some other factor (perhaps price or income).

FIGURE 7.3: SUMMARY OF MORE COMMONLY USED FORECASTING METHODS

Technique	Moving Average	Exponential Smoothing	Trend Analysis	Regression Analysis
Description	Each point of a moving average of a time series is the arithmetic or weighted average of a number of consecutive points of the series, where the number of data points is chosen so that the effects of seasonals or irregularity or both are eliminated.	Similar to moving average, except that more recent data points are given more weight. Descriptively, the new forecast is equal to the old one plus some proportion of the past forecasting error. Effective when there are random demand and no seasonal fluctuations in the data series.	Fits a trend line to a mathematical equation and then projects it into the future by means of this equation. There are several variations: the slope-characteristic method, polynomials, logarithms, and so on.	Functionally relates sales to other economic, competitive, or internal variables and etimates an equation using the least-squares technique. Relationships are primarily analyzed statistically, although any relationship could be selected for testing on a rational ground.
Accuracy:				
Short-term (0–3 months)	Poor to good	Fair to very good	Very good	Good to very good
Medium-term (3 months–2 years)	Poor	Poor to good	Good	Good to very good

FIGURE 7.3 (cont.)

Technique	Moving Average	Exponential Smoothing	Trend Analysis	Regression Analysis
Long-term (2 year and over)	Very poor	Very poor	Good	Poor
Identification of turning point	Poor	Poor	Poor	Very good
Typical application	Inventory control for low-volume items	Production and inventory control, forecasts of sales, and financial data.	New product forecasts (particularly intermediate and long-term).	Forecasts of sales by product classes, forecasts of income and other financial data.
Data required	A minimum of two years of sales history if seasonals are present. Otherwise, fewer data. (Of course, the more history the better.) The moving average must be specified.	The same as for a moving average.	Varies with the technique used. However, a good rule of thumb is to use a minimum of five years' annual data to start. Thereafter, the complete history.	Several years' quarterly history to obtain good, meaningful relationships. Mathematically necessary to have two more observations than there are independent variables.

	Very minimal	Minimal	Varies with application	Varies with application
Cost of forecasting with a computer				
Is calculation possible without a computer?	Yes	Yes	Yes	Yes
Time required to develop an application and make forecasts	1 day—	1 day—	1 day—	Depends on ability to identify relationships

Source: Reprinted by permission of the Harvard Business Review. An exhibit from "How to Choose the Right Forecasting Technique" by John C. Chambers, Satinder K. Mullick and Donald D. Smith (July/August 1971). Copyright © 1971 by the President and Fellows of Harvard College; all rights reserved.

The coefficient of determination is computed from the following formula:

$$r^2 = 1 - \frac{\Sigma(y - \hat{y})^2}{\Sigma(y - \bar{y})^2}$$

In simple regression, you can use this shortcut formula:

$$r^2 = \frac{(n\Sigma xy - [\Sigma x][\Sigma y])^2}{(n\ \Sigma x^2 - [\Sigma x]^2)(n\Sigma y^2 - [\Sigma y]^2)}$$

EXAMPLE 7.10

Refer to the table in Example 7.7. With $y^2 = 4,359$, you can compute r^2 using the shortcut formula as follows:

$$r^2 = \frac{(1,818)^2}{(3,228)\ ([12][4,359] - [225]^2)}$$

$$= \frac{1,305,124}{(3,228)(52,308 - 50,625)}$$

$$= \frac{3,305,124}{(3,228)(52,308 - 50,625)}$$

$$= \frac{3,305,124}{(3,228)(1,683)} = \frac{3,305,124}{5,432,724}$$

$$= 0.6084$$

INTERPRETATION: About 60.84% of the variation in total sales is explained by advertising, and the remaining 39.16% is still unexplained. This relatively low r^2 indicates that lots of room for improvement still exists in the estimated sales forecast equation $y = \$10.5836 + \$0.5632x$.

EXAMPLE 7.11

Now examine the data presented in Example 7.9. The r^2 is computed as follows:

$$r^2 = \frac{9^2}{(50)\ [(5)(9.58) - (6.80)]^2}$$

$$= \frac{81}{50(47.9 - 46.24)}$$

$$= \frac{81}{50 \cdot 1.66} = \frac{81}{83} = 0.9759$$

CONCLUSION: A very high r^2 (0.9759) indicates that the trend line is an excellent fit, and there is a growing trend in EPS over time.

How can I measure the accuracy of management predictions?

You can use the standard error of the estimate, designated s_e, and defined as the standard deviation of the regression. The formula for s_e is

$$s_e = \sqrt{\frac{\Sigma(y - \hat{y})^2}{n - 2}} = \sqrt{\frac{\Sigma y^2 - a\Sigma y - b\Sigma xy}{n - 2}}$$

Confidence interval relates to the probability that the sampled result accurately portrays the population. If you want the prediction to be 95-percent confident, compute a confidence interval.

Confidence interval $= y + z(s_e)$

where

z = normal standard variate, which is determined from the normal distribution table according to the manager's desired confidence level

EXAMPLE 7.12

Refer again to Example 7.7. The standard error of the estimate is computed as follows:

$$s_e = \sqrt{\frac{(4,359) - (10.5836)(225) - (0.5632)(3,414)}{12 - 2}}$$

$$= \sqrt{\frac{54.9252}{10}} = \sqrt{5.49252} = 2.3436$$

If you want your prediction to be 95% confident, the confidence interval would equal the estimated sales ± 2(2.3436). The computations are $16.2156 ± 2(2.3436) = $16.2156 ± 4.6872, or

$11.5284 ~ $20.9028

How can I test the appropriateness of the coefficients?

The standard error of the coefficient, designated s_b, gives an estimate of the range within which the true coefficient may actually be. The standard error of the coefficient is calculated as follows:

$$s_b = \frac{s_e}{\sqrt{\Sigma(x - \bar{x})^2}}$$

or, in shortcut form,

$$s_b = \frac{s_e}{\sqrt{\Sigma x^2 - \overline{x}\Sigma x}}$$

The t statistic shows the statistical significance of x in explaining y. It is determined by dividing the estimated coefficient b by its standard error s_b:

$$t \text{ statistic} = \frac{b}{s_b}$$

The t statistic really measures how many standard errors the coefficient is away from zero. RULE OF THUMB: Any value of t greater than $+2$ or -2 is acceptable. The higher the t value, the more significant is b and therefore the greater your confidence in the coefficient as a predictor.

NOTE: You can also find the t value from Table 7.1.

EXAMPLE 7.13

Once again, refer to Example 7.7. Note the following:

$$s_e = 2.3436$$
$$\Sigma x^2 = 2,792$$
$$\overline{x} = 14.5$$
$$\Sigma x = 174$$

The standard error of the regression coefficient (0.5632) is computed as follows:

$$s_b = \frac{2.3436}{\sqrt{2,792 - (14.5)(174)}}$$
$$= \frac{2.3426}{\sqrt{2,792 - 2,523}}$$
$$= \frac{2.3436}{\sqrt{269}} = \frac{2.3436}{16.40} = 0.143$$

The t statistic $= b/s_b = 0.5632/0.143 = 394$

CONCLUSION: Since $t = 3.94 > 2$, the coefficient b is statistically significant.

7.4.2 Multiple Regression

Multiple regression involves more than one independent or explanatory variable. You need to take note of the following statistics when doing multiple regression:

- t statistic
- r-bar squared ($\overline{r}^2$) *and F* statistic

TABLE 7.1 VALUES OF t_p FOR SPECIFIED PROBABILITIES P AND DEGREES OF FREEDOM v

THIS TABLE SHOWS

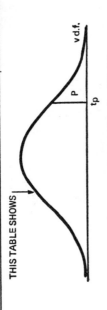

Degrees of Freedom v	Level of Significance P for One-Sided Statements												
	0.45	0.40	0.35	0.30	0.25	0.20	0.15	0.10	0.05	0.025	0.01	0.005	0.0005
1	0.158	0.325	0.510	0.727	1.000	1.376	1.963	3.078	6.314	12.706	31.821	63.657	636.692
2	0.142	0.289	0.445	0.617	0.816	1.061	1.386	1.886	2.920	4.303	6.965	9.925	31.598
3	0.137	0.277	0.424	0.584	0.765	0.978	1.250	1.638	2.353	3.182	4.541	5.841	12.924
4	0.134	0.271	0.414	0.569	0.741	0.941	1.190	1.533	2.132	2.776	3.747	4.604	8.610
5	0.132	0.267	0.408	0.559	0.727	0.920	1.156	1.476	2.015	2.571	3.365	4.032	6.869
6	0.131	0.265	0.404	0.553	0.718	0.906	1.134	1.440	1.943	2.447	3.143	3.707	5.959
7	0.130	0.263	0.402	0.549	0.711	0.896	1.119	1.415	1.895	2.365	2.998	3.499	5.408
8	0.130	0.262	0.399	0.546	0.706	0.889	1.108	1.397	1.860	2.306	2.896	3.355	5.041

TABLE 7.1 (cont.)

Degrees of Freedom v	Level of Significance P for One-Sided Statements														
	0.45	0.40	0.35	0.30	0.25	0.20	0.15	0.10	0.05	0.025	0.01	0.005	0.0005
9	0.129	0.261	0.398	0.543	0.703	0.883	1.100	1.383	1.833	2.262	2.821	3.250	4.781
10	0.129	0.260	0.397	0.542	0.700	0.879	1.093	1.372	1.812	2.228	2.764	3.169	4.587
11	0.129	0.260	0.396	0.540	0.697	0.876	1.088	1.363	1.796	2.201	2.718	3.106	4.437
12	0.128	0.259	0.395	0.539	0.695	0.873	1.083	1.356	1.782	2.179	2.681	3.055	4.318
13	0.128	0.259	0.394	0.538	0.694	0.870	1.079	1.350	1.771	2.160	2.650	3.012	4.221
14	0.128	0.258	0.393	0.537	0.692	0.868	1.076	1.345	1.761	2.145	2.624	2.977	4.140
15	0.128	0.258	0.393	0.536	0.691	0.866	1.074	1.341	1.753	2.131	2.602	2.947	4.073
16	0.128	0.258	0.392	0.535	0.690	0.865	1.071	1.337	1.746	2.120	2.583	2.921	4.015
17	0.128	0.257	0.392	0.534	0.689	0.863	1.069	1.333	1.740	2.110	2.567	2.898	3.965
18	0.127	0.257	0.392	0.534	0.688	0.862	1.067	1.330	1.734	2.101	2.552	2.878	3.922
19	0.127	0.257	0.391	0.533	0.688	0.861	1.066	1.328	1.729	2.093	2.539	2.861	3.883
20	0.127	0.257	0.391	0.533	0.687	0.860	1.064	1.325	1.725	2.086	2.528	2.845	3.850
21	0.127	0.257	0.391	0.532	0.686	0.859	1.063	1.323	1.721	2.080	2.518	2.831	3.819
22	0.127	0.256	0.390	0.532	0.686	0.858	1.061	1.321	1.717	2.074	2.508	2.819	3.792

23	0.127	0.256	0.390	0.532	0.685	0.858	1.060	1.319	1.714	2.069	2.500	2.807	3.767
24	0.127	0.256	0.390	0.531	0.685	0.857	1.059	1.318	1.711	2.064	2.492	2.797	3.745
25	0.127	0.256	0.390	0.531	0.684	0.856	1.058	1.316	1.708	2.060	2.485	2.787	3.725
26	0.127	0.256	0.390	0.531	0.684	0.856	1.058	1.315	1.706	2.056	2.479	2.779	3.707
27	0.127	0.256	0.389	0.531	0.684	0.855	1.057	1.314	1.703	2.052	2.473	2.771	3.690
28	0.127	0.256	0.389	0.530	0.683	0.855	1.056	1.313	1.701	2.048	2.467	2.763	3.674
29	0.127	0.256	0.389	0.530	0.683	0.854	1.055	1.311	1.699	2.045	2.462	2.756	3.659
30	0.127	0.256	0.389	0.530	0.683	0.854	1.055	1.310	1.697	2.042	2.457	2.750	3.646
40	0.126	0.255	0.388	0.529	0.681	0.851	1.050	1.303	1.684	2.021	2.423	2.704	3.551
60	0.126	0.254	0.387	0.527	0.679	0.848	1.046	1.296	1.671	2.000	2.390	2.660	3.460
120	0.126	0.254	0.386	0.526	0.677	0.845	1.041	1.289	1.658	1.980	2.358	2.617	3.373
∞	0.126	0.253	0.385	0.524	0.674	0.842	1.036	1.282	1.645	1.960	2.326	2.576	3.291

t_P is the value of the student's t random variable such that the probability of obtaining a sample t value at least as large as t_P is P. The value of P must be doubled if two-sided statements are made using the same t_P value.

Source: This table is taken from Table III of Fisher and Yates, Statistical Tables for Biological, Agricultural and Medical Research, published by Oliver and Boyd, Edinburgh, and by permission of the authors and publishers.

- Multicollinearity
- Autocorrelation (or serial correlation)

What does the t statistic show?

Even though the *t* statistic was discussed in the previous section, we take it up again because it is even more valid in multiple regression. The *t* statistic shows the significance of each independent variable in predicting the dependent variable. In multiple regression, the *t* statistic is defined as follows:

$$t \text{ statistic} = \frac{b_i}{s_{b_i}}$$

where

$i = i$th independent variable

RULE OF THUMB: It's best to have a large *t* statistic (either positive or negative) for each independent variable. Generally, a value greater than $+2$ or less than -2 is acceptable. You can usually eliminate variables with a low *t* value without substantially decreasing r^2 or increasing the standard error. Table 7.2 provides t- value for a specified level of significance and degrees of freedom.

How do I measure goodness of fit?

For multiple regressions, goodness of fit is best represented by *r*-bar squared ($\bar{r}^2$), shown as follows:

$$\bar{r}^2 = 1 - (1 - r^2)\frac{n - 1}{n - k}$$

where

n = number of observations
k = number of coefficients to be estimated

An alternative to the *r*-bar squared would be the *F* test. The *F* statistic is defined as follows:

$$F = \frac{\Sigma(\hat{y} - \bar{y})^2/k}{\Sigma(y - \hat{y})^2/n - k - 1}$$

$$= \frac{\text{Explained variation} / k}{\text{Unexplained variation} / n - k - 1}$$

Values for *F* for specified probabilities and degrees of freedom are given in Table 7.3. If the *F* statistic is greater than the table value, you can conclude that the regression equation is statistically significant in overall terms.

NOTE: Virtually all computer programs for regression analysis show $\bar{r}^2$ and an *F* statistic.

TABLE 7.2 STUDENT'S t DISTRIBUTION

Degree of freedom $= n - k - 1$	Probability														
	0.9	0.8	0.7	0.6	0.5	0.4	0.3	0.2	0.1	0.05	0.02	0.01	0.001
1	0.158	0.325	0.510	0.727	1.000	1.376	1.963	3.078	6.314	12.706	31.821	63.657	636.619
2	0.142	0.289	0.445	0.617	0.816	1.061	1.386	1.886	2.920	4.303	6.965	9.925	31.598
3	0.137	0.277	0.424	0.584	0.765	0.978	1.250	1.638	2.353	3.182	4.541	5.841	12.924
4	0.134	0.271	0.414	0.569	0.741	0.941	1.190	1.533	2.132	2.776	3.747	4.604	8.610
5	0.132	0.267	0.408	0.559	0.727	0.920	1.156	1.476	2.015	2.571	3.365	4.032	6.869
6	0.131	0.265	0.404	0.553	0.718	0.906	.134	1.440	1.943	2.447	3.143	3.707	5.959
7	0.130	0.263	0.402	0.549	0.711	0.896	1.119	1.415	1.895	2.365	2.998	3.499	5.408
8	0.130	0.262	0.399	0.546	0.706	0.889	1.108	1.397	1.860	2.306	2.896	3.355	5.041
9	0.129	0.261	0.398	0.543	0.703	0.883	1.100	1.383	1.833	2.262	2.821	3.250	4.781
10	0.129	0.260	0.397	0.542	0.700	0.879	1.093	1.372	1.812	2.228	2.764	3.169	4.587
11	0.129	0.260	0.396	0.540	0.697	0.876	1.088	1.363	1.796	2.201	2.718	3.106	4.437
12	0.128	0.259	0.395	0.539	0.695	0.873	1.083	1.356	1.782	2.179	2.681	3.055	4.318
13	0.128	0.259	0.394	0.538	0.694	0.870	1.079	1.350	1.771	2.160	2.650	3.012	4.221
14	0.128	0.258	0.393	0.537	0.692	0.868	1.076	1.345	1.761	2.145	2.624	2.977	4.140
15	0.128	0.258	0.393	0.536	0.691	0.866	1.074	1.341	1.753	2.131	2.602	2.947	4.073

TABLE 7.2 (cont.)

Degree of freedom $= n - k - 1$	Probability														
	0.9	0.8	0.7	0.6	0.5	0.4	0.3	0.2	0.1	0.05	0.02	0.01	0.001
16	0.128	0.258	0.392	0.535	0.690	0.865	1.071	1.337	1.746	2.120	2.583	2.921	4.015
17	0.128	0.257	0.392	0.534	0.689	0.863	1.069	1.333	1.740	2.110	2.567	2.898	3.965
18	0.127	0.257	0.392	0.534	0.688	0.862	1.067	1.330	1.734	2.101	2.552	2.878	3.922
19	0.127	0.257	0.391	0.533	0.688	0.861	1.066	1.328	1.729	2.093	2.539	2.861	3.883
20	0.127	0.257	0.391	0.533	0.687	0.860	1.064	1.325	1.725	2.086	2.528	2.845	3.850
21	0.127	0.257	0.391	0.532	0.686	0.859	1.063	1.323	1.721	2.080	2.518	2.831	3.819
22	0.127	0.256	0.390	0.532	0.686	0.858	1.061	1.321	1.717	2.074	2.508	2.819	3.792
23	0.127	0.256	0.390	0.532	0.685	0.858	1.060	1.319	1.714	2.069	2.500	2.807	3.767
24	0.127	0.256	0.390	0.531	0.685	0.857	1.059	1.318	1.711	2.064	2.492	2.797	3.745
25	0.127	0.256	0.390	0.531	0.684	0.856	1.058	1.316	1.708	2.060	2.485	2.787	3.725
26	0.127	0.256	0.390	0.531	0.684	0.856	1.058	1.315	1.706	2.056	2.479	2.779	3.707
27	0.127	0.256	0.389	0.531	0.684	0.855	1.057	1.314	1.703	2.052	2.473	2.771	3.690
28	0.127	0.256	0.389	0.530	0.683	0.855	1.056	1.313	1.701	2.048	2.467	2.763	3.674
29	0.127	0.256	0.389	0.530	0.683	0.854	1.055	1.311	1.699	2.045	2.462	2.756	3.659
30	0.127	0.256	0.389	0.530	0.683	0.854	1.055	1.310	1.697	2.042	2.457	2.750	3.646

40	0.126	0.255	0.388	0.529	0.681	0.851	1.050	1.303	1.684	2.021	2.423	2.704	3.551
60	0.126	0.254	0.387	0.527	0.679	0.848	1.046	1.296	1.671	2.000	2.390	2.660	3.460
120	0.126	0.254	0.386	0.526	0.677	0.845	1.041	1.289	1.658	1.980	2.358	2.617	3.373
∞	0.126	0.253	0.385	0.524	0.674	0.842	1.036	1.282	1.645	1.960	2.326	2.576	3.291

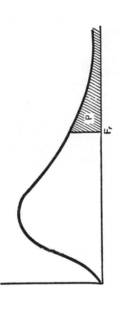

Values of F_r for Probabilities P

In Table 7.2 the level of significance P is 0.05 for the first entry of n_1, and 0.01 for the second entry of n_2. For example, an $n_1 = 5$ and $n_2 = 16$ results in an F value of 2.85 for a 0.05 significance level.

How can I be sure the independent variables are unrelated?

When you use more than one independent variable in a regression equation, the variables themselves may be correlated. *Multicollinearity* occurs when these variables interfere with each other. When this is the case, you may produce spurious (accidental) or inaccurate forecasts.

Here's how to recognize multicollinearity:

- The t statistics of two seemingly important independent variables are suspiciously low
- The estimated coefficients on independent variables have signs opposite from what you would logically expect

You can solve the problem of multicollinearity two ways:

- Drop one of the highly correlated variables from the regression
- Change the structure of the equation by (1) dividing all variables by some factor that will leave the basic economic logic but will remove multicollinearity; (2) estimating the equation on a "first-difference" basis; or (3) combining the collinear variables into a new variable that equals their weighted sum

What is autocorrelation?

Autocorrelation indicates a correlation between successive errors. In other words, it usually shows that an important part of the variation of the dependent variable has not been explained. WHAT TO DO: When autocorrelation exists, search for other independent variables to include in the regression equation.

The Durbin–Watson statistic provides the standard test for autocorrelation. Table 7.4 provides values of the Durbin–Watson statistic for specified sample sizes and independent variables. Generally, you can interpret the statistic as follows:

Durbin–Watson Statistic	Autocorrelation
Between 1.5 and 2.5	No autocorrelation
Below 1.5	Positive autocorrelation
Above 2.5	Negative autocorrelation

An example showing applications of all the tests discussed in this section can be found in Section 7.6.

TABLE 7.3 F DISTRIBUTION

$n_1 =$ degrees of freedom for numerator $= k$

	1	2	3	4	5	6	7	8	9	10	11	12
1	161	200	216	225	230	234	237	239	241	242	243	244
	4,052	**4,999**	**5,408**	**5,625**	**5,764**	**5,559**	**5,928**	**5,981**	**6,023**	**6,054**	**6,082**	**6,106**
2	18.51	19.00	19.16	19.25	19.30	19.33	19.36	19.37	19.38	19.39	19.40	19.41
	98.49	**99.01**	**99.17**	**99.25**	**99.30**	**99.33**	**99.34**	**99.36**	**99.38**	**99.40**	**99.41**	**99.42**
3	10.13	9.55	9.28	9.12	9.01	8.94	8.88	8.84	8.81	8.78	8.76	8.74
	34.12	**30.81**	**29.46**	**28.71**	**28.24**	**27.91**	**27.67**	**27.49**	**27.34**	**27.23**	**27.13**	**27.06**
4	7.71	6.94	6.59	6.39	6.26	6.16	6.09	6.04	6.00	5.96	5.93	5.91
	21.20	**18.00**	**16.69**	**15.98**	**15.52**	**15.21**	**14.98**	**14.80**	**14.66**	**14.54**	**14.45**	**14.37**
5	6.61	5.79	5.41	5.19	5.05	4.95	4.88	4.82	4.78	4.74	4.70	4.68
	16.26	**13.27**	**12.06**	**11.39**	**10.37**	**10.67**	**10.45**	**10.27**	**10.15**	**10.05**	**9.96**	**9.89**
6	5.99	5.14	4.76	4.53	4.39	4.28	4.21	4.15	4.10	4.06	4.03	4.00
	13.74	**10.92**	**9.78**	**9.15**	**8.76**	**8.47**	**8.26**	**8.10**	**7.98**	**7.87**	**7.79**	**7.72**
7	5.59	4.74	4.35	4.12	3.97	3.87	3.79	3.73	3.68	3.63	3.60	3.57
	12.25	**9.55**	**8.45**	**7.85**	**7.44**	**7.19**	**7.00**	**6.84**	**6.71**	**6.62**	**6.54**	**6.47**
8	5.32	4.48	4.07	3.84	3.69	3.58	3.50	3.44	3.39	3.34	3.31	3.28
	11.26	**8.64**	**7.69**	**7.01**	**6.63**	**6.37**	**6.19**	**6.03**	**5.91**	**5.82**	**5.74**	**5.67**

TABLE 7.3 (cont.)

					n_1 = degrees of freedom for numerator = k							
	1	2	3	4	5	6	7	8	9	10	11	12
9	5.12	4.26	3.86	3.63	3.48	3.37	3.29	3.23	3.18	3.13	3.10	3.07
	10.66	**8.02**	**6.99**	**6.42**	**6.06**	**5.30**	**5.62**	**5.47**	**5.35**	**5.26**	**5.18**	**5.11**
10	4.96	4.10	3.71	3.48	3.33	3.22	3.14	3.07	3.02	2.97	2.94	2.91
	10.04	**7.54**	**6.55**	**5.99**	**5.64**	**5.39**	**5.21**	**5.06**	**4.95**	**4.85**	**4.78**	**4.71**
11	4.84	3.98	3.59	3.36	3.20	3.09	3.01	2.95	2.90	2.86	2.82	2.79
	9.65	**7.20**	**6.22**	**5.67**	**5.32**	**5.07**	**4.88**	**4.74**	**4.63**	**4.54**	**4.46**	**4.40**
12	4.75	3.88	3.49	3.26	3.11	3.00	2.92	2.85	2.80	2.76	2.72	2.69
	9.33	**6.93**	**5.95**	**5.41**	**5.04**	**4.82**	**4.65**	**4.50**	**4.39**	**4.30**	**4.22**	**4.16**
13	4.67	3.80	3.41	3.18	3.02	2.02	2.84	2.77	2.72	2.67	2.63	2.60
	9.07	**6.70**	**5.74**	**5.20**	**4.86**	**4.62**	**4.44**	**4.30**	**4.19**	**4.10**	**4.02**	**3.96**
14	4.60	3.74	3.34	3.11	2.96	2.85	2.77	2.70	2.65	2.60	2.56	2.53
	8.86	**6.51**	**5.56**	**5.03**	**4.69**	**4.46**	**4.28**	**4.14**	**4.03**	**3.94**	**3.86**	**3.80**
15	4.54	3.68	3.29	3.06	2.90	2.79	2.70	2.64	2.59	2.55	2.51	2.48
	8.62	**6.36**	**5.42**	**4.89**	**4.56**	**4.32**	**4.14**	**4.00**	**3.89**	**3.80**	**3.73**	**3.67**
16	4.49	3.63	3.24	3.01	2.85	2.74	2.66	2.59	2.54	2.49	2.45	2.42
	8.53	**6.23**	**5.29**	**4.77**	**4.44**	**4.20**	**4.03**	**3.89**	**3.78**	**3.69**	**3.61**	**3.55**

n_2												
17	4.45	3.59	3.20	2.96	2.81	2.70	2.62	2.55	2.50	2.45	2.41	2.38
	8.40	6.11	5.18	4.67	4.34	4.10	3.93	3.79	3.68	3.59	3.52	3.45
18	4.41	3.55	3.16	2.93	2.77	2.66	2.58	2.51	2.46	2.41	2.37	2.34
	8.26	6.01	5.09	4.58	4.25	4.01	3.86	3.71	3.60	3.51	3.44	3.37
19	4.38	3.52	3.13	2.90	2.74	2.63	2.55	2.48	2.43	2.38	2.34	2.31
	8.18	5.98	5.01	4.50	4.17	3.94	3.77	3.63	3.52	3.43	3.36	3.30
20	4.35	3.49	3.10	2.87	2.71	2.60	2.52	2.45	2.40	2.35	2.31	2.28
	8.10	5.86	4.94	4.43	4.10	3.87	3.71	3.56	3.45	3.37	3.30	3.23
21	4.32	3.47	3.07	2.84	2.68	2.57	2.49	2.42	2.37	2.32	2.28	2.25
	8.02	5.78	4.87	4.37	4.04	3.81	3.65	3.51	3.40	3.31	3.24	3.17
22	4.30	3.44	3.05	2.82	2.66	2.55	2.47	2.40	2.35	2.30	2.26	2.23
	7.94	5.72	4.82	4.31	3.99	3.76	3.69	3.45	3.35	3.26	3.18	3.12
23	4.28	3.42	3.03	2.80	2.64	2.53	2.45	2.38	2.32	2.28	2.24	2.20
	7.88	5.64	4.76	4.28	3.94	3.71	3.54	3.41	3.30	3.21	3.14	3.07
24	4.26	3.40	3.01	2.78	2.62	2.51	2.43	2.36	2.30	2.26	2.22	2.18
	7.82	5.61	4.72	4.22	3.90	3.67	3.50	3.36	3.25	3.17	3.09	3.03
25	4.24	3.38	2.99	2.76	2.60	2.49	2.41	2.34	2.28	2.24	2.20	2.16
	7.77	5.57	4.68	4.13	3.86	3.63	3.46	3.32	3.21	3.13	3.05	2.99
26	4.22	3.37	2.98	2.74	2.59	2.47	2.39	2.32	2.27	2.22	2.18	2.15
	7.72	5.83	4.64	4.14	3.82	3.59	3.42	3.29	3.17	3.09	3.02	2.96

n_2 = degrees of freedom for denominator = $n - k - 1$

TABLE 7.3 (cont.)

	n_1 = degrees of freedom for numerator = k											
	14	16	20	24	30	40	50	75	100	200	500	∞
1	245	246	248	249	250	251	252	253	253	254	254	254
	6,142	**6,169**	**6,208**	**6,334**	**6,258**	**6,286**	**6,302**	**6,323**	**6,334**	**6,352**	**6,361**	**6,364**
2	19.42	19.43	19.44	19.45	19.46	19.47	19.47	19.48	19.49	19.49	19.50	19.50
	99.43	**99.44**	**99.45**	**99.46**	**99.47**	**99.48**	**99.48**	**99.49**	**99.49**	**99.49**	**99.50**	**99.50**
3	8.71	8.69	8.66	8.64	8.62	8.60	8.58	8.57	8.56	8.54	8.54	8.53
	26.92	**26.83**	**26.69**	**26.60**	**26.50**	**26.41**	**26.35**	**26.27**	**26.23**	**26.18**	**26.14**	**26.12**
4	5.87	5.84	5.80	5.77	5.74	5.71	5.70	5.68	5.66	5.65	5.64	5.63
	14.24	**14.15**	**14.02**	**13.93**	**13.83**	**13.74**	**13.69**	**13.61**	**13.57**	**13.52**	**13.48**	**13.46**
5	4.64	4.60	4.56	4.53	4.50	4.46	4.44	4.42	4.40	4.38	4.37	4.36
	9.77	**9.68**	**9.55**	**9.47**	**9.38**	**9.29**	**9.24**	**9.17**	**9.13**	**9.07**	**9.04**	**9.02**
6	3.96	3.92	3.87	3.84	3.81	3.77	3.75	3.72	3.71	3.69	3.68	3.67
	7.60	**7.52**	**7.39**	**7.31**	**7.23**	**7.14**	**7.09**	**7.02**	**6.99**	**6.94**	**6.90**	**6.88**
7	3.52	3.49	3.44	3.41	3.38	3.34	3.32	3.29	3.28	3.25	3.24	3.23
	6.35	**6.27**	**6.15**	**6.07**	**5.98**	**5.90**	**5.85**	**5.78**	**5.75**	**5.70**	**5.67**	**5.65**
8	3.23	3.20	3.15	3.12	3.08	3.05	3.03	3.00	2.98	2.96	2.94	2.93
	5.56	**5.48**	**5.36**	**5.28**	**5.20**	**5.11**	**5.06**	**5.00**	**4.96**	**4.91**	**4.88**	**4.86**

9	3.02 **5.00**	2.98 **4.92**	2.93 **4.80**	2.90 **4.73**	2.86 **4.64**	2.82 **4.56**	2.80 **4.51**	2.77 **4.45**	2.76 **4.41**	2.73 **4.36**	2.72 **4.33**	2.71 **4.31**
10	2.86 **4.60**	2.82 **4.52**	2.77 **4.41**	2.74 **4.33**	2.70 **4.25**	2.67 **4.17**	2.64 **4.12**	2.61 **4.05**	2.59 **4.01**	2.56 **3.96**	2.55 **3.93**	2.54 **3.91**
11	2.74 **4.29**	2.70 **4.21**	2.65 **4.10**	2.61 **4.02**	2.57 **3.94**	2.53 **3.86**	2.50 **3.80**	2.47 **3.74**	2.45 **3.70**	2.42 **3.66**	2.41 **3.62**	2.40 **3.60**
12	2.64 **4.50**	2.60 **3.98**	2.54 **3.86**	2.50 **3.78**	2.46 **3.70**	2.42 **3.61**	2.40 **3.56**	2.36 **3.49**	2.35 **3.46**	2.32 **3.41**	2.31 **3.38**	2.30 **3.36**
13	2.55 **3.85**	2.51 **3.78**	2.46 **3.67**	2.42 **3.59**	2.38 **3.51**	2.34 **3.42**	2.32 **3.37**	2.28 **3.30**	2.26 **3.27**	2.24 **3.21**	2.22 **3.18**	2.21 **3.16**
14	2.48 **3.70**	2.44 **3.62**	2.39 **3.51**	2.35 **3.43**	2.31 **3.34**	2.27 **3.26**	2.24 **3.21**	2.21 **3.14**	2.19 **3.11**	2.16 **3.06**	2.14 **3.02**	2.13 **3.00**
15	2.43 **3.56**	2.39 **3.48**	2.33 **3.36**	2.29 **3.29**	2.25 **3.20**	2.21 **3.12**	2.18 **3.07**	2.15 **3.00**	2.12 **2.97**	2.10 **2.92**	2.08 **2.89**	2.07 **2.87**
16	2.37 **3.45**	2.33 **3.37**	2.28 **3.25**	2.24 **3.18**	2.20 **3.10**	2.16 **3.01**	2.13 **2.96**	2.09 **2.89**	2.07 **2.86**	2.04 **2.80**	2.02 **2.77**	2.01 **2.75**
17	2.33 **3.35**	2.29 **3.27**	2.23 **3.16**	2.19 **3.08**	2.15 **3.00**	2.11 **2.92**	2.08 **2.86**	2.04 **2.79**	2.02 **2.76**	1.99 **2.70**	1.97 **2.67**	1.96 **2.65**
18	2.29 **3.27**	2.25 **3.19**	2.19 **3.07**	2.15 **3.00**	2.11 **2.91**	2.07 **2.83**	2.04 **2.78**	2.00 **2.71**	1.98 **2.68**	1.95 **2.62**	1.93 **2.59**	1.92 **2.57**

TABLE 7.3 (cont.)

n_1 = degrees of freedom for numerator = k

	14	16	20	24	30	40	50	75	100	200	500	∞
19	2.26	2.21	2.15	2.11	2.07	2.02	2.00	1.96	1.94	1.91	1.90	1.88
	3.19	**3.12**	**3.00**	**2.92**	**2.84**	**2.76**	**2.70**	**2.63**	**2.60**	**2.54**	**2.51**	**2.49**
20	2.23	2.18	2.12	2.08	2.04	1.99	1.96	1.92	1.90	1.87	1.85	1.84
	3.13	**3.05**	**2.94**	**2.86**	**2.77**	**2.69**	**2.63**	**2.56**	**2.53**	**2.47**	**2.44**	**2.42**
21	2.20	2.15	2.09	2.05	2.00	1.96	1.93	1.89	1.87	1.84	1.82	1.81
	3.07	**2.99**	**2.88**	**2.80**	**2.72**	**2.63**	**2.58**	**2.51**	**2.47**	**2.42**	**2.38**	**2.36**
22	2.18	2.13	2.07	2.03	1.98	1.93	1.91	1.87	1.84	1.81	1.80	1.78
	3.02	**2.94**	**2.83**	**2.75**	**2.67**	**2.58**	**2.53**	**2.46**	**2.42**	**2.37**	**2.33**	**2.31**
23	2.14	2.10	2.04	2.00	1.96	1.91	1.88	1.84	1.82	1.79	1.77	1.76
	2.97	**2.89**	**2.78**	**2.70**	**2.62**	**2.53**	**2.48**	**2.41**	**2.37**	**2.32**	**2.28**	**2.26**
24	2.13	2.09	2.02	1.98	1.94	1.89	1.86	1.82	1.80	1.76	1.74	1.73
	2.93	**2.85**	**2.74**	**2.66**	**2.58**	**2.49**	**2.44**	**2.36**	**2.33**	**2.27**	**2.23**	**2.21**
25	2.11	2.06	2.00	1.96	1.92	1.87	1.84	1.80	1.77	.174	1.72	1.71
	2.89	**2.81**	**2.70**	**2.62**	**2.54**	**2.45**	**2.40**	**2.32**	**2.29**	**2.23**	**2.19**	**2.17**
26	2.10	2.05	1.99	1.95	1.90	1.85	1.82	1.78	1.76	1.72	1.70	1.69
	2.86	**2.77**	**2.66**	**2.58**	**2.50**	**2.41**	**2.36**	**2.28**	**2.25**	**2.19**	**2.15**	**2.13**

TABLE 7.4 DURBIN–WATSON VALUES

LEVEL OF SIGNIFICANCE: 0.01

Number of residuals T	K = 1		K = 2		K = 3		K = 4		K = 5	
	d_L	d_U	d_L	d_U	d_L	d_U	d_L	d_U	d_L	d_U
15	1.08	1.36	0.95	1.54	0.82	1.75	0.69	1.97	0.56	2.21
16	1.10	1.37	0.98	1.54	0.86	1.73	0.74	1.93	0.62	2.15
17	1.13	1.38	1.02	1.54	0.90	1.71	0.78	1.90	0.67	2.10
18	1.16	1.39	1.05	1.53	0.93	1.69	0.82	1.87	0.71	2.06
19	1.18	1.40	1.08	1.53	0.97	1.68	0.86	1.85	0.75	2.02
20	1.20	1.41	1.10	1.54	1.00	1.68	0.90	1.83	0.79	1.99
21	1.22	1.42	1.13	1.54	1.03	1.67	0.93	1.81	0.83	1.96
22	1.24	1.43	1.15	1.54	1.05	1.66	0.96	1.80	0.86	1.94
23	1.26	1.44	1.17	1.54	1.08	1.66	0.99	1.79	0.90	1.92
24	1.27	1.45	1.19	1.55	1.10	1.66	1.01	1.78	0.93	1.90
25	1.29	1.45	1.21	1.55	1.12	1.66	1.04	1.77	0.95	1.89
26	1.30	1.46	1.22	1.55	1.14	1.65	1.06	1.76	0.98	1.88
27	1.32	1.47	1.24	1.56	1.16	1.65	1.08	1.76	1.01	1.86
28	1.33	1.48	1.26	1.56	1.18	1.65	1.10	1.75	1.03	1.85
29	1.34	1.48	1.27	1.56	1.20	1.65	1.12	1.74	1.05	1.84

TABLE 7.4 (cont.)

LEVEL OF SIGNIFICANCE: 0.01

Number of residuals T	K = 1		K = 2		K = 3		K = 4		K = 5	
	d_L	d_U	d_L	d_U	d_L	d_U	d_L	d_U	d_L	d_U
30	1.35	1.49	1.28	1.57	1.21	1.65	1.14	1.74	1.07	1.83
31	1.36	1.50	1.30	1.57	1.23	1.65	1.16	1.74	1.09	1.83
32	1.37	1.50	1.31	1.57	1.24	1.65	1.18	1.73	1.11	1.82
33	1.38	1.51	1.32	1.58	1.26	1.65	1.19	1.73	1.13	1.81
34	1.39	1.51	1.33	1.58	1.27	1.65	1.21	1.73	1.15	1.81
35	1.40	1.52	1.34	1.58	1.28	1.65	1.22	1.73	1.16	1.80
36	1.41	1.52	1.35	1.59	1.29	1.65	1.24	1.73	1.18	1.80
37	1.42	1.53	1.36	1.59	1.31	1.66	1.25	1.72	1.19	1.80
38	1.43	1.54	1.37	1.59	1.32	1.66	1.26	1.72	1.21	1.79
39	1.43	1.54	1.38	1.60	1.33	1.66	1.27	1.72	1.22	1.79
40	1.44	1.54	1.39	1.60	1.34	1.66	1.29	1.72	1.23	1.79
45	1.48	1.57	1.43	1.62	1.38	1.67	1.34	1.72	1.29	1.78
50	1.50	1.59	1.46	1.63	1.42	1.67	1.38	1.72	1.34	1.77

Note: This table displays the values of the Durbin–Watson d for sample sizes T and explanatory variables K^1 where $K^1 = K - 1$.

LEVEL OF SIGNIFICANCE: 0.05

Number of residuals T	K = 1		K = 2		K = 3		K = 4		K = 5	
	d_L	d_U	d_L	d_U	d_L	d_U	d_L	d_U	d_L	d_U
15	0.81	1.07	0.70	1.25	0.59	1.46	0.49	1.70	0.39	1.96
16	0.84	1.09	0.74	1.25	0.63	1.44	0.53	1.66	0.44	1.90
17	0.87	1.10	0.77	1.25	0.67	1.43	0.57	1.63	0.48	1.85
18	0.90	1.12	0.80	1.26	0.71	1.42	0.61	1.60	0.52	1.80
19	0.93	1.13	0.83	1.26	0.74	1.41	0.65	1.58	0.56	1.77
20	0.95	1.15	0.86	1.27	0.77	1.41	0.68	1.57	0.60	1.74
21	0.97	1.16	0.89	1.27	0.80	1.41	0.72	1.55	0.63	1.71
22	1.00	1.17	0.91	1.28	0.83	1.40	0.75	1.54	0.66	1.69
23	1.02	1.19	0.94	1.29	0.86	1.40	0.77	1.53	0.70	1.67
24	1.04	1.20	0.96	1.30	0.88	1.41	0.80	1.53	0.72	1.66
25	1.05	1.21	0.98	1.30	0.90	1.41	0.83	1.52	0.75	1.65
26	1.07	1.22	1.00	1.31	0.93	1.41	0.85	1.52	0.78	1.64
27	1.09	1.23	1.02	1.32	0.95	1.41	0.88	1.51	0.81	1.63
28	1.10	1.24	1.04	1.32	0.97	1.41	0.90	1.51	0.83	1.62
29	1.12	1.25	1.05	1.33	0.99	1.42	0.92	1.51	0.85	1.61
30	1.13	1.26	1.07	1.34	1.01	1.42	0.94	1.51	0.88	1.61

TABLE 7.4 (cont.)

LEVEL OF SIGNIFICANCE: 0.01

Number of residuals T	K = 1		K = 2		K = 3		K = 4		K = 5	
	d_L	d_U	d_L	d_U	d_L	d_U	d_L	d_U	d_L	d_U
31	1.15	1.27	1.08	1.34	1.02	1.42	0.96	1.51	0.90	1.60
32	1.16	1.28	1.10	1.35	1.04	1.43	0.98	1.51	0.92	1.60
33	1.17	1.29	1.11	1.36	1.05	1.43	1.00	1.51	0.94	1.59
34	1.18	1.30	1.13	1.36	1.07	1.43	1.01	1.51	0.95	1.59
35	1.19	1.31	1.14	1.37	1.08	1.44	1.03	1.51	0.97	1.59
36	1.21	1.32	1.15	1.38	1.10	1.44	1.04	1.51	0.99	1.59
37	1.22	1.32	1.16	1.38	1.11	1.45	1.06	1.51	1.00	1.59
38	1.23	1.33	1.18	1.39	1.12	1.45	1.07	1.52	1.02	1.58
39	1.24	1.34	1.19	1.39	1.14	1.45	1.09	1.52	1.03	1.58
40	1.25	1.34	1.20	1.40	1.15	1.46	1.10	1.52	1.05	1.58
45	1.29	1.38	1.24	1.42	1.20	1.48	1.16	1.53	1.11	1.58
50	1.32	1.40	1.28	1.45	1.24	1.49	1.20	1.54	1.16	1.59

7.5 MEASURING THE ACCURACY OF YOUR FORECASTS

One of the most important aspects of any forecast is the amount of error associated with it. DEFINITION:

Error = Actual − Forecast

What measures are commonly used for summarizing errors?

Two measures are commonly used to summarize errors: mean absolute deviation (MAD) and mean squared error (MSE). MAD is defined as the average error, or

$$MAD = \frac{\Sigma \mid actual - forecast \mid}{n}$$

Note: Vertical lines indicate absolute values (or positive values)

MSE is the average of squared errors, expressed as follows:

$$MSE = \frac{\Sigma(actual - forecast)^2}{n - 1}$$

EXAMPLE 7.14

Company Z reports the following sales data:

Time Period	Actual	Forecast	Error	|Error|	(Error)^2
1	$217	$215	2	2	4
2	213	216	−3	3	9
3	216	215	1	1	1
4	210	214	−4	4	16
5	213	211	2	2	4
6	219	214	5	5	25
7	216	217	−1	1	1
8	212	216	−4	4	16
				22	76

Computations for MAD and MSE are

$$\text{MAD} = \frac{\Sigma \mid \text{error} \mid}{n} = \frac{22}{8} = 2.75$$

$$\text{MSE} = \frac{\Sigma(\text{error})^2}{n-1} = \frac{76}{8-1} = 10.86$$

How do I choose the best forecasting equation?

Choosing among alternative forecasting equations basically involves two steps:

- Eliminate the obvious losers
- Select a winner from among the remaining contenders

You can eliminate the losers by asking these questions:

- Does the equation make sense either intuitively or theoretically? If not, then eliminate.
- Does the equation have independent variables with low t statistics? If so, they should be reestimated or dropped in favor of equations in which all independent variables are significant. This test will probably eliminate equations facing problems with multicollinearity.
- How about a low $\bar{r}^2$? This statistic can be used to rank the remaining equations and to select the best candidates. REMEMBER THIS: A low $\bar{r}^2$ could mean (1) a wrong functional form was fitted (linear, quadratic, etc.); (2) an important independent variable or variables is or are missing; or (3) other combinations of independent variables might be more desirable.

Here's how to select the best equation:

- Given equations that survive all previous tests, the equation with the Durbin–Watson statistic closest to 2.0 can provide a basis for selection.
- The equation whose prediction accuracy is best as measured by MAD or MSE generally provides the best basis for forecasting.

7.6 HOW TO USE THE COMPUTER FOR MULTIPLE REGRESSION

Are computers helpful for statistical analyses?

Software packages can greatly assist decision makers and forecasters with a variety of statistical analyses.

How does the computer handle multiple regression?

Here's an example of how a computer handles multiple regression. REMEMBER THIS: Each software package is different. For this example, we use STATPAK, one of the easiest programs to use. In Figure 7.4, you'll find a computer listing containing the input data and output results using three independent variables. To help you, illustrative comments have been added where applicable.

EXAMPLE 7.15

Cypress Consumer Products Corporation wishes to develop a forecasting model for its dryer sales by using multiple regression analysis. The marketing department prepared the following sample data that appears in the following table using three independent variables: sales of washers, disposable income, and savings.

Month	Sales of Washers (x_1)	Disposable Income (x_2)	Savings (x_3)	Sales of Dryers (y)
	(000)	(000)	(000)	(000)
January	$45	$16	$71	$29
February	42	14	70	24
March	44	15	72	27
April	45	13	71	25
May	43	13	75	26
June	46	14	74	28
July	44	16	76	30
August	45	16	69	28
September	44	15	74	28
October	43	15	73	27

The Forecasting Equation. From the STATPAK output, you can see that

$$\hat{y} = -45.796 + 0.597x_1 + 1.177x_2 + 0.405x_3$$

Suppose expectations for November are as follows:

x_1 = sales of washers = $43,000
x_2 = disposable income = $15,000
x_3 = savings = $75,000

FIGURE 7.4 THE STATPACK PROGRAM

RUN ***STATPACK
STATPACK

ARE YOU A STATPACK EXPERT
?* NO

THE RESPONSE 'SOS' MAY BE ENTERED IN ORDER TO GAIN ADDITIONAL IN-
FORMATION ABOUT THE RESPONSE NEEDED BY STATPACK. SOS MAY BE EN-
TERED ONLY IF THE QUESTION IS FOLLOWED BY THE CHARACTERS ?*

SPECIFY THE NAMES OF THE INPUT AND OUTPUT FILES(FORM:IN,OUT)
?* *,   *(Indicates that all input and output will be on the screen or printer.)*

WHAT ANALYSIS DO YOU WISH TO PERFORM
?* MULTIPLE REGRESSION

HOW MANY ROWS IN YOUR DATA MATRIX   *(How many observations?)*
?* 10

HOW MANY COLUMNS   *(How many variables?)*
?* 4

NOW, ENTER EACH ROW
?45,16,71,29
?42,14,70,24

```
?44,15,72,27
?45,13,71,25
?43,13,75,26
?46,14,74,28
?44,16,76,28   (Entered incorrectly)
?45,16,69,23
?44,15,74,28
?43,15,73,27

DO YOU WISH TO PRINT THE DATA JUST READ IN
?* NO

DO YOU WISH TO CHANGE SOME VALUES
?* YES

TYPE EDIT CODE
?* SOS

THE FOLLOWING CODES SIGNIFY TYPES OF EDIT FEATURES..
    0—NO MORE EDIT
    1—REPLACE AN INDIVIDUAL VALUE
    2—REPLACE AN ENTIRE ROW
    3—ADD A ROW
    4—DELETE A ROW
    5—SORT DATA (DESCENDING)
    6—SORT DATA (ASCENDING)
```

FIGURE 7.4 (cont.)

?* 1

TYPE ROW NUMBER, COLUMN NUMBER, AND NEW VALUE
?7,4,30   *(Corrected input value for July.)*

TYPE EDIT CODE
?* 0

DO YOU WISH TO PRINT THE DATA MATRIX
?* YES

45.000	16.000	71.000	29.000
42.000	14.000	70.000	24.000
44.000	15.000	72.000	27.000
45.000	13.000	71.000	25.000
43.000	13.000	75.000	26.000
46.000	14.000	74.000	28.000
44.000	16.000	76.000	30.000
45.000	16.000	69.000	28.000
44.000	15.000	74.000	28.000
43.000	15.000	73.000	27.000

SPECIFY THE DEPENDENT VARIABLE
?' 4

HOW MANY INDEPENDENT VARIABLES
?' 3

SPECIFY THESE VARIABLES
?1,2,3

VARIABLE	REG.COEF.	STD.ERROR COEF.	COMPUTED T
1	0.59697	0.08113	7.35866
2	1.17684	0.08007	13.99748
139 3	0.40511	0.04223	9.59200

143	INTERCEPT	-45.79634
144	MULTIPLE CORRELATION	0.99167
145	STD. ERROR OF ESTIMATE	0.28613

ANALYSIS OF VARIANCE FOR THE REGRESSION

SOURCE OF VARIATION	D.F.	SUM OF SQ.	MEAN SQ.	F VALUE
ATTRIBUTABLE TO REGRESSION	3	29.109	9.703	118.515
DEVIATION FROM REGRESSION	6	0.491	0.082	
TOTAL	9	29.600		

267

The forecasted sales for this month would be

$$\hat{y} = -45.796 + 0.597(43) + 1.177(15) + 0.405(75)$$
$$= -45.796 + 25.671 + 17.655 + 30.375$$
$$= 27.905 \text{ or } \$27,905$$

The Coefficient of Determination. Note that the STAT-PAK output gives the value of r, not r^2 (nor $\bar{r}^2$ for that matter). For this example,

$r = 0.99167$; thus
$r^2 = (0.99167)^2 = 0.983$

For multiple regression, $\bar{r}^2$ is more appropriate. Thus

$$\bar{r}^2 = 1 - (1-0.983)\frac{(10-1)}{(10-3)}$$
$$= 1 - 0.017 \left(\frac{9}{7}\right)$$
$$= 1 - 0.0219 = 0.978$$

CONCLUSION: 97.8 percent of total variation in sales of dryers is explained by the three independent variables. The remaining 2.2 percent remains unexplained by this equation.

The Standard Error of the Estimate (s_e). From the output, s_e is shown to equal 0.28613, which measures the dispersion of actual sales around the estimated equation.

Computed t. From the output, t statistics are for the three variables as follows:

x_1 : 7.35866
x_2 : 13.99748
x_3 : 9.59200

Remember the rule of thumb that a t value greater than 2.0 is acceptable. Here, all values are greater than 2.0. Strictly speaking, with $n-k-1 = 10-3-1 = 6$ degrees of freedom, and a level of significance of, say, 0.01, the t value from Table 7.2 = 3.707. CONCLUSION: All three independent variables are statistically significant.

F Test. From the output, $F = 118.515$. At a 0.01 level of significance, this F value is far above 9.78. CONCLUSION: The regression as a whole is highly significant.

Conclusions. Based on these statistical considerations, you can conclude that

• The estimated equation is a good fit
• All three independent variables are highly significant

- The regression as a whole is highly significant
- The model can be used as a forecasting equation with a high degree of confidence

8

Making Use of Quantitative Decision Making

Quantitative methods (or models), also known as operations research or management science, refer to sophisticated mathematical and statistical techniques for solving problems pertaining to managerial planning and decision making. Numerous such techniques are available, six of which are discussed in this chapter. They are

- Decision making under uncertain conditions
- Decision theory
- Linear programming
- Learning curve
- Inventory planning and control
- Queuing models

8.1 DECISION MAKING UNDER UNCERTAIN CONDITIONS

Under what conditions are decisions made?

Decisions are made under conditions of certainty or uncertainty (risk). Under certainty implies that for each decision there is only one event and therefore only one outcome for each action. Under uncertainty, which is more common realistically, several events are involved for each action and with each a different probability of occurrence. WHAT TO DO: Under uncertainty, it's often helpful to compute the following:

- Expected value
- Standard deviation
- Coefficient of variation

What does expected value tell me?

For decisions involving uncertainty, the concept of expected value ($\overline{A}$) provides a rational means for selecting the best course of action. Expected value is defined as a weighted mean using the probabilities as weights. It is found by multiplying the probability of each outcome by its payoff:

$$\overline{A} = \overline{Z}A_x P_x$$

where:

A_x = outcome for the xth possible event
P_x = the probability of occurrence for that outcome

What is the significance of the standard deviation?

The standard deviation (σ) measures the dispersion of a probability distribution (see also Section 7.1). It can be defined as the square root of the mean of the squared deviations from the expected value; thus

$$\sigma = \sqrt{\sum_{x=1}^{n} (A_x - \overline{A})^2 \, P_x}$$

Standard deviation is commonly used as an absolute measure of risk. RULE OF THUMB: The higher the standard deviation, the higher the risk.

What does the coefficient of variation mean?

The coefficient of variation (cv) is a measure of relative dispersion, or relative risk. You can compute it by dividing the standard deviation by the expected value:

$$cv = \frac{\sigma}{\overline{A}}$$

EXAMPLE 8.1

Investment Projects A and B have the following probability distribution of cash inflows in each of the next four years:

	Cash Inflows			
Probability	(.2)	(.3)	(.4)	(.1)
Project A	$ 50	200	300	400
Project B	$100	150	250	850

The expected value of the cash inflow is computed as follows:

Project A

$$\overline{A} = \$500(.2) + \$200(.3) + \$300(.4) + \$400(.1) = \$230$$

Project B

$$\overline{A} = \$100(.2) + \$140(.3) + \$240(.4) + \$850(.1) = \$250$$

The standard deviations are computed as follows:

Project A

$$\sigma = \sqrt{\begin{array}{l}([\$50 - \$230]^2 \, [0.2] + [200 - 230]^2 \, [0.3] \\ + \, [300 - 230]^2 \, [0.4] + [400 - 230]^2 \, [0.1])\end{array}}$$

$$\sigma = \$107.70$$

Project B

$$\sigma = \sqrt{\begin{array}{l}([\$100 - 250]^2 \, [0.2] + [150 - 250]^2 \, [0.3] \\ + \, [250 - 250]^2 \, [0.4] + [850 - 250]^2 \, [0.1])\end{array}}$$

$$\sigma = \$208.57$$

The coefficients of variation are computed as follows:

Project A

$$cv = \frac{\$107.70}{\$230} = 0.47$$

Project B

$$cv = \frac{\$208.57}{\$250} = 0.83$$

CONCLUSIONS: Project B is riskier than Project A because its standard deviation is greater. And, because its coefficient of variation is also greater, the degree of risk is also greater for Project B.

8.2 DECISION THEORY

What is decision theory?

Decision theory refers to a systematic approach to making decisions, particularly under conditions of uncertainty. While the statistics mentioned in Section 7.1 are essential for making your best choice, the decision problem can best be approached by using a payoff table or decision matrix. This consists of three basic components:

- *The row.* Each row represents a set of available alternative courses of action.
- *The column.* Each column represents the "states of nature," or conditions that are likely to occur and over which you have no control.
- *The entries.* These appear in the body of the table and represent the outcome of the decision, known as payoffs. These may be in the form of costs, revenues, profits, or cash flows.

What is the role of expected value in decision theory?

By computing the expected value of each action, you will be able to pick the best one.

Suppose you can obtain a perfect prediction of which event will occur. The expected value with such perfect information would be the total expected value of selected actions. Thus, expected value of perfect information (EVPI) can be computed as follows:

EVPI = expected value with perfect information
minus expected value with existing
information

EXAMPLE 8.2

The daily demand for strawberries is expressed by the following probability distribution:

daily demand	0	1	2	3
probability	.2	.3	.3	.2

Assume

$$\text{unit cost} = \$3$$
$$\text{selling price} = \$5 \text{ (i.e., profit on sold unit} = \$2)$$
salvage value
on unsold units = \$2
(i.e., loss on
unsold unit = \$1)

The company can stock 0, 1, 2, or 3 units. Problem: How many units should be stocked daily? Assume that units from one day cannot be sold on the next. The payoff table can be constructed as follows:

| | STATE OF NATURE | | | | |
| | Demand (Probability) | | | | Expected |
Stock	0 (.2)	1 (.3)	2 (.3)	3 (.2)	Value (A)
0	$0	$0	$0	$0	$0
Actions 1	−1	2	2	2	1.40
2	−2	1[a]	4	4	1.90[b]
3	−3	0	3	6	1.50

[a] Profit for (stock 2, demand 1) = (no. units sold)
(profit per unit) −
(no. units unsold)
(loss per unit)
= (1)($5 − 3)
− (1)($3 − 2)
= $2 − 1 = $1

[b] Expected value for (stock 2) = − 2(.2) + 1(.3)
+ 4(.3) + 4(.2)
= $1.90

With perfect information, you can make the following analysis:

| | STATE OF NATURE | | | | |
| | Demand (Probability) | | | | Expected |
Stock	0 (.2)	1 (.3)	2 (.3)	3 (.2)	Value (Ā)
0	$0				0
1		2			.6
Actions 2			4		1.2
3				6	1.2
					$3.0

CONCLUSIONS: The optimal stock action is stock 2, with the highest expected value of $1.90. Thus, with existing information, the best you can do is to select stock 2 units to obtain $1.90. With perfect information, you could make as much as $3. Therefore, the expected value of perfect information (EVPI) = $3.00 − $1.90, or $1.10. This is the maximum price you should be willing to pay for additional information.

8.3 LINEAR PROGRAMMING AND SHADOW PRICES

8.3.1 Linear Programming

What is linear programming?

Linear programming (LP) is concerned with optimal allocation of limited resources among competing activities. Specifically, it's a technique used to maximize revenue, contribution margin, or profit, or it is used to minimize a cost function subject to constraints.

What does linear programming consist of?

Linear programming consists of two important components:

- Objective function
- Constraints that typically are inequalities

Here's an example: A company wishes to find an optimal product mix in order to maximize its total contribution without violating restrictions imposed by the availability of resources. Or, it may want to determine a least-cost combination of input materials while satisfying production requirements, maintaining required inventory levels, staying within production capacities, and using available employees. The objective function is to minimize production costs. The constraints are production requirements, inventory levels, production capacity, and available employees.

What are applications of linear programming?

In addition to the preceding example, some applications for which you can use LP follow.

CHECKLIST OF APPLICATIONS
FOR LINEAR PROGRAMMING

- Selecting an investment mix
- Blending chemical products
- Scheduling flight crews
- Assigning jobs to machines
- Determining transportation routes
- Determining distribution or allocation patterns

What is involved in the formulation of linear programming?

To formulate the LP problem, first define the "decision variables" that you are trying to solve. Next, express the objective function and constraints in terms of these decision variables. NOTE: All expressions must be in linear form.

EXAMPLE 8.3

Company J produces two products, A and B. Both require time in two processing departments, the Assembly Department and the Finishing Department. Data for the two products are given as follows:

	PRODUCTS		Available
Processing	A	B	Hours
Assembly	2	4	100
Finishing	3	2	90
Contribution margin per unit	$25	$40	

The company wants to find the most profitable mix of these two products. First define the decision variables as follows:

A = the number of units of Product A to be produced

B = the number of units of Product B to be produced

The objective function is to maximize the total contribution margin (CM), expressed as follows:

Total CM = $\$25A + \$40B$

Then, formulate the constraints as inequalities, as follows:

- Assembly constraint: $2A + 4B \leq 100$
- Finishing constraint: $3A + 2B \leq 90$
- Nonnegativity constraints: $A, B \geq 0$

The LP model would be constructed as follows:

- Maximize total CM = $25A + 40B$
- Subject to $2A + 4B \leq 100$
  $3A + 2B \leq 90$
  $A, B \geq 0$

How do I solve LP problems?

There are several methods available for solving LP problems. Here are two common ones:

- *The simplex method.* This is most commonly used method of solving LP problems. It uses an algorithm, which can be defined as an iterative method of computation, to move from one solution to another until it reaches the best one.

- *The graphical method.* This solution is easier to use but is limited to problems involving two or at most three decision variables.

To use the graphical method, follow these five steps:

- Change inequalities to equalities
- Graph the equalities
- Identify the correct side for the original inequalities
- After all this, identify the feasible region or area of feasible solutions wherein values of the decision variables satisfy all the restrictions simultaneously
- Determine the contribution margin at all corners in the feasible region

EXAMPLE 8.4

Using Example 8.3, obtain the feasible region by going through steps one through four. This is shown as the shaded area in Figure 8.1. Then evaluate all the corner points within the feasible region in terms of their CM. Computations follow.

	Corner Points A	B	Contribution Margin $25A + $40B
(a)	30	0	$25(30) + $40(0) = $ 750
(b)	20	15	25(20) + 40(15) = 1,100
(c)	0	25	25(0) + 40(25) = 1,000
(d)	0	0	25(0) + 40(0) = 0

CONCLUSION: Corner *b* (20*A*, 15*B*) produces the most profitable solution.

FIGURE 8.1: GRAPHICAL SOLUTION

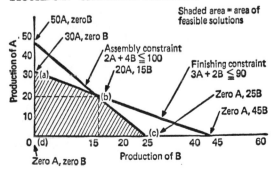

8.3.2 Shadow Prices

What are shadow prices?

If you have solved an LP problem, you might still wish to know whether it pays to add capacity in hours in a particular department. For example, you would be interested to know the monetary value to the company by adding, say, an hour per week of assembly time. This value is the additional contribution margin that could be earned, or the shadow price of a given resource. Shadow prices constitute a form of *opportunity cost* if you consider it as the contribution margin that would be lost by not adding capacity.

To justify a decision in favor of a short-term capacity expansion, you must be sure the shadow price exceeds the actual price of the expansion. Here's how to compute shadow prices (or opportunity costs):

- Add one hour (or preferably more) to the constraint under consideration

- Resolve the problem and find the maximum CM

- Compute the difference between CM of the original LP problem and the CM determined in the previous step; this is the shadow price

NOTE: Other methods, such as using the dual problem, are available to compute shadow prices.

EXAMPLE 8.5

Use the data from the previous example to compute the shadow price of the assembly capacity. To facilitate graphing, add eight hours of capacity to this department. The new assembly constraint is shown in Figure 8.2.

	Corner Points A	B	Contribution Margin $25A + $40B
(a)	30	0	$25(30) + $40(0) = $ 750
(b)	18	18	25(18) + 40(18) = 1,170
(c)	0	27	25(0) + 40(27) = 1,080
(d)	0	0	25(0) + 40(0) = 0

The new optimal solution, Corner *b* (18*A*, 18*B*) has a total CM of $1,170 per week. The shadow price of the

FIGURE 8.2: GRAPHICAL SOLUTION

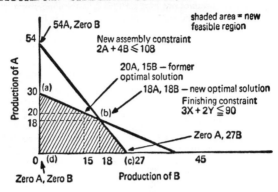

assembly capacity = $1,170 − $1,100 = $70. YOUR
CONCLUSION: The company should be willing to pay
up to $70 to obtain an additional eight hours per week,
or $8.75 per hour per week.

8.3.3 How to Use the Computer for Linear Programming

How does the computer handle linear programming?

Here's an example of how a computer can help solve
a linear programming problem. For this example, we
use EASYLP.

EXAMPLE 8.6

CSULB Company makes two products: snowmobiles
and outboard motors. The selling price and variable
manufacturing and selling expense data are given as
follows:

	Snowmobiles	Outboard Motors
Selling price	$1,400	$1,000
Variable cost	1,200	700
Contribution margin	$ 200	$ 300

Production is carried out in a single plant. Parts for each product are first produced in the machining department and then moved to the assembly line.

	Snowmobiles	Outboard Motors
Standard machining time	10 hours	30 hours
Standard assembly time	20	20
Total capacity of machining department	150	200

Each unit of snowmobile requires 300 units of material no. 444, and each unit of outboard motor requires 500 units. Currently, 4,800 units are available.

The company wants to determine (1) the most profitable mix of these products and (2) the shadow price for each scarce resource, that is, machining time, assembly time, and material.

The Optimal Solution. From EASYLP output:

x_1 = the number of units of snowmobiles to be produced = 7.5
x_2 = the number of units of outboard motors to be produced = 2.5

NOTE: If you must have an integer solution, you should use the integer programming method.

The Shadow Prices. Shadow prices are as follows:

For machining time	$5.00
For assembly time	7.50
For material	0.00

INTERPRETATION: The company would be willing to pay $5 and $7.50 to buy one additional hour of machining time and assembly time, respectively. By not buying, the company would lose $5 and $7.50 in potential contribution. On the other hand, the company is unwilling to pay anything for material. Why? Adding one extra unit of material no. 444 will not bring any additional contribution to the company.

8.4 LEARNING CURVE

How does the learning curve work to estimate labor hours?

The learning curve is based on the proposition that labor hours decrease in a definite pattern as labor operations are repeated. Statistical findings show that as the cumulative output doubles, the cumulative average input will be reduced by some constant percentage, ranging from 10 to 40 percent. Thus, the learning curve is an expression of this phenomenon as it applies to labor hours needed per unit produced.

How do I properly express the learning curve relationship?

The curve is usually designated by its compliment. That is, if the rate of reduction is 20 percent, then you would refer to the curve as an 80-percent learning curve.

The following illustrates the 80-percent learning curve relationship:

QUANTITY (IN UNITS)		TIME (IN HOURS)	
Per lot	Cumulative	Total Cumulative	Average time per unit
15	15	600	40.0
15	30	960	32.0 (40.0 × 0.8)
30	60	1,536	25.6 (32.0 × 0.8)
60	120	2,460	20.5 (25.6 × 0.8)
120	240	3,936	16.4 (20.5 × 0.8)

TAKE NOTE: As production quantities double, the average time needed per unit reduces by 20 percent from its immediately previous time.

EXAMPLE 8.7

Stanley Electronics Products, Inc., finds that new-product production is affected by an 80% learning curve. The company has just produced 50 units at 100 hours per unit. Costs were as follows:

Materials @ $20	$1,000
Labor and labor-related costs	
Direct labor (100 hr @ $8)	800
Variable overhead (100 hr @ $2)	200
	$2,000

The company has just received a contract for another 50 units. Management wants to add a 50% markup to the cost of materials, labor, and labor-related costs. You can compute the price for this job as follows:

The learning curve table shows the following:

Quantity	Total Time (in hours)	Average Time (per unit)
50 units	100	2 hours
100	160	1.6 (80% × 2 hr)

The new 50-unit job requires 60 total hours of production time.

Contract Price Computations

Materials @ $20	$1,000
Labor and labor-related costs	
Direct labor (60 hr @ $8)	480
Variable overhead (60 hr @ $2)	120
	$1,600
Markup (50%)	800
Contract price	$2,400

In what other ways can I use the learning curve?

CHECKLIST OF APPLICATIONS FOR THE LEARNING CURVE

- Scheduling labor requirements
- Making capital budgeting decisions
- Setting incentive wage rates

8.5 INVENTORY PLANNING AND CONTROL

Why are inventory planning and control important?

The purpose of inventory planning and control is to develop policies that will achieve an optimal inventory investment. You can do this by determining the optimal inventory level necessary to minimize related costs.

What kinds of costs are associated with inventory?

Inventory costs fall into three categories. They are

- *Order costs.* These include all costs associated with preparing a purchase order.
- *Carrying costs.* These include storage costs for inventory items plus opportunity cost (that is, the cost incurred by investing in inventory).
- *Shortage (stockout) costs.* These are costs incurred when an item is out of stock. They include the lost contribution margin on sales plus lost customer goodwill.

When and how much should I order?

Several inventory planning and control models are available that try to answer these questions. Three such models are

- Economic order quantity (EOQ)
- Reorder point (ROP)
- Determination of safety stock

How does the Economic Order Quantity (EOQ) model work?

The EOQ model determines the order size that minimizes the sum of carrying and ordering costs.

ASSUMPTIONS: Demand is assumed to be known with certainty and to remain constant throughout the year. Order cost is also assumed to be fixed. Also, unit carrying costs are assumed to be constant. Since demand and lead time (time interval between placing an order and receiving delivery) are assumed to be determinable, no shortage costs exist.

EOQ is computed as follows:

$$EOQ = \sqrt{\frac{2 \text{ (annual demand) (ordering cost)}}{\text{carrying cost per unit}}}$$

Total inventory costs

$$= \text{carrying cost per unit} \times \frac{EOQ}{2}$$

$$+ \text{ order cost} \times \frac{\text{annual demand}}{EOQ}$$

$$\text{Total number of orders per year} = \frac{\text{annual demand}}{EOQ}$$

EXAMPLE 8.8

Oakman, Inc. buys sets of steel at $40 per set from an outside vendor. Oakman will need 6,400 sets evenly throughout the year. Management desires a 16% return on its inventory investment (cost of capital). In addition, rent, insurance, taxes, etc. for each set in inventory comes to $1.60. The order cost is $100.

The carrying cost per set = $1.60 + 16%(40) = $8.00.

Thus,

$$EOQ = \sqrt{\frac{2 \, (6,400) \, (100)}{\$8.00}}$$
$$= \sqrt{160,000} = 400 \text{ sets}$$

Total inventory costs = $8.00
                         (400/2) + $100 (6400/400)
                       = $1,600 + $1,600 = $3,200

Total number
  of annual orders = 6,400/400
                   = 16 orders.

How do I determine the reorder point?

Reorder point tells you when to place an order. However, this method requires that you know the lead time from placing to receiving an order.

Reorder point is computed as follows:

ROP = lead time × average usage per unit of time.

This tells you the level of inventory at which a new order should be placed. NOTE: If you need a safety stock, then add this amount to the ROP model.

EXAMPLE 8.9

Using the preceding example, assume lead time is constant at one week. There are 50 working weeks in the year. Reorder point is computed as follows:

$$\text{Reorder point} = 1 \text{ week} \times \frac{6,400}{50 \text{ weeks}}$$
$$= 1 \times 128 = 128 \text{ sets}$$

CONCLUSION: When the inventory level drops to 128 sets, a new order should be placed.

Figure 8.3 shows this inventory system when the order quantity equals 400 sets.

FIGURE 8.3: BASIC INVENTORY SYSTEM

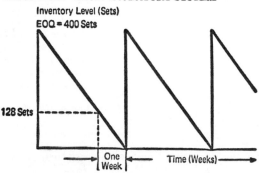

When are these models realistic to use?

The EOQ model described here is appropriate for a pure inventory system; that is, for single-item, single-stage inventory decisions for which joint costs and constraints can be ignored. EOQ and ROP assume that both lead time and demand rates are constant and known with certainty. CAUTION: This may be unrealistic. Still, these models have been proved useful in inventory planning for many companies. There are, for instance, many businesses for which these assumptions hold to some extent. They include:

- Subcontractors who must supply parts on a regular basis to a primary contractor;

- Automobile dealerships, in which demand varies from week to week but tends to even out over a season

CAUTION: When demand is not known precisely and/ or other complications arise, you should not use these models. You should instead refer to probabilistic models.

What about quantity discounts?

EOQ does not take quantity discounts into account, which is often unrealistic in actual practice. Usually the more you order, the lower the unit price you pay. A typical price discount schedule follows:

Order Size	Unit Cost
$0 < E < 500$	$ 40.00
$500 < E < 1000$	39.90
$1000 < E$	39.80

where E = order size

WHAT TO DO: With the price discounts shown here, you must include unit costs in your cost model as follows:

$$\text{Total costs} = \text{total inventory costs} + \text{cost of product}$$
$$= \text{carrying cost per unit}$$
$$\times \frac{E}{2} + \text{order cost}$$
$$\times \frac{\text{annual demand}}{E}$$
$$+ \text{unit price} \times \text{annual demand}$$

Use these three steps to find the economic order size with price discounts:

- Compute the EOQ when price discounts are ignored and the corresponding costs using the new cost after discount.
- Compute the costs for those quantities greater than EOQ at which price reductions occur.
- Select the value of E that results in the lowest annual cost.

EXAMPLE 8.10

Using the information from the previous two examples and the discount schedule shown previously, try to determine the economic order size. Recall that EOQ = 400. The further you move from point 400, the greater will be the sum of the ordering and carrying points. Thus, 400 is the only candidate for the minimum total cost value within the first price range. The only candidate within the $39.90 price range is $E = 500$, and $E = 1,000$ is the only candidate within the $39.80 range. The evaluation of these three points follows, and they are illustrated in Figure 8.4.

FIGURE 8.4: COSTS FOR PRICE DISCOUNT PROBLEM

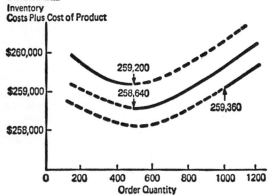

CONCLUSION: The economic order quantity with price discounts is 500. The manufacturer is justified in going to the first price break, but the extra carrying cost of the second price break more than outweighs the savings in ordering and in the cost of the product itself.

ANNUAL COSTS WITH VARYING ORDER SIZES

Order Size	400	500	1,000
Ordering cost $\dfrac{(\$100 \times 6{,}400)}{\text{order size}}$	$ 1,600	$ 1,280	$ 640
Carrying cost $\dfrac{(\$8 \times \text{order size})}{2}$	1,600	2,000	4,000
Product cost (unit price × 6,400)	256,000	255,360	254,720
Total cost	$259,200	$258,640	$259,360

What can I do when lead time and demand are uncertain?

When lead time and demand are uncertain, you must carry extra units of inventory, called *safety stock*, as protection against possible stockouts.

Service level can be defined as the probability that demand will not exceed supply during lead time. Thus, a service level of 90 percent implies a probability of 90 percent that demand will not exceed supply during lead time. To determine the optimal level of safety stock size, you might want to measure costs of not having enough inventory, or stockout costs. Here are three cases for computing the safety stock. The first two do not recognize stockout costs; the third case does.

Case 1: Variable usage rate, constant lead time

$$\text{ROP} = \text{Expected usage during lead time} + \text{safety stock}$$
$$= \bar{u}\,\text{LT} + z\,\sqrt{\text{LT}}\,(\sigma_u)$$

where

$\bar{u}$ = average usage rate
LT = lead time
σ_u = standard deviation of usage rate
z = standard normal variate as defined in Table 8.1

For a normal distribution, a given service level amounts to the shaded area under the curve to the left of ROP in Figure 8.5.

FIGURE 8.5: SERVICE LEVEL

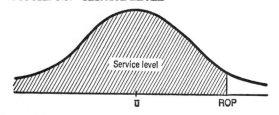

Service level

$\bar{u}$ ROP

EXAMPLE 8.11

Ken's Pizza uses large cases of tomatoes at an average rate of 50 cans per day. Usage can be approximated by a normal distribution with a standard deviation of five cans per day. Lead time is four days. Thus:

$$\overline{u} = 50 \text{ cans per day}$$
$$\sigma_u = 5 \text{ cans}$$
$$LT = 4 \text{ days}$$

How much safety stock is necessary for a service level of 99%? And what is the ROP?

For a service level of 99%, $z = 2.33$ (from Table 8.1). Thus:

$$\text{Safety stock} = 2.33 \sqrt{4}\ (5) = 23.3 \text{ cans}$$
$$\text{ROP} = 50(4) + 23.3 = 223.3 \text{ cans}$$

FIGURE 8.6: SERVICE LEVEL = 99%

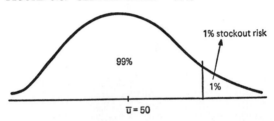

Case 2: Constant usage rate, variable lead time

For constant usage with variable lead time, the reorder point is computed as follows:

$$\begin{aligned}
\text{ROP} &= \text{expected usage during lead time} \\
&\quad + \text{ safety stock} \\
&= \overline{u}\ \overline{LT} + zu\ \sigma_{LT}
\end{aligned}$$

where

u = constant usage rate
$\overline{LT}$ = average lead time
σ_{LT} = standard deviation of lead time

EXAMPLE 8.12

The local hamburger shop uses 10 gallons of cola per day. Lead time is normally distribution with a mean of six days and a standard deviation of 2 days. Thus,

$$u = 10 \text{ gallons per day}$$
$$\overline{LT} = 6 \text{ days}$$
$$\sigma_{LT} = 2 \text{ days}$$

How much safety stock should be carried to achieve a service level of 99%, and what is the ROP?

Safety stock = 2.33(10)(2) = 46.6 gallons
ROP = 10(6) + 46.6 = 106.6 gallons

(Note: 2.33 = z at 99% service level.)

TABLE 8.1: VALUES OF z_P FOR SPECIFIED PROBABILITIES P

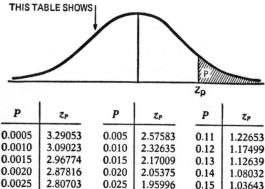

P	z_P	P	z_P	P	z_P
0.0005	3.29053	0.005	2.57583	0.11	1.22653
0.0010	3.09023	0.010	2.32635	0.12	1.17499
0.0015	2.96774	0.015	2.17009	0.13	1.12639
0.0020	2.87816	0.020	2.05375	0.14	1.08032
0.0025	2.80703	0.025	1.95996	0.15	1.03643
0.0030	2.74778	0.030	1.88079	0.16	0.99446
0.0035	2.69684	0.035	1.81191	0.17	0.95417
0.0040	2.65207	0.040	1.75069	0.18	0.91537
0.0045	2.61205	0.045	1.69540	0.19	0.87790
0.0050	2.57583	0.050	1.64485	0.20	0.84162
0.006	2.51214	0.06	1.55477	0.25	0.67449
0.007	2.45726	0.07	1.47579	0.30	0.52440
0.008	2.40892	0.08	1.40507	0.35	0.38532
0.009	2.36562	0.09	1.34076	0.40	0.25335
0.010	2.32635	0.10	1.28155	0.45	0.12566

z_P is the value of the standardized normal (mean = 0, standard deviation = 1) random variable z such that the probability of obtaining a sample z value at least as large as z_P is P. The value of P must be doubled if two sided statements are made using the same z_P value.

Source: Croxton/Cowden/Bolch, *Practical Business Statistics*, 4th Ed., © 1969, p. 393. Reprinted by permission of Prentice-Hall, Inc., Englewood Cliffs, N.J.

Case 3: Incorporation of stockout costs

This case specifically recognizes the cost of stockouts or shortages, which can be quite expensive. Lost sales, disgruntled customers, idle machines, and disrupted production scheduling are examples of internal and external costs caused by stockouts.

WHAT TO DO: You can use the probability approach to determine the optimum stock size in the presence of stockout costs. Here's an example:

EXAMPLE 8.13

Refer to Example 8.9. The total usage over a one-week period is estimated as follows:

Total Use	Probability
78	.2
128	.4
178	.2
228	.1
278	.1
	1.0

A stockout cost is estimated at $12 per set. Recall that the carrying cost is $8 per set. Computation of safety stock is shown on page 292.

CONCLUSIONS: The table shows that total costs are minimized at $1,200 when a safety stock of 150 sets is maintained. Thus, ROP = 128 sets + 150 sets = 278 sets.

8.6 QUEUING (WAITING LINE) MODELS

What is the purpose of queuing theory?

Queuing, or waiting line, theory investigates the everyday hassle of waiting in line. If you are an operating, marketing or production manager, you could apply this tool should waiting time involve you.

Like EOQ, queuing theory involves minimization of overall costs; that is, the sum of waiting costs borne by customers or businesses and the cost of providing extra service facilities and/or attendants.

What are the applications of queuing theory?

The applications of queuing theory are numerous. For example, you may want to determine the number of doctors that should be on call at a clinic.

Safety Stock Levels in Units	Stockout and Probability	Average Stockout in Units	Average Stockout Costs	No. of Orders	Total Annual Stockout Costs	Carrying Costs	Total
0	50 with .2 100 with .1 150 with .1	35[a]	$420[b]	16	$6,720[c]	0	$6,720
50	50 with .1 100 with .1	15	180	16	2,880	400[d]	3,280
100	50 with .1	5	60	16	960	800	1,760
150	0	0	0	16	0	1,200	1,200

[a] 50(.2) + 100(.1) + 150(.1) = 10 + 10 + 15 = 35 units

[b] 35 units × $12.00 = $420

[c] $420 × 16 times = $6,720

[d] 50 units × $8.00 = $400

292

What are some queuing models?

Before investigating queuing models, you need to know three things. They are

- Your company's experience with the daily ebb and flow of customers
- The probability assumptions as the nature of this process unfolds; for example, what are the chances of experiencing an unusually large bunching of arrivals
- Determination of costs associated with waiting and improving the rate of service

There are many queuing models from which you can choose. One, called the Single Channel Exponential Service Time Model, assumes a Poisson arrival rate and infinite source. For this model, use the following symbols:

A = mean arrival rate
S = mean service rate

Management scientists have developed the following equations for this single-channel model:

- System utilization = probability that the servers are busy = $\dfrac{A}{S}$
- Average number in the system = number of units in the queue plus number being served = $\dfrac{A}{(S-A)}$
- Average number waiting for service to begin = number of units in the queue = $\dfrac{A^2}{S(S-A)}$
- Average time spent waiting in the system = queue time plus service time = $\dfrac{1}{S-A}$
- Average time spent waiting before service begins = time in queue = $\dfrac{A}{S(S-A)}$
- Percent of idle time = $1 - \dfrac{A}{S}$

EXAMPLE 8.14

Los Alamitos Car Wash is an automatic operation with a single bay. On a typical Saturday morning, cars arrive at a mean rate of nine per hour, with arrivals tending to follow a Poisson distribution. Service time, including

manual drying time, is assumed to be exponentially distributed. Past experience suggests that the mean service
time should average five minutes. Thus

A = 9 cars per hour
S = 1 per 5 minutes or 12 per hour

You can determine the following:

- System utilization = $\dfrac{9}{12}$ = 75%. This means the
  system is busy 75% of the time.
- Average number of cars in line and service =
  $\dfrac{9}{12-9}$ = 3 cars
- Average number of cars in line = $\dfrac{9^2}{12(12-9)}$ =
  $\dfrac{81}{36}$ = 2.25 cars
- Average time cars spend waiting in line and for
  service = $\dfrac{1}{12-9}$ = ⅓ hour or 20 minutes
- Average time cars spend waiting for service =
  $\dfrac{9}{12(12-9)}$ = 9/36 = ¼ or 15 minutes
- Percent of idle time = 1 − 0.75 = 0.25 or 25%

Index

NOTES

NOTES

NOTES

NOTES

NOTES

NOTES

NOTES

NOTES

NOTES

NOTES

Use this handy form
to order additional copies of
The Vest-Pocket MBA

Also Available On 15-Day Free Trial

Just check the box(es) below and fill out ordering information on reverse side.